INTRODUCTION TO
OIL AND GAS
ENVIRONMENTAL PROJECT MANAGEMENT

INTRODUCTION TO
OIL AND GAS
ENVIRONMENTAL PROJECT MANAGEMENT

Tim Marler

PennWell Publishing Company
Tulsa, Oklahoma

Copyright © 1994 by
PennWell Publishing Company
1421 South Sheridan/P.O. Box 1260
Tulsa, Oklahoma 74101

Marler, Tim
Introduction to oil and gas environmental project management / Tim Marler
p.   cm.
Includes bibliographical references and index.
ISBN 0-87814-430-7
1. Petroleum industry and trade–Environmental aspects. 2. Gas industry–Environmental aspects. 3. Industrial management–Environmental aspects.
TD195.P4M363   1994
363.73' 82–dc20

Printed in the United States of America

1   2   3   4   5   98   97   96   95   94

TO:

The Lord, who gave me whatever wits I may have. Also, to my wife, Teresa, and children, Calista, Andrea, and Aaron, who helped me keep them during the writing of this book.

CONTENTS

Acknowledgements   *x*
Acronyms   *xi*
Measurements   *xiv*
Preface   *xv*
Introduction   *xviii*

Photo Section

Appendix A   *141*
Appendix B   *154*
Glossary of Terms   *179*
Index   *184*

---

1   **ENVIRONMENTAL MANAGEMENT STRATEGIES**   **1**
         AND THE NEW INDUSTRY ORDER
The New Reality
Diminished Domestic Presence
of Major Companies
The New Home Front
Organization Strategies, Internal and Outsourced
Auditing As a Part of Management Strategy Status
Cleanup Funds
OBO: Terror in the Economy Bin
To Accentuate the Positive
Summary

---

2   **FEELING BLUE ABOUT GREENPEACE?**   **11**
Where Are We and How Did We Get Here?
Environmental Regulation
Clean Water Act
Clean Air Act

Resource Conservation and Recovery Act (RCRA)
Exemption is Not Absolution
Safe Drinking Water Act
Comprehensive Environmental Response
Compensation, and Liability Act
Superfund Amendments and
Reauthorization Act, Title III
Toxic Substances Control Act
Naturally Occurring Radioactive Material
Summary

3   ENVIRONMENTAL AUDITS IN THE OIL PATCH   25
Audit Purpose
What is Phase 1?
Phase 2
Example A
Example B
Phase 1 Procedure
Common Oilfield Facilities and
Their Related Environmental Concerns
Industry Standardization

4   SOIL SAMPLING - A PRIMER   39
Soil Development
Soil Structuring
Sample Parameters (Non-Organic)
Sample Analysis (Organic)
Reporting Requirements
Soil Sampling

5   GROUNDWATER CONTAMINATION   55
Potential Impact of Oilfield Activities
on Groundwater
Background Information
Oilfield Contamination Sources and Indicators

Evaluation and Risk Analysis
Groundwater Sampling
Monitoring Well Network Design
How Big is Big?

**6   NATURALLY OCCURRING   75
        RADIOACTIVE MATERIAL (NORM)**
The Problem
Background Information
Units
NORM Surveying and Testing Equipment
Surveying and Testing
New EPA Developments
Disposal Options
Personnel Training
Summary
Example

7   THAT'S THE PITS   91
Analysis
Pit Evaluation

8   REMEDIATION OPTIONS   101
Groundwater Remediation
Pit Remediation
Pit Closure Options
Soil Amendments
Summary

9   CASE HISTORIES   115
Scenario 1
Scenario 2
Scenario 3
Scenario 4
Scenario 5

ACKNOWLEDGEMENTS

The author would like to gratefully thank and acknowledge those who have benefitted him intellectually and provided much of the knowledge and training that made this book possible. Isaac Newton once said that, if he had seen farther than other men, it was because he had stood on the shoulders of giants.

First, Dr. Lloyd Deuel (of SASI) and Dr. George Holliday (of Holliday Environmental Services, Inc.), have been invaluable over the years as a resource in the area of soil analysis. Much of the understanding needed to write this book, particularly Chapter Four, I owe to them. Second, Radiation Technical Services, and especially Mr. Shane Bradley, have provided excellent training and information. Also, Mr. Morris Hall has been a good friend and has taught me much about groundwater as well as encouraging me during some tough situations.

ACRONYMS

The following acronyms are useful to know when dealing with environmental issues. Most of them are used in the book, but some are added simply because they are useful to know. This listing is by no means intended to be comprehensive.

AEC	Atomic Energy Commission
AFIT	After Federal Income Tax
ALARA	As Low As Reasonably Achievable
AMU	Atomic Mass Units
APCD	Air Pollution Control District
API	American Petroleum Institute
AQD	Air Quality Division
AST	Aboveground Storage Tank
ASTM	American Society for Testing and Materials
BFIT	Before Federal Income Tax
BTEX	Benzene, Toluene, Ethylbenzene, Xylenes
CAA	Clean Air Act
CASRN	Chemical Abstracts Service Registry Number
CEC	Cation Exchange Capacity
CERCLA	Comprehensive Environmental Response, Compensation, and Liability Act
CERCLIS	Comprehensive Environmental Response, Compensation, and Liability Information System
CFR	Code of Federal Regulations
CMT	Cement
CPM	Counts Per Minute
CSG	Casing
CWA	Clean Water Act
CZMA	Coastal Zone Management Act
DEC	Dept. of Environmental Conservation
DEP	Dept. of Environmental Protection
DEQ	Dept. of Environmental Quality
DER	Dept. of Environmental Resources
DMR	Discharge Monitoring Report
DNR	Department of Natural Resources
DOD	Dissolved Oxygen Demand
DOE	Department of Energy

DOT	Department of Transportation
DPM	Decays Per Minute
EC	Electrical Conductivity
ECRA	Environmental Cleanup Responsibility Act
EHS	Extremely Hazardous Substance
EIS	Environmental Impact Statement
EPA	Environmental Protection Agency
EPCRA	Emergency Planning and Community Right-to-Know Act (SARA Title III)
ERNS	Emergency Response Notification System
ESA	Endangered Species Act
ESA	Environmental Site Assessment
ESP	Exchangeable Sodium Percentage
FEMA	Federal Emergency Management Agency
FIFRA	Federal Insecticide, Fungicide, and Rodenticide Act
FOIA	Freedom of Information Act
FR	Federal Register
FWKO	Free Water Knockouts
GC	Gas Chromatography
HAZMAT	Hazardous Materials
HRS	Hazard Ranking System
IR	Infrared Spectroscopy
IRIS	Integrated Risk Information System
IRS	Internal Revenue Service
JOA	Joint Operating Area
LEPC	Local Emergency Planning Committee
LQG	Large Quantity Generator
LSO 29-B	Louisiana Statewide Order 29-B
LUST	Leaking Underground Storage Tank
MCL's	Maximum Contamination Levels
MIT	Mechanical Integrity Test
MMS	Minerals Management Service
MMBOE	Million Barrels of Oil Equivalent
MSDS	Material Safety Data Sheet
NESHAP	National Emission Standards for Hazardous Air Pollutants
NORM	Naturally Occurring Radioactive Material
NOW	Non-hazardous Oil Field Waste
NPDES	National Pollutant Discharge Elimination System
NPL	National Priority List
OBO	Operated By Others

OCC	Oklahoma Corporation Commission
OPA	Oil Pollution Act
OSHA	Occupational Safety and Health Administration
P&S	Purchase and Sale
PCB	Polychlorinated Biphenyls
PIT	Pressure Integrity Test
PPB	Parts Per Billion
PPM	Parts Per Million
PRP	Potentially Responsible Party
RCRA	Resource Conservation and Recovery Act
RI/FS	Remedial Investigation/Feasibility Study
RP	Responsible Party
RRC	Texas Railroad Commission
RQ	Reportable Quantity
SAR	Sodium Absorption Ratio
SARA	Superfund Amendments and Reauthorization Act
SDWA	Safe Drinking Water Act
SEPC	State Emergency Planning Commission
SERC	State Emergency Response Commission
SIC	Standard Industrial Classification
SPCC	Spill Prevention, Control, and Countermeasure
SQG	Small Quantity Generators
SWD	Salt Water Disposal
TCLP	Toxicity Characteristic Leaching Procedure
TD	Total Depth
TDS	Total Dissolved Solids
TNRCC	Texas Natural Resource Conservation Commission
TOC	Total Organic Carbon
TPH	Total Petroleum Hydrocarbons
TPQ	Threshold Planning Quantity
TSCA	Toxic Substances Control Act
TSD	Treatment, Storage, and Disposal
UIC	Underground Injection Control
USC	United States Code
USDA	United States Department or Agriculture
USDW	Underground Source of Drinking Water
UST	Underground Storage Tank
VOA	Volatile Organic Analysis
VOC	Volatile Organic Compound
WPA	Wetlands Protection Act

MEASUREMENTS

Barrels **Bbl**

Curies **Ci**

MicroRoentgens per Hour **µR/hr.**

Milliequivalents per 100 grams **Meq/100 gm**

Milligrams per Kilogram (solid) **Mg/Kg**

Milligrams per Liter (liquid) **Mg/L**

Million Barrels of Oil **MMBO**

Million Barrels of Oil Equivalent **MMBOE**

MilliRems **mR**

Parts Per Billion **PPB**

Parts Per Million **PPM**

Parts Per Thousand **PPT**

PicoCuries Per Gram **pCi/Gm**

Standard Unit **s.u.**

PREFACE

When the reader finishes this book, he may be tempted to do something rash like hanging himself with his necktie or throwing himself on his tie tack (better yet, throwing the nearest Greenpeace member on his tie tack). Therefore, in an effort to head off such an eventuality, it is worth noting right up front that not all changes are bad. Some of what is blowing in the wind is favorable.

Much of the relief effort centers around tax abatement as an oil and gas incentive program. At the federal level, the Department of Energy (DOE) is studying the potential beneficial effects of allowing companies to expense geological and geophysical expenditures, according to a March 28, 1994, article in the _Oil & Gas Journal_. The same article notes that the Independent Petroleum Association of America (IPAA) has petitioned the the Commerce Dept. for relief from low priced oil imports under the 1962 Trade Expansion Act. Energy Secretary, Hazel O'Leary asked the Commerce Dept. to expedite its review of the petition, her concern being a trend toward increasing dependence on foreign oil imports.

Senator David Boren (D. Oklahoma) is in favor of a tax credit for marginal producers that would phase out with increasing oil prices. Other industry representatives would like to see a tax on imported products. It seems that there is an element in Washington that would like to see domestic oil and gas production get a shot in the arm. The question is whether they can sling enough weight to get something accomplished in a timely fashion amidst the ongoing madness.

One example of a success story at the state level is the recent (1989) tax abatement program initiated in Texas that encourages operators to go back and do recompletion and workovers on marginal wells for secondary and tertiary recovery, thus avoiding premature abandonment. Once again, supply-side economics proves to be viable. A recent _Oil & Gas Journal_ article reports that the Texas Railroad Commission (RRC) has calculated that the production incentive program has generated a ratio of 2:1 in regard to dollars realized by the state versus dollars spent. The abatement program grants a 50% tax exemption for 10 years for all oil produced from new secondary and tertiary recovery programs. According to _O&GJ's_ report, the program has added 945 MMBO to Texas reserves in 4 years.

Additionally, Oklahoma has, in May 1994, passed legislation to provide drilling and production incentive by tax abatement. According to a June 1994 article in *OGJ*, substantial tax benefits can accrue to operators who: 1) bring a well back on stream that has been off production for 2 years or more; 2) do certain qualifying recompletion and workovers that increase production, and/or; 3) drill new wells to depths greater than 15,000 ft.

Apart from being a sterling example of how supply-side economics works, these tax programs also have an indirect, but positive, environmental utility. Wellbores that might have sat unattended and deteriorating and might have become a groundwater contamination problem have been refurbished with new tubulars and put into service.

Sometimes the concern for environmental issues does lead to a profitability boon for some people and companies. California, which did not until the 1990s (surprisingly enough) have a strict well abandonment rule, has implemented one with somewhat unexpected results. Operators have had to make decisions about thousands of idle or temporarily abandoned wells for the first time in that state's history. The surprising thing is not that hundreds of wells have been plugged, but that a large number of profitable workovers were discovered and a upward surge in the workover rig count resulted. Likewise, the production in California has been buoyed by these workovers.

It is also very interesting (and hopeful) to note that, at the time of this writing, environmental activist groups are experiencing drops in membership. Organizations such as Greenpeace, the Sierra Club, and the Audubon Society are having to trim costs and budgets. This would seem nearly astounding considering the current names on the political map in Washington, D.C. These groups have soul mates (ostensibly) at the very highest echelons of government. Why then do they seem to be in decline? No one really knows, and some of these groups are reported to be hiring consultants to get at that answer. My theory, for what it's worth, is that these activists are feeling the impact of talk show hosts such as Marlin Maddoux and Rush Limbaugh who are bucking the dominant media culture. For the first time, many Americans are hearing the truth about the agendas being put forward by these organizations. In the past, many well-intentioned citizens contributed to environmentalist groups under the misapprehension that they were just "conservationist organizations." It is becoming apparent to many that the direction of these groups and their constituency is far beyond conservation or even sanity.

So...could it be that the tide is turning? We'll see. It is still my belief that business planning must be based on a worst case scenario. Mind you, the decision to *enter* business or a business deal must be based on optimism or at least realism but the planning of *how* to conduct that business must take into account the down-side. Thinking that environmental regulation will decrease is probably not very responsible thinking. There is room to hope, however, that the extent to which that regulatory burden is increased can be minimized.

Try to keep that in mind as you read the rest of this little tome.

INTRODUCTION

U.S. upstream oil and gas interests are currently faced with the necessity of modifying exploration and production activities to comply with emerging environmental regulations. A few major and independent oil companies are adopting a position that the best business strategy for dealing with environmental liabilities is to act affirmatively and aggressively. Others are trying to spend minimal amounts in order to give the appearance of compliance. And some still are strenuously resisting what they regard to be an onerous and unwarranted restriction on their productivity.

In the midst of all this, banks are loaning money for the drilling of wells and the acquisition of producing properties, knowing that their financial risks related to environmental liability are very high. Landowners are increasingly and justifiably concerned about inheriting the costs for cleanups after the operator has departed. In addition, there are thousands of non-operating working interest owners who lack any real technical capability or regulatory expertise to deal with the situation, yet are held to be responsible for environmental problems that may occur on their properties. Some people are selling ... Others are buying ... A great number are financially insolvent. In short, everything is in flux. There are great risks and potential catastrophes as well as great rewards. How does one know which is which?

You had better know, and you had better be able to document it!

What is the condition of that oil property on your "north forty?" The field you are *selling* ... can you prove in court in two years that it was clean when you sold it? You may get the opportunity. So, you are *buying* a field ... is it really such a good deal? Are you aware that the new equation for arriving at the bottom line on a field's worth has to account for environmental liabilities? And you, our lender friend, are you really going to loan hundreds of thousands of dollars on a pig-in-a-poke without having taken a thorough look at the associated environmental risks?

Tough Questions ... Tough Times.

At this juncture in time, the ugly specter of Resource Conservation and Recovery Act (RCRA) reauthorization looms over the oil patch. After doing some comparative cost estimation, I have found that if the oil field exemption from hazardous waste is eliminated, the cost to deal with the same remediation would probably be inflated three to five times. The unwary surface owner, buyer, or seller may wind up paying for the sins of others, and the cost could be phenomenal! There will also be a corresponding increase in the intensity and stringency of regulation when the word *hazardous* is invoked. Estimates of initial industry expenditures to achieve compliance with regulations under RCRA Subtitle C run as high as $56 billion.

There is a message in all this. The things that made one a good operator 15 years ago no longer suffice. The industry and those affected parties, such as landowners and non-operating working interest owners, will be feeling the repercussions of this situation for the foreseeable future and it *will* get worse.

A leading environmental manager with a major oil company said, "Historically, industry responded to environmental regulation with caution. Caution, in many cases, became an accepted mode of response. The common practice was, 'Let's stall. Things will get better. This environmental thing will go away. The public will lose interest. The law is so bad it will have to change for the better. Besides, someone is going to find a really inexpensive technology in the next few years, and our costs will be less if we just put this whole thing off.'" However, this cautious approach fails to recognize certain realities.

Are you ready for the new sweeping changes which will occur in the future? Will your investments have the same bottom line value after environmental liabilities are considered?

There are several approaches to managing your environmental problems. A popular option is to use the "ostrich" approach. In this mode, the PRP (a term meaning 'potentially responsible party' used by regulatory agencies and lawyers to apply to persons being sued and prosecuted) elects to go on with business as usual just hoping it will all go away. Then, one day, the phone rings...

A variation on the ostrich approach is the "bull in the ring." One can choose to become combative, surly, and charge the red cape. There are few things more inspiring to see than a gallant entrepreneur charging at an underpaid, under-motivated, quietly resentful public"servant" with all guns blazing, banners flying, and veins bulging. I must admit that I believe more of this should be done, but...one must pick one's battlefield. It is useful to keep in mind that the usual fate of the bull is less than glamorous. Actually, in all seriousness, there is a better way to handle the regulatory problem. Facts and data are far more effective than blustering. There is no need to have shirts printed up with the word WELCOME on the back. It is preferable to stand firm on issues armed with plenty of defensible data.

May I suggest that we use our heads? Frankly, if you want to be in the oil business at the end of this decade, you had better make up your mind to *manage* your problem. A plan of action is essential. I doubt that Field Marshall Erwin Rommel was that fond of desert landscapes, but he learned to make the situation and terrain work for him.

Given the present political climate, there is now only one prudent way for an oil and gas operator or non-operating working interest owner to consider the future. The regulatory environment will almost certainly become much more hostile for the oil industry in a shorter period of time than some of us ever anticipated. Here is a consideration for your perusal: It is very possible that the RCRA exemption currently enjoyed by the oil industry will be lost or diminished in the near future. Congress and the White House are now controlled, to some extent, by interests that would (right or wrong) militate to reclassify oil and gas wastes as *hazardous* materials.

In essence, you will probably have closer regulation than you have ever experienced in times past. Even if reclassification of oil field waste does *not* occur, you can expect the heat to be turned up. Expect private litigation to mount catastrophically. The author is involved in a job right now that will, very possibly, result in fines to the operator, non-operating working interest owners, and mineral interests, as well as a lawsuit in the millions of dollars.

Bottom line...you have more (and less expensive) options right now than you will probably have for quite some time. You are in a race against time, and there is every prudent reason to begin to act now to identify, quantify, and deal with your problems.

This book will not make an expert of anyone in any of the subjects upon which it touches. It is intended as an overview to help the reader focus on the environmental issues that are relevant to the oil patch. Perhaps, by reading this work, the reader will have a clearer and firmer grasp of the scope and seriousness of the environmental aspect of the "oil bidness."

Admittedly, the air quality issue remains a question mark. There are emerging regulations on a state-by-state basis that will affect the industry. Whereas, E&P operations were more or less overlooked previously, the 1990 Clean Air Act Amendments will pull operators into that regulatory arena in the short term. Environmental managers in several firms are seeking to get a handle on how their organization's operations are likely to be affected from a cost standpoint. A full treatment of the air issue can be found in Merritt Nicewander's *Clean Air Act Permitting Guidance Manual*, published by PennWell Books and should fill in the gaps left in this work.

Environmental Management Strategies and the New Industry Order

THE NEW REALITY

Since 1986, the U.S. oil industry has been on a roller coaster ride that seems to be all down and no up. Those who experienced the gloom of $9/bbl oil have some difficulty even remembering the more prosperous days of the late 1970s and early 1980s. Things are different in any number of ways: attitudes, investor recalcitrance, regulatory climate, and so on.

The world is awash in a sea of oil (poor choice of words in an environmental book). Prices have never recovered to the $30+/bbl that was once unquestioned. In fact, even during the recent Persian Gulf war where two of the premier oil producers were locked in combat, the price (after one brief panic spike) settled back and scarcely bobbled. Virtually every internal price forecast of major oil companies tentatively puts forward a slow ramp up for prices at the wellhead. No one believes in another boom anymore. Oil, in some respects, is another post-WWII boom industry that grew with a growing manufacturing and industrial base. Like the steel industry in the 1970s, it is being transformed into a new type of entity.

The domestic oil industry of the future gives every appearance of being smaller, leaner, and dominated by independents.

MAJORS' U.S. EXODUS

One glaring difference today is the continued decreasing presence of the major oil companies in the U.S. One after another, they have shifted the focus of their E&P budgets to overseas investment. Large organizations are looking for "elephants in the long grass": something that will cause a shimmer in their stock prices. The author has looked at large portions of the inland domestic playground and must admit that the giant projects are few and far between. One million bbl of oil equivalent (MMBOE) is still attainable, but if your corporate template is 5 MMBOE the picture becomes a good deal less cheerful. A look at the field size distribution curves for any number of domestic plays (be it Anadarko basin or the Gulf Coast Yegua-Wilcox) tells a grim story. The big ones have, for the most part, passed into history.

Whether the overseas strategy will yield sufficient fruit to make it worthwhile remains to be seen. Frankly, outside of the established producing areas such as the Middle East and the North Sea, the real success seems to have been limited thus far. Many factors militate against a U.S.company's success in overseas exploration or at least serve to increase the risk. Political instability is pandemic. It is hard to assess in some countries who will be in the seat of power tomorrow or even who is there today.

Likewise, countries are seeking to exercise increased control over their natural resources and believe that they (selfish wretches that they are) should be the primary beneficiary and not a foreign company. In short, getting a concession is not the same game that it was 40 years ago. Development economics intrudes itself and renders uneconomic fields that would set off a leasing stampedeif they were in the U.S. If you have to build a pipeline across Nigeria to produce your crude, you are apt to look at the economics really hard before proceeding.

Furthermore, and more to the point of this book, there is now an international awareness of environmental issues, so companies that are operating in some countries are beginning to run into tricky situations. In one instance I know of, a large independent was seeking to take over a very mature field in another country. A clause in the transfer agreement made the American company responsible for any environmental problems caused by its operation, excluding any preexisting conditions. That sounds fair enough, but the reality was that the country in question required the use of environmental firms that were on its approved list.

To sign such an agreement, one would need to be very thorough and look at all possibilities, but the U.S. company was required to use a consulting firm with a vested interest in the country in question which has a vested interest in not finding all the problems. The solution in such a case requires hiring trusted expertise to duplicate and quality check the national contractor. Alternatively, you can trust the good will of the host government.

Right now many developing countries are little interested in the environmental issue. They need cash. Central and Eastern Europe, Russia, and other nations are in a state of flux. They have some pretty terrible environmental problems, but survival takes precedence over green thinking. For the time being, they are attempting to attract foreign investment, so the environmental financial burden is not being levied upon operators as severely in those countries as in the U.S.

It will be interesting to see if American E&P companies that move into developing countries begin to encounter retroactive environmental regulation as the host country stabilizes. It would be advisable to have a pretty good environmental baseline on the condition of your operating areas at the time you move in and begin operations. It might not save you anything, but then again, it could.

THE NEW HOME FRONT

Well, the majors' departure is perceived by many to be a boon to the independent oil companies that will inherit the U.S. oil patch for the time being. Lease bonuses should be more affordable, and fields will be sold to independents who can operate with a lower overhead. In fact, the brokers who were putting together deals in the mid-1980s for producing properties have been swept away by a massive 'going out of business sale' on the part of the majors.

There are, however, some drawbacks to this situation. First, a great deal of money invested in drilling opportunities in the past came from major oil companies. As they depart, a great deal of the capital resource also departs. An additional negative associated with the departure of the major oil companies is the potential for an associated loss of lobbying dollars that have been spent to combat onerous regulations. U.S. major oil companies have spent considerable funds lobbying and campaigning against further restrictive regulation of the industry. If they are substantially divested of their domestic E&P interests, their incentive to spend money lobbying against E&P regulation may be proportionally reduced.

Independents must realize that the shift in focus for the majors and the divestiture of producing properties is more than just a response to cash flow in the traditional sense. They are dumping (or trying to dump) their exposure to environmental liability. Make no mistake about it, they want to distance themselves from liability associated with increased environmental awareness and regulation.

Environmental regulation of E&P is increasing, and independents will carry an increasing share of the cost of that regulation. It might be wise to review certain clauses of these purchase and sale (P&S) agreements that have been signed and see what the purchaser signed up for.

Likewise, the changes can be seen as a scale change. It seems that the companies who were, in the past, referred to as large independents will begin to be thought of as the new domestic "majors." Could it be that large independents will, in the future, replace the majors in the minds of regulatory agencies as the cash cows?

The industry is still encountering instability as it deals with seemingly constant changes occurring not just in price forecasts but in regulatory climate. New regulations are appearing almost monthly and, for those who operate in multiple states, the volume of change can result in crisis management and siege mentality. Is there a way to make the best of this situation? How does one take advantage of these changes and profit from them?

ORGANIZATIONAL STRATEGIES

In order to deal with the growing environmental requirements, companies, even independents, are developing strategies that are designed to cope. A relatively new creature has emerged from this flux. He is called the "Environmental Coordinator" or, sometimes, the "Environmental Manager." The idea here is to assign the entire growing body of environmental responsibility and centralize it within one internal sub-organization. There is a plethora of organizational charts that could be drawn to illustrate what various companies are doing to contain and manage the regulatory problem. However, there are a couple of key issues that must be considered in regard to these internal strategies.

First, it has been the author's observation that many of these internal organizations are like a Hollywood set. There is a good facade, but no substance. In order to function, the environmental organization *must* be empowered. Many oil company executives, frankly, resent having to deal with this issue and are paying it only lip service. Paper organizations with figureheads exist, but these organizations have little or no budget and no decision-making capability. In the author's line of work, these figurehead managers are referred to as "the Designated Prison Inmate."

In other cases, internal environmental organizations are set up (either unwittingly, through inexperience, or by design) with a built-in conflict of interest. For instance, it is not uncommon for the Environmental Manager (who functions by making gut-wrenching decisions that often involve loss of revenue and production shut-ins) to be reporting to the Production Manager (who gets his bonuses from the yearly production/revenue stream). A charitable man might attribute this to inexperience with a new aspect of the business. A less charitable man might…Well, let's just say he might see it somewhat differently.

This leads to another question that is bound to cause discomfort. How high up the management ladder does an environmental problem need to be communicated and how high (and low) does personal liability reach? The corporate veil is no longer an "iron curtain." Officers of some corporations have been prosecuted, and regulatory agencies can choose to try to pierce the corporate veil if they feel that their investigations warrant such an action. In addition to avoiding apparent conflicts of interest, this question should be considered in adopting an environmental strategy. A legal opinion may be necessary in order to get a picture of where case law has taken this issue.

Much though we would like to find ways to see "crisis as opportunity," environmental constraints are, for producers, mostly a drain and an impediment to cash flow. This will tempt many to be somewhat less than enthusiastic about establishing a viable environmental strategy. I have heard stories of environmental engineers and managers being asked to omit key data from reports. A conversation with one Environmental Coordinator indicated, to my surprise, item after item that was not being handled by his work process. Finally, upon being directly asked, "What exactly are you doing, then?" the employee replied, "I guess our management has made the decision to wait and get caught."

By no means are the negatives listed above implied to be universal throughout the industry. Most companies are making a legitimate effort to grapple with this very real problem. Highly restrictive environmental regulation is relatively new to the industry, and it comes at a bad time. The domestic oil industry has suffered setback after setback since 1986. Cash flow is a problem for most companies and it is being hit with demands for large environmental expenditure.

Not everyone can accommodate an internal staff to deal with the these issues. Some readers are small independents with small ways but potentially big liabilities. For you, the best recourse may be to establish a relationship with a good environmental attorney and have a close relationship with a consultant or consultants to help you deal with their problems. With "outsourcing," careful cost control can put the company ahead and still provide adequate coverage of the environmental issues. This is becoming more true as the cost and liability of having full-time employees skyrockets. This involves letting someone into your business, however, which can be uncomfortable for many businessmen. In the consulting business, character counts. You had better get an attorney and consultant who will tell you the truth and not what you want to hear. It is true that "In the multitude of counselors there is safety," but that statement assumes the reliability and character of the counselors.

AUDITING AS PART OF MANAGEMENT STRATEGY

Any management strategy for dealing with the environmental aspect of the E&P business must utilize an auditing program. There are two basic types of audits: Property Transfer and Compliance. A discussion of property transfer considerations follows, and a detailed consideration of them is included in a later chapter, but it is useful at this point to discuss compliance auditing. Compliance audits are designed to insure that current operations are within the boundaries of existing and pending regulations as well as designed to catalog existing problems. A good auditing program will allow the systematic and proactive development of a serial approach to dealing with known problems.

Many companies have taken the position that compliance auditing should be minimized with the reasoning that, "If we know about it we have to do something about it" (yes, and the author has heard lawyers say it, too). While there may be some justification for that way of thinking, it is not reliably true and, in the mid to long term, not knowing could result in fines, prosecution, and catastrophic cost.

The fact is that most companies are driven by fear, and no one wants to be the bearer of bad tidings. Managers tend to be told what their subordinates think they want to hear. It bears repeating that the very design of an organization can reinforce this atmosphere. Moreover, it sometimes happens that an employee rises though the ranks precisely because he is selfish and highly ambitious. Such an individual is apt to care more for his career than for the well-being of the company. He can, and does, hurt the company, but in the past those losses were somewhat hard to quantify. In the regulatory arena, there is potential for those losses to become highly quantifiable. This environmental and regulatory battlefield will test the corporate character and the character of individual employees to the limits. Is your company up to the test?

In the case of companies that are in an acquisition mode, one way to control and limit environmental cramps is to avoid ingestion. Property transfer audits are an essential management method. Unbelievably, some are still purchasing properties without any appraisal of the associated environmental risks. However, most are beginning to spend some money on this aspect of acquisition.

What does an audit do for you? Well, in brief, if you are the purchaser, it makes you aware of the liability issues associated with the property and causes you to make a better informed decision. Likewise, it should, if properly heeded and executed, allow the purchaser to avail himself of the Comprehensive Environmental Response, Compensation, and Liability Act's (CERCLA) "Innocent Purchaser Defense." Third, it documents the baseline condition of the property at the time of sale, which can answer questions that may arise down the road. Finally, it can and should be used as a negotiation tool.

If you are the seller, it is equally important that you have a baseline documentation of the condition of the property at the time of sale. If you took care of your field, the day may come when you will have to prove it. Likewise, litigation case law indicates that the trend is more and more toward full disclosure.

It will be rare indeed to find a mature producing property with no associated environmental liabilities. The question is, "How much? and what is the associated financial exposure?" I contend that any evaluation of the economics of a property that does not include the environmental liability (on a risked basis) is not valid. Real property transfers have for quite some time involved environmental audits as a matter of requirement (by lenders). As incredible as it may seem, however, the same lenders have been loathe to require audits for oil and gas properties. That is a result of brinkmanship.

Bankers have long been aware that they were blindly lending their depositors money on investments that could be potential disasters, but no one wanted to be the first to begin requiring audits. Why? Because they are in the business of making money by lending it, and the fear has been that, "If our bank begins to require this first, then potential customers will go to another bank where getting the loan will be easier." Even in the lending arena things are changing, though. Lender liability laws plus the repossession of some known environmental liabilities have caused the lending community to sit up and take notice.

A phenomenon that I have found disturbing, to say the least, is that many P&S agreements are being written and signed that make the purchaser responsible and liable for everything including, possibly, the Chicago Fire. On the surface these P&S agreements appear to allow for price adjustments or withdrawal based upon environmental problems. What they in fact prove to be is an "as-is-where-is" contract. Purchasers are being told that they must not only accept the property as is with all attendant liability, but must *indemnify* the seller for all past environmental problems and practices. This seems hardly rational and amounts to the seller saying that he has a moral right to hold a purchaser as a human shield. Incredibly, these contracts are still being signed, although more and more companies are proving to be willing to walk away from those kinds of deals.

Elimination of liability is probably a forlorn hope on the part of these sellers, anyway. Regulatory agencies are as apt to make the decision to go back in the chain of title as they are to go after the current owner. It is my opinion that many of these small purchasers will simply default on their agreement to spend their resources defending the seller anyway, because they just do not have that kind of money. It is a fact that one simply cannot contractually eliminate environmental liability. One major oil company I know of appears to be committed to cleaning up its messes before the property leaves its hands. This appears to be the wiser course of action to insure that the liability does not return like a boomerang.

LOSS OF STATUS

Another change has occurred that is less perceptible but very real. Oil has lost some of its prestige in oil producing states. As the industry has declined, it has become less and less significant as a revenue source both to government and the private sector. As result, the power of the regulatory agencies that had stewardship over the E&P world has declined somewhat in respect to other state regulatory agencies. Frankly, the decline of these state agencies will probably mean more stringent regulation of E&P. Those who have been in the industry for a long time will understand what I mean.

An agency that regulates an industry ultimately draws its life from that industry. Therefore, an affinity develops for the industry in question (sort of like the Stockholm syndrome involving hostages and their captors). When, in the process of turf wars between regulatory agencies, that first agency loses ground, other agencies that have no such affinity impinge on the hapless industry. The author believes that the Oil and Gas E&P industry can look for more scrutiny from state and federal agencies that have heretofore had little impact on E&P.

Likewise, one representative of a private business with which I have dealt said, "Used to, when people came in and said, 'We've got oil business for you,' everyone jumped. Now we say, 'Who cares?'" The oil industry once was the proverbial 800-lb gorilla. Now it has taken in its waistband considerably. This will take some real getting used to, having to be just another industry in places where one used to be king.

CLEANUP FUNDS

Another relatively new development in the regulatory arena is the establishment of oil field cleanup funds. Since 1986, abandoned sites and associated complaints have become common. In response to the situation, legislatures and regulatory agencies in some oil producing states are creating funds from which mony can be disbursed to remediate orphaned sites.

In 1991, the Texas Legislature passed Senate Bill 1103, which established a $10 million fund for oil field cleanup. Originally, it was aimed at plugging abandoned, orphaned wells, but it has since been expanded to encompass comprehensive cleanup efforts. Under the Texas Natural Resources Code §§91, the cleanup fund is supported entirely by fees, penalties, and reimbursements collected from the oil and gas industry.

Lest someone think that this gets him off the hook for cleanup, it should be understood that the first procedure (before fund money is used to begin remediation) is to attempt to locate and cause the operator to clean up his mess. It should be noted that everyone legally operating in the industry is paying for this cleanup effort.

Since Texas Senate Bill 1103, the state of Louisiana has followed suit by passing the "Louisiana Oilfield Site Restoration Law Act 404." Under this act, a trust fund has been established that is funded primarily by fees and assessments against E&P operations. Once again, everyone legally operating in Louisiana is paying for this cleanup effort, whether they have contaminated or not.

OBO: TERROR IN THE ECONOMY BIN

At least a word should be said about the status of non-operated working interest positions. In the past, many larger companies would seek out smaller companies to actually operate in the drilling and production phase. The reason for this is easily understood in economic terms. Smaller companies can operate at far lower overhead expense ratios and thus increase the profit margin on the field. However, the same qualities that allowed them to operate more inexpensively also meant that they were more apt to cut corners or lack the resources to deal with environmental issues.

The fact is that no one in the larger companies has been monitoring these kinds of operations from an environmental standpoint. It simply was not part of the day to day surveillance activities of large companies, so it fell into the crack. Chickens are starting to come home to roost in the Operated By Others (OBO) realm. There have been some notable nasty surprises. This will increase.

In the new industry, the ability to operate inexpensively can no longer be the sole consideration in choosing a partner in a Joint Operating Area JOA or in development and production of a field. What you do not know can cost you big bucks. Partners must be carefully selected with their environmental track record in view. Owning 70% of a mess (of which you know little or nothing) is a ticking time bomb. It is best to avoid these situations through foresight, but, since the industry is in transition, many such established relationships already exist. In such established cases, it would be advisable to investigate the environmental conditions of those properties and establish ongoing surveillance.

To accentuate the positive, it is not all gloom. There are also desires on the part of some elements within oil producing states to resuscitate the industry from its deep, prolonged malaise, and tax abatements have been used. In Texas, tax abatements have been used to encourage independents to reenter old wellbores and recommence production. Oklahoma has recently weighed in with similar legislation.

SUMMARY

The U.S. oil business has changed. The new giant domestic fields will be few and far between. The regulatory environment will probably continue to become more restrictive. Environmental lawsuits and surface landowner scrutiny will inevitably increase as royalty payments decrease. If internal staffing and coordination are the route you choose to go in order to manage the environmental issues, then here are some recommendations:

- Avoid organizational structuring that gives even the appearance of conflict of interest.

- Adopt commitment to doing the right thing from the top down. This does not mean capitulation to every regulatory demand. Many environmental situations are stupid and counterproductive, but where the law is clear, subordinates must be convinced that the upper management is dead set on taking the high road.

- Character matters. Motive is everything. Place people in the key positions who will do what is right for the right reason.
- Empower your environmental people to act. They need a budget and signature authority.

If you are not interested in internal staffing to manage the problem, the following recommendations are made:

- Get a good environmental attorney and consultant (or consultants) and invest time in developing a team relationship between them that will cause things to flow smoothly and mesh with your work process. Ditto on the character and motive comment above.
- Do not just bring them in to put out brush fires, but let them help you plan your business.
- Make time to listen to them.

Feeling Blue About Greenpeace? **2**

WHERE WE ARE AND HOW WE GOT HERE

Environmental work is the complete and utter triumph of acronyms over common sense. Finding one's way through the bewildering array of regulatory agencies and abbreviations requires a calm head and a *Concise Lexicon of EnviroSpeak – English: English – EnviroSpeak*. It is annoying to have to deal with this cryptic language, but the truth is that the environmental industry sprang from the loins of a bulging federal bureaucracy, so why expect otherwise?

The entire industry came into existence by Congressional fiat. Certainly, Congress did not pass a law that said "There shall be an environmental industry," but they might as well have. While looking into routes to becoming an environmental consultant to the oil industry, I approached several large environmental consulting firms with the idea. In every case, their response was the same. "Are there new regulations to force the oil industry to clean up?" they would ask. The person who asked the question was frequently an ex-government bureaucrat who had left government to cash in on the opportunity provided by the new environmental regulations. In many cases, my perception was that their leaving government was the closest these people had ever come to actual capitalism.

Well, OK, so we have environmental regulation that has spawned an entire sub-culture whose language apparently consists solely of acronyms. "RI/FS, CERCLA AMFA ECRA, but, on the other hand, MMPA VOC UST?" What's that? You didn't understand that? Well then, can you conjugate the verb "to RCRA?" Pretty poor performance. You must not be as interested as we are in saving the planet! And so it goes...

How did this madness start? Honestly, there was some (I say *some*) legitimate concern in the beginning of the environmental movement, because pollution was, in fact, occurring. Some legitimate concern is still warranted. No right thinking person enjoys the thought of natural beauty being despoiled and human health being threatened.

Organizations began to be formed in the 1960s and 1970s for the purpose of "saving the earth," many of which were lunatic in nature. Their ranks were bolstered by upper middle-class rich kids needing a cause, 60s radicals looking for a place to employ their agitation skills, pantheists, socialist utopians, etc., and a movement was well under way. Essentially, these people were and are attempting to forge a world in which they would be unable to live, but reason does not enter into this debate very often. Very little of the "save the earth" crowd's strident platform has any basis in science or even reality. The logging industry is decimated and building material prices have reached astronomical proportions because of these people's ornithological fantasies. Our federal government is being pressured to ratify international treaties and laws based upon "global warming," for which there is no conclusive proof. Actually, in some scientific circles, it is argued that there is no proof at all. The fact is though, that between their lobbying, some outright ecoterrorism, and the willing complicity of a media culture that subscribes to the component philosophies of the movement, they have brought about societal and legislative action.

The oil industry, by contrast, has not been terribly successful in selling its position. Nevertheless, the regulatory climate for E&P could be a lot worse (no kidding). E&P has been spared having to comply with some regulation which virtually every other industry has had to learn to cope with. Additionally, state regulators in most oil producing states are still relatively sympathetic to the oil industry. So, let's dry up that whining, pluck up our courage, and manfully explore this world of regulations, regulators, terms, acronyms, and abbreviations. Let's look into what they mean to you, the producer, and get a feel for how this system works. The statement that "knowledge is power" is true, even if it was said by a white Eurocentric male. If these regulations cannot be made to work for you, then, at the very least, you need to know a little bit about them in order to minimize the potential for their deleterious effect on your business. Despite what some may say, investing money in environmental expenditure and abiding by the regulations will probably not boost your cash flow. Frankly, the main focus here is to avoid massive financial hemorrhage as result of failure to play the game well. There is little high side to playing the game well, but a great deal of potential laced to playing it poorly.

ENVIRONMENTAL REGULATION

Federal environmental regulations are created under the auspices of acts of Congress. When, through whatever avenue, legislation is introduced and passed by Congress, responsibility for implementation of that body of law is assigned to a federal agency, usually the EPA. That agency then studies the issue and finalizes the regulations that will be used to define compliance with the new law. The study period can be lengthy, but when the regulations are put in place, they will be published in the Code of Federal Regulations (CFR).

Some of the new regulations will be enforced and stewarded directly by the EPA. If a state has, through the benevolence of the federal government, retained primacy, it will administer the regulation of the law with the stipulation that the state regulations must be *at least* as stringent as those of the EPA. In this way, it all sort of comes rolling "downhill" and lands on you.

Most of the regulatory interaction in the oil patch occurs between the industry and the oil producing states. Regulation is not new to the oil industry. Situations like reservoir damage stemming from overproduction caused by unchecked drilling at Spindletop field gave rise to regulation in the form of drilling and proration units, allowables, and the like by states anxious to protect their resources (and their tax base). The Texas Railroad Commission, the Oklahoma Corporation Commission, and the Louisiana Office of Conservation, as well as others, have been on the scene for quite some time. What has changed is the ascendancy of supreme federalism and the rise to power of the EPA. These older state organizations are now largely reduced to the mediumistic practice of "channeling" the EPA. You probably won't find open mirth in the halls of these institutions over the situation, either. It is being foisted upon them just as it is on you. The Feds build the stagecoach and then hitch the state agencies to it and drive it (with a whip, if necessary).

For background, we will go over some of the pertinent federal acts that have produced environmental regulation that affects the E&P world. The listing here is not intended to be exhaustive, but to show you the source of some of the regulation with which you have to deal.

CLEAN WATER ACT (CWA)

This act, administered by the EPA, is intended to regulate the discharge of hazardous pollutants into the nation's *surface* waters. The CWA is the authority under which the Spill Prevention Control and Countermeasure (SPCC) Plans are administered. Additionally, the National Pollutant Discharge Elimination System (NPDES) is authorized under the CWA. It is important to understand that the CWA does not recognize the oil industry's RCRA exemption

SPCC PLANS. Since the CWA prohibits the discharge of oil in harmful quantities upon or into the navigable waters of the United States, all non-transportation related onshore and offshore facilities that deal with production of or drilling for oil, gathering, storing, refining, transferring, distributing, or consuming oil and/or oil products must have an SPCC plan. There are specific exemptions. A facility whose geographic location makes discharge into navigable federal waters unlikely would be exempt. Likewise, facilities with minimal storage capacity would be exempt. Underground storage tanks of less than 42,000 gal. would be exempt as well as aboveground storage tanks with capacities of less than 1,320 gal. (provided that no individual tank on the site has greater than 660 gal. capacity).Copies of this plan must be kept available for inspection. They need not be prepared by an engineer, but they must be certified by a Professional Engineer. Within the last year or so, the EPA has retained a private consulting firm to make surprise inspections (sometimes by helicopter) to check SPCC plans.

NPDES PERMITS. Under the CWA, the only way someone can legally discharge pollutants into the waters of the U.S. from any point source is to have an NPDES permit. Production discharge pits are permitted under this regulation. Over the past several years, the state of Louisiana has been particularly aggressive in closing production pits. Operators are having to convert to salt water injection wellse as their permits expire. This program is sometimes administered by the relevant state agency such as the Oklahoma Corporation Commission (OCC) or the Louisiana Department of Natural Resources (LDNR).

CLEAN AIR ACT (CAA)

Administered by the EPA and intended to regulate the emission of hazardous air contaminants the original act was passed in 1970, but the more recent development is the passage of the Clean Air Act Amendments of 1990. Oil producing states had to scramble to get their regulations in line by the deadline in order to maintain primacy. The amendments contain seven titles that deal with various regulatory programs. Estimates of compliance cost (nationwide) run as high as $25 billion/yr. These amendments greatly expand the EPA's authority. Clean Air Act Amendments include a number of titles that cover subjects such as Non-attainment Areas, Mobile Sources and Clean Fuels, Air Toxics, Acid Rain, Chlorofluorocarbons, Permits, and Enforcement. At this time, much attention is focused on Title V (Permit Program), which is modeled after the NPDES permit.

RESOURCE CONSERVATION AND RECOVERY ACT (RCRA)

RCRA was enacted by Congress in 1976 to regulate the generation, storage, transportation, treatment, and disposal of hazardous waste. It was amended in 1980 and in 1984. One hears much about RCRA in the oil patch along with reference to the Oil & Gas Exploration and Production Exemption. This bears some further discussion as some in the industry are making more of this exemption than perhaps they should. Others are simply bewildered by it.

At issue are the different regulatory requirements imposed on substances regulated under RCRA Subtitle C, which is a comprehensive (and fairly complicated) program that mandates "cradle to grave" management of hazardous wastes. "Cradle to grave" refers to managing the waste (considered by the EPA as being owned by the generator) from generation to disposal. Under RCRA C, many wastes are "listed" wastes and are presumed to be hazardous by virtue of the fact that they are listed. Listed wastes are divided into these categories:

- Source-Specific Wastes, which include industry specific wastes, such as refining wastes.

- Generic Wastes, which are wastes from common industrial processes such as solvents that are not limited to one specific industry.

- Commercial Chemical Products, which include products that are manufactured and commercially marketed, such as creosote or certain pesticides.

In addition to listed wastes, a waste under RCRA C may be "characteristically hazardous." If a waste exhibits any of the four hazardous characteristics discussed in 40 CFR §261.20, it is considered hazardous for regulatory purposes. The four key characteristics are ignitability, corrosivity, reactivity, and toxicity.

Wastes that are not hazardous by any of these criteria are considered to be solid wastes and are regulated under a separate heading that is RCRA Subtitle D. This brings us to the oil field exemption, which is regulated under RCRA D. Thus far, the reader may be uncertain as to what difference that could make. We will explore the ramifications further, but the bottom line is money. If the industry were

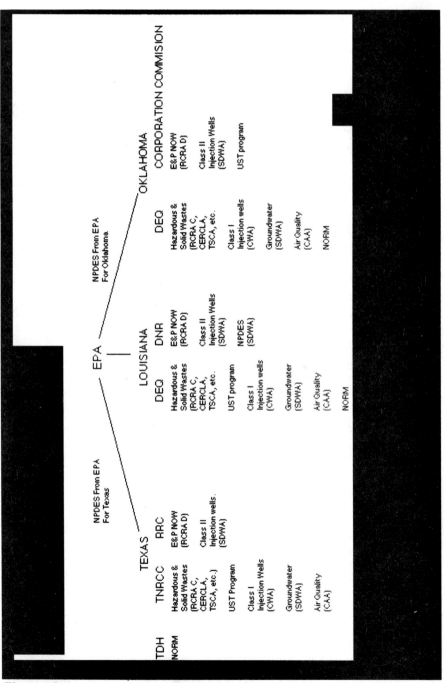

Figure 2-1
How key state regulatory agencies' programs relate to federal regulations.

regulated under Subtitle C, there would be wistful looks and dreamy eyes as wizened old men sat and played checkers and reminisced about the good old days when they were under RCRA D and their hearts were young and full of delight. These old men would be about, say...40 years of age, but really grey. They would be playing checkers because they wouldn't be in the oil business any more. Estimates of up front expenditure required of upstream oil and gas to get into compliance with RCRA C range from about $3 billion to $60 billion depending on how much of the exemption would be lost.[1] Gulp.

Briefly, the industry arrived at its present RCRA treatment in a series of steps. In 1980, when RCRA was amended for the first time, the new amendments exempted E&P wastes from the hazardous waste provisions of RCRA C and directed a study of the E&P wastes. The results of that study were brought before Congress in December 1987, and the regulatory determination was made public on June 30, 1988. Comments pertaining to the regulatory determination were published in the *Federal Register* on July 6, 1988. Those comments in the *Federal Register* clarified the EPA's position that several E&P wastes were exempt from RCRA C and that other oil field wastes were not included in the intent of the 1980 amendment.

In a nutshell, the criteria that decided whether or not a waste should be regulated under RCRA C as a hazardous waste was whether or not the waste was "tied to the wellhead." In other words, certain wastes such as produced salt water and oil were intrinsic to the E&P process and as such were to be regulated as Non-hazardous Oil Field Waste (NOW). On the contrary, there are a number of substances in use in the oil field operation that are generic in the sense that they have a wider application. Therefore, wastes such as painting wastes, waste solvents, pesticide wastes, etc. are not exempt.

As it currently stands, a waste generated in an oil field upstream of the downstream end of the gathering system that is intrinsically derived from the production of oil and gas is exempt from regulation under RCRA C. With oil, the exemption carries through the end of the primary separation process. In the case of gas, the exemption is extended to the downstream end of the gas plant.

EXEMPTION IS NOT ABSOLUTION

So far, so good. What you have heard so far, you could have heard elsewhere. It is what follows that is less understood and more sobering. Perhaps a personal vignette would be in order to set the stage for the following discussion. Upon finding severe soil contamination with oil and brine, I reported the results. A company representative said, "There's nothing that says we have to clean that up. We have an exemption!" You see, in his mind, the RCRA exemption grants total absolution. The fact that the regulatory agency in his state with whom he was most accustomed to interacting had fuzzy regulations on that precise subject allowed him to adjust his thinking to live only in the world of RCRA.

If one carefully reviews the purpose of RCRA, he will find that it is designed to deal with generation, storage, transportation, disposal, recordkeeping, etc. In the strict sense of the interpretation, it does not necessarily exempt the operator from cleanup in the case of a spill. In other words, as long as that sludge is in the bottom of the tank, it is NOW. If that NOW is spilled, the world becomes a good deal less certain. In fact, in EPA's discussion of its regulatory determination found in the July 6, 1988 *Federal Register*, the agency mentions the Safe Drinking Water Act (SDWA). The implication is that the potential gaps left in the regulatory control of the situation through exempting E&P waste are filled by other bodies of regulation such as CWA, SDWA, and CERCLA.

When the waste goes on the ground it is now viewed as a contamination incident. If it is affecting groundwater, your waste has now run afoul of the SDWA. If it is in a place where it can eventually contaminate navigable federal waters, your waste is a CWA issue.

Let's walk through a scenario using CERCLA as an example. A large spill of a mixture of exempt waste occurs and there are no clear state regulations as to cleanup requirements under the auspices of RCRA D. EPA originally held the position that oil field waste is exempt from CERCLA liability. However, a legal memorandum, dated March 19, 1992, was issued in which the EPA took the position that the 42 USC §9601 does not necessarily render a RCRA D substance exempt from CERCLA liability. It may be considered a "hazardous substance," which is an extremely broad term with no prescribed thresholds – much broader than "hazardous waste." CERCLA's clear and present danger language can be invoked and, *voila*! You have CERCLA liability. True, CERCLA does have an exemption for "petroleum or any fraction thereof," but in the scenario above a mixture of exempt wastes was spilled. Brine may not be exempt in every given case,, although a recent court case, Jastram vs. Phillips Petroleum, 1994, found that brine is not subject to CERCLA liability as a hazardous substance. CERCLA's "mixture rule," however, declares that if a non-hazardous waste stream is mixed with a hazardous waste stream, the entire waste stream becomes hazardous.

Bottom line? RCRA D status is not absolution. A similar scenario to the above could be constructed for CWA or SDWA or even other regulatory bodies. There will be those who will declare the above discussion to be a non-real world scenario. So, consider this: while other state regulatory agencies, such as the Louisiana DNR and the Texas RRC, are going about the business of developing and implementing regulations based on the RCRA exemption, other agencies are moving to take the logic of the above scenario in their enforcement policies. Louisiana's Department of Environmental Quality (DEQ) has, within its laws that create liability for hazardous "substance" remedial action, very broad authority to order cleanups. Currently, the Louisiana DEQ regulations focus not on TCLP as an indicator but upon the concept of a "hazardous threat to the environment, human health, and/or property." This is real world, and regulatory actions are proceeding right now that embody this broad authority concept. The author just recently did an audit of a property wherein the regulatory search turned up a nearby production pit in the Comprehensive Environmental Response, Compensation, and Liability Information System (CERCLIS) files.

All of this is a long way of saying, "be careful." Environmental regulations are plentiful, and your perspective must be circumspect. Tunnel vision can get you blindsided.

In a continuing development, groundwater contaminant action levels were proposed in the July 1990 Federal Register as Subpart S (40 CFR 264-265) and were supposed to be finalized in December 1993. These action levels were derived from Maximum Contaminant Levels (MCL) regulated under SDWA and are intended to address groundwater monitoring concerns at RCRA Treatment Storage and Disposal Facilities. At the time of this writing, only a small portion of Subpart S has become final, and the action levels were not part of the finalized portion. However, individual states have latitude within their hazardous waste programs to utilize Subpart S levels even though they have not become final. The author has been informed by regulators in one oil producing state that they would probably consider Subpart S action levels in their enforcement.

While the industry RCRA C exemption has created a cost benefit, it also has created, or at least perpetuated, a confusion of regulatory agencies. Since E&P companies have to deal with both exempt and non-exempt waste, they are in the position of having to deal with multiple regulatory agencies. One-stop shopping for regulation is not the norm in the oil patch. This RCRA dichotomy can be confusing. In Texas, for instance, NOW issues are under RRC authority. Hazardous and solid waste issues, on the other hand, are handled by the Texas Natural Resource Conservation Commission (TNRCC). In Oklahoma, the Corporation Commission handles most E&P functions, but hazardous waste is the domain of the DEQ, which is under the Department of Health.

This is common in the larger oil producing states where one agency establishes its program under the auspices of RCRA D, while another marches under the banner of RCRA C. There is inevitable overlap between these agencies and frequent "turf wars." Where no clear memorandum of understanding exists between agencies, the operator can be caught in difficult and frustrating situations.

SAFE DRINKING WATER ACT (SDWA)

The SDWA was passed in 1974 with the intent of regulating contaminant levels in drinking water. Approximately one half of the population of the United States gets its drinking water from groundwater and half from other sources, so there is some overlap between this and the CWA. In any event, groundwater ultimately discharges into waters that can impact federal waters.

Part C of the SDWA specifically requires the EPA to ensure protection of the nation's *underground* water resources. MCLs have been established for particular substances in drinking water, and those levels can be found in 40 CFR 141. Standards for contaminant levels for other substances are under study. Federal mandates are providing impetus for individual states to further develop their own programs.

Most oil producing states *are* moving to further establish their groundwater protection program. The Louisiana DEQ Groundwater Protection Division has broad authority under LAC 33:I.3919 to order remedial action and has been active in doing so.

One program of SDWA that relates strongly to E&P is the Underground Injection Control (UIC) Program. Within the UIC Program, a special classification was developed for wells that inject oil field related fluids. Such wells are categorized as Class II injection wells. In most, if not all major oil producing states that have retained primacy over UIC, the agency that handles NOW issues will have jurisdiction of the Class II UIC program. In Louisiana, for instance, the DNR will control the Class II well permitting and testing. The parallel organization in Oklahoma is the Pollution Abatement Division of the Corporation Commission. A 1987 Memorandum of Understanding assigned Class II jurisdiction within the State of Texas to the RRC. Federal regulations that pertain to the UIC program are in 40 CFR 147. There are some key issues involved in the Class II requirements. Those issues include:

- A restriction of injected waste. Only exempt waste may be injected. Therefore, the injection of solvents (as an example) would not be permitted.
- A prohibition against a Class II well endangering underground drinking water sources.
- A permitting requirement for wells not otherwise permitted by rule.
- Periodic testing. States must require periodic mechanical integrity tests (MIT) or tracer surveys.

Groundwater issues are, as with RCRA, an area of regulatory agency jurisdiction that can confuse operators. In Oklahoma, for instance, operators will be most familiar with the Corporation Commission, Oil and Gas Conservation Division, but groundwater issues will mainly be under the stewardship of the Health Department's Department of Environmental Quality (DEQ). In Texas, RRC has oversight of the Exploration and Production issues, but the TNRCC handles groundwater contamination issues.

The important thing to see is that these federally mandated programs become the wind in the sails of the "ship of state" for individual states . If appropriate state agencies do not already exist to carry out these federal mandates, they must be created. In other cases, existing agencies must be expanded or organized to carry out their new mission.

COMPREHENSIVE ENVIRONMENTAL RESPONSE, COMPENSATION AND LIABILITY ACT CERCLA)

CERCLA is commonly known as "Superfund." Just being able to quote the full text of this acronym may qualify one as an environmental professional. CERCLA became law in 1980 and originally was intended (in some minds) to provide for the cleanup of *inactive and abandoned* hazardous waste sites. Just as a tale grows in the telling, government programs tend to grow with time. What in fact happened is that the program has become established with a mission to identify sites on or from which hazardous waste releases have occurred and to insure that the responsible parties (RPs) or the taxpayer or both remediate the problem.

This body of regulation has, in the past, been less troublesome for the oil patch and is nightmarishly complex. Consequently, it has not received the attention that has been afforded RCRA. That will probably change. CERCLA will begin, increasingly, to affect and play a role in the world of E&P as the industry continues to deteriorate and additional problems are found in and around abandoned fields. Additionally, as already discussed under the RCRA heading, there are cases where agencies might use certain provisions of CERCLA to enforce cleanups at oil field sites.

As mandated under CERCLA, the EPA has a review process by which potential Superfund sites are evaluated and ranked. Sites that have been identified and are under evaluation are placed in a site listing called CERCLIS. During the evaluation, the goal is to place the site in a priority ranking for site remediation needs. There are three main aspects of this decision making process that are considered:

- The sites are evaluated using the "Hazard Ranking System."
- The sites are evaluated in light of the individual state's priority assessment of the site.
- An evaluation is made of the degree to which the site constitutes a significant threat to the human health, human welfare, and/or the environment.

Once a regulatory determination is made, the worst sites are assigned to the National Priorities Listing (NPL), which is like an environmental version of 'America's Most Wanted.' Next begins some really serious expenditure of tax money and things get exciting. The EPA's first resort is to locate Potentially Responsible Parties (PRPs). Once named, all the parties begin suing each other and frantically pointing the finger in other directions. If there is any money left after the lawsuits that the lawyers have not gotten, it will be confiscated by the EPA for cleanup. It is unlikely that there will be any money left after the lawyers, so the EPA next turns to tax money which has already been (wisely, with much forethought) confiscated from private citizens by the federal government. It is elegant, really.

OK, forget what I just said. Why dwell on reality when we can meditate on the way things are *supposed* to work in the program? Here is how it is supposed to work: After the PRPs are identified, the burden of proof is on them to prove that they did *not* contribute to the site. If you are identified, you will be spending money. This has happened. Individuals and companies have been identified as PRPs simply on the basis of having a business association with the property. Under CERCLA, the EPA has very broad authority to act and recover costs for cleanup. Only sites on the NPL are eligible for Superfund-financed remediation, but the EPA can choose to clean up the site using public funds and then sue the RP or RPs to recover the cost. Also, it can order PRPs to clean up the site. CERCLA does allow PRPs who were drawn into the cost of site remediation to sue other PRPs who did not participate. Here is a scary thought: one single PRP may be held responsible and forced to cough up even if his contribution to the whole problem was very small.

What materials are regulated under CERCLA? There is insufficient room in this work to detail that answer, but the answer is very broad. Unlike RCRA, which specifies the term "hazardous waste" and has defined regulatory threshold levels, CERCLA has been used in a different way. The term "hazardous substances" identified in CERCLA has a broader definition and may not in all cases require any threshold concentration in order to trigger remediation liability. In CERCLA, hazardous substance definition includes any substance listed under the CWA, Toxic Substances Control Act (TSCA), RCRA, etc. More than 700 substances are listed under CERCLA. There is a specific exemption for petroleum (including natural gas liquids and liquefied natural gas). However, be warned that wastes that are specifically exempt from RCRA C hazardous waste classification, may constitute a hazardous substance under CERCLA.

CERCLA's "mixture rule" is important to understand. Dilution of hazardous waste is not an acceptable practice, and if hazardous waste is introduced into a NOW waste stream, the entire mixture can be considered to be hazardous. There is good reason to manage wastes so as to avoid this possibility (Photo 2-1).

Likewise, CERCLA's "Innocent Landowner Provision" is worth reviewing. As things stand, the EPA can list individuals and companies as PRPs even on circumstantial evidence. What if you buy a property that becomes included in a Superfund site, you did not even own the property when the contamination occurred, and yet find yourself named a PRP (maybe the only one). The answer is, "Tough luck...You should have looked before you leapt." Recognizing this possibility, the Innocent Landowner Defense has come into existence. In other words, if you bought the property after making "all appropriate inquiry," then you will be held harmless. The question is, "What constitutes 'all appropriate inquiry?'" There is further discussion of this in the chapter on audits, but generally the idea is that if something could have reasonably expected to have been found, it should have been found. You had better do that audit, but if you choose not to do so, the drill has been outlined for you above.

It was mentioned above that the EPA consults with the individual state in assessing potential NPL sites. Most oil producing states have programs, as a part of their overall hazardous and solid waste programs, that correspond with CERCLA.

SUPERFUND AMENDMENT AND REAUTHORIZATION ACT, TITLE III, EMERGENCY PLANNING AND COMMUNITY RIGHT-TO-KNOW ACT (SARA TITLE III OR EPCRA)

SARA Title III was passed in 1986 as an amendment to CERCLA and requires notification to state and local officials by owners/operators of facilities that store, use, and release hazardous and extremely hazardous chemicals. Regulatory thresholds are established for extremely hazardous substances that can be found in 40 CFR Part 355, Appendix A.

Fulfillment of the requirements under this act involves the notification of the proper authorities that certain chemicals are on site. Also, there are reporting requirements for releases and recordkeeping (inventory control) requirements.

Although E&P facilities were not originally included in Title III coverage, they were included in 1988. E&P sites, which are classified as Standard Industrial Classification (SIC) Code 13, are subject to three major requirement areas:

- They are subject to emergency planning/notification provisions. An owner/operator of a facility which has on site an extremely hazardous substance (EHS) in excess of the threshold planning quantity (TPQ) must submit a written notice to the State Emergency Response Commission (SERC) and the Local Emergency Planning Commission (LEPC). Spill reporting is also required under this portion of Title III.

- They must submit material safety data sheets (MSDS). The owner/operator must send a list of the hazardous chemicals (present in quantities of 10,000 lb or more) or the MSDSs for each of them to the LEPC and the local fire department that services the facility. The threshold quantity for EHSs is 500 lb or more.

- They must comply with emergency and hazardous chemical reporting requirements. As of March 1989, all oil and gas E&P facilities must submit an inventory of all chemicals that have been present on the site at levels above their TPQs during the pre-ceding year. These must be submitted to the SERC, LEPC, and the local fire department.

Other SIC Codes (20-39) that correspond to manufacturing must comply with the toxic chemical release reporting provisions of Title III, but E&P is not obligated to do so at this time. Failure to submit the appropriate information can result in stringent regulatory measures. Operators who violate reporting requirements can be fined as much as $10,000. Failure to submit the annual chemical inventory can result in fines as much as $25,000.

TOXIC SUBSTANCES CONTROL ACT (TSCA)

TSCA was enacted in 1976 to regulate the manufacture, use, and disposal of certain toxic chemical substances. Polychlorinated biphenyls (PCB) and asbestos are two materials that pertain to the oil patch and are regulated by TSCA; 40 CFR Parts 710 and 761 discuss the regulation of PCBs. As a part of the purpose noted above for TSCA, there are prescribed recordkeeping and labeling requirements stipulated.

Penalties for failure to comply with this act are draconian. Both civil and criminal penalties can be assessed for as much as $25,000/day. Compliance is advisable.

NATURALLY OCCURRING RADIOACTIVE MATERIA L (NORM)

NORM is a departure from the norm (pardon the pun) in terms of regulatory evolution. In most cases the driving force behind increased regulation has been federal mandates. In this case, however, the oil producing states seem to have jumped out ahead of the Feds. Right now, the EPA is scratching its collective head about NORM and the implications of it for its program, and it is difficult to tell what EPA's entry (if any) into these radium-infestedwaters will do to the regulatory outlook.

At the time of this writing, all the major oil producing states have NORM regulations in place. NORM is discussed more fully in its own chapter. The lack of a single motive force and unifying principle (i.e., the EPA) makes *detailed* discussion of the NORM regulations outside the scope of this book because they vary significantly from state to state. Suffice it to say that it can be an expensive problem to have.

SUMMARY

The preceding discussion is by no means exhaustive. There are other federal environmental regulations that could be discussed, but the intent here was to hit the major issues and to give the reader an idea of the scope of his regulatory problem. Likewise, it is important for the reader to understand the danger of tunnel vision. An environmental problem affects, in real terms, a natural system. The protection of this system has been approached piecemeal by the passage of Congressional acts and the development of corresponding regulations. RCRA attacks one portion of the problem from a specific angle. TSCA plugs another gap. CERCLA closes the back door. They are all designed to protect that integrated natural system, so they all dovetail...and there you are, neatly sewn up in the regulatory fabric. The point is that if you have a problem, there is probably by now a regulation that has you covered.

Just because there is an oil field RCRA exemption does not mean that you are totally immune to regulatory incursion into your business or even to hazardous waste regulation. Many are finding that out the hard way.

It is also important to glean that, while the driving force in regulation may be at the federal level, the actual regulation which you as an operator, producer, driller, lender, etc. will encounter, will be mostly at the state level. Most oil producing states have an agency that will deal specifically with Non-hazardous Oilfield Waste issues. Yet there are other agencies in those same states with very different regulatory goals and philosophies which will play a role in your business.

Figure 2-1 is a very generalized organizational chart to show an example of the relationship between regulatory domains and regulatory agencies. Texas, Oklahoma, and Louisiana are selected as an example of how it works. Other states may vary slightly in their breakouts of responsibility.

---

[1]Jody Perkins, Costs to the Petroleum Industry of Major New and Future Federal Government Environmental Regulations - Discussion Paper #070, (Washington, D.C., American Petroleum Institute, 1991).

Transfer Audits for 3
Producing Properties

Just about everybody would like to give away their liability and get paid a premium price to do it. A whole multitude of people would like carte blanche to operate poorly and shoddily, high-grade the property, and implicate someone else in the problem. It is a nasty world, despite what German philosophers of centuries past and modern day Pollyannas may assert. Rarely does the phrase "caveat emptor" have greater depth of significance than in the sale or purchase of an oil and gas field.

Many of these fields that are now on the sale block were in operation for decades before anyone gave much thought to environmental consideration. The activities in these fields have, by their very nature, been intrusive and environmentally risky.

Think about it for a moment. Holes have been drilled through the drinking water supply and hydrocarbons have been brought up the same (leaking?) annulus to the surface where they have been spilled. Salt water has been pumped into unlined pits only to seep back through the soil toward the fresh water aquifer. "Sins" have been committed, and they will be visited upon the buyer to the third and fourth position in the chain of title.

Perhaps, if no one was looking hard at the situation, the operator and working interest owners might go glibly on with their life, but that is no longer the case. People are looking. Attorneys have found (amazingly) that lawsuits can be profitable. Landowners do not want to get stuck with damaged property and environmental problems with which they will have to deal. Other landowners who are, shall we say, more "entrepreneurial," will see an opportunity to profit at your expense. If you are buying the property, you may very well be the last in the chain of title before the property goes back to the land or mineral owner. We will see in this section how that can have powerful implications for your profitability.

Regulators at the state level are getting increasing heat from the federal regulators, the effect of which is tending to tighten enforcement. They also are looking over your shoulder, and environmental regulation will continue to grow as a factor in the oil industry. Should you doubt the veracity of this, I fear that reading this book will be of little value to you and that you might more profitably spend your time talking to your attorney.

Now, let's imagine this scenario: You sold Gusher field to Grunge Oil Inc. You were pretty proud of it and felt that you kept it neat and tidy. Time passes. (In the movies you would now be seeing the hands on the clock going 'round and 'round and pages falling from the calender.)

Just as the leaves are turning, the air is becoming crisp, and you are thinking about that little 16 gauge automatic you've been seeing at the sporting goods store, someone knocks at your door. It is your friendly local regulator who informs you that a complaint and a lawsuit has been filed over a contamination incident on Gusher field. Farmer Bob's prize Holsteins are burping condensate. He has grisly pictures of cows with brown, oily mustaches. "All very interesting," you say. "But what has this to do with me?" you ask in charming innocence. It appears that Grunge is claiming that you share responsibility. Can you prove that you do not? Hmmmm?

Let's not forget the banking industry. Mr. Otto Lookcloser extended $3 million to Grunge to buy the field. It turns out that the groundwater remediation is going to cost $3.76 million. Grunge is going to have to default. Mr. Lookcloser now has three options. He can write it off and watch $3 million of his depositors' funds swirl down the toilet bowl. Or he can foreclose and become the owner of an identified environmental nightmare. On the other hand, he can jump in and try to bail out Grunge in the forlorn hope of somehow recouping the loss.

All the above is intended to set the stage for the following discussion of transfer auditing. You had better be thorough. Your due diligence had better be diligent. Without the environmental factor worked in, you have no idea of the value of the property. Your defense is impaired in future liability collisions unless you have a "snapshot in time" or, in other words, documentation of the environmental condition of the property at the time of transfer.

AUDIT PURPOSE

The operative phrase here is "snapshot in time." An audit, properly done, is intended to identify your environmental liability and help you better assess the real value of the asset being purchased (or sold). A property transfer audit is a tool for negotiation, an insurance policy, and an advance preparation of the technical aspect of your legal case. In addition, it is intended to help the buyer qualify under the "innocent purchaser" provision of CERCLA.

In commercial real estate transactions, audits are routine and required by lenders. This will probably become the rule in the oil field ere much time passes. A general rule of thumb would be that a commercial real estate audit would cost 3-5% of the purchase price. Everyone is unhappy about paying this amount but should consider ways to creatively handle the expenditure. *It will become a routine part of the cost of doing business.*

WHAT IS PHASE ONE?

It is important to remember that there is, as yet, no legal definition of what constitutes a Phase One audit even though certain voluntary standards are now being adopted. Like beauty, the definition lies in the eyes (and mind) of the beholder. Therefore, it is important to have an understanding of the issues that routinely need to be addressed in an oil and gas audit and the issues that may arise under special circumstances. These issues will be discussed in the next chapter.

Even now, many people are still confused about some of the jargon related to environmental work. For instance, there is a vast difference between an environmental audit and an environmental impact statement, yet many are not aware of the fact. An environmental audit describes the condition of a property and problems, either historic or current that might be associated with it. An impact statement deals with how a proposed activity may affect the environmental condition of a property. These two items are tangentially related at best, yet they continue to be confused.

Generally speaking, a phase one audit will not involve intrusive activity such as drilling, boring, or sampling. It will be more involved with file searches, visual inspection and documentation. The logic (there apparently is some) is that a first phase of investigation should be done and distilled. This first phase should then guide in the implementation of the second phase. Through looking at the history and current condition of the property, one can get a better idea whether (or not) to place and where to place sampling locations and monitoring wells.

PHASE TWO

After the more qualitative analysis of the first phase, samples of the soil, water, and possibly even air are needed to further quantify contamination types and levels. Frankly, two phases of soil sampling are frequently going to be needed. The first phase should be a protocol that "casts a wide net." Its purpose is to identify the *types* of contamination present. A second phase might then be needed in order to assess the *level and extent* of contamination by those materials identified in the first sampling. Like the elements of an audit, sampling will be discussed in its own chapter. To quantitatively determine remedial necessity and design, it is simply not enough to have a sample that indicates chromium contamination, you must know how much and how deep and how extensive. This third level of investigation is rarely practicable in a property transfer of an oil field, however, and estimates and decisions will usually be predicated upon methodologies other than a detailed sampling grid.

EXAMPLE A: PHASE ONE AUDIT

Let us create an imaginary example that will illustrate Phase One and Phase Two and how to approach an environmental audit in an orderly and timely fashion. We will look at a scenario that is not uncommon. "Little Nell Oil" has signed a purchase agreement to buy a production well and tank battery from "Snidely Whiplash and Associates." It is decided that the property must be investigated environmentally as part of the due diligence process. A Phase One audit is ordered. The following is an excerpt from that report. Some of the terms in this example will not be recognizable to the uninitiated, but are explained in the appropriate chapters of this book.

SITE #2
WHIPLASH GRIMES 'A' TANK BATTERY
SITE DESCRIPTION
EQUIPMENT

The tank battery at this location is consists of two heater treaters (one out of service), a boot tank, and two 500 bbl oil storage tanks. A large oil stain on the south side of the boot tank indicates that the tank has overflowed. A flange on the active heater was leaking brine. No identification signs were displayed at the site.

SOIL CONTAMINATION

An accumulation of standing water (probably produced brine) and free oil (about 35° gravity API) was observed in the south and southwest portion of the site inside the firewall (Figure 3-1).

The soil in the area of the battery appears to be a very sandy soil and probably exhibits a low Cation Exchange Capacity (CEC). Ground vegetation looks normal around the facility. Down gradient, southwest of the tank battery, however, there are trees that are turning brown.

Top of the fresh water is reported at about 100 ft in this area. Perched aquifers are common.

PROBLEM ANALYSIS

There appears to have been a problem with the salt water disposal system for the lease which has resulted in a spill of brine and hydrocarbons onto the soil inside the firewall. There may be linkage between the brown and discolored trees and the leaked brine and oil. This facility may be acting as a point source for a contamination front.

RECOMMENDATIONS

1.   Sample soil down gradient from the tank battery for CEC, SAR, ESP, EC, TPH, TOC, and Cl.

2.   Sample soil upgradient from the facility to establish background conditions.

It is normally the practice to provide photographic documentation of the condition of the site, which has not been provided here, since the problem is hypothetical. There would, of course, be further documentation to support the assessment of the baseline condition and history of the site, but the above example will suffice for our purpose at hand.

We will continue with our investigation of the site in Example B, the Phase Two audit.

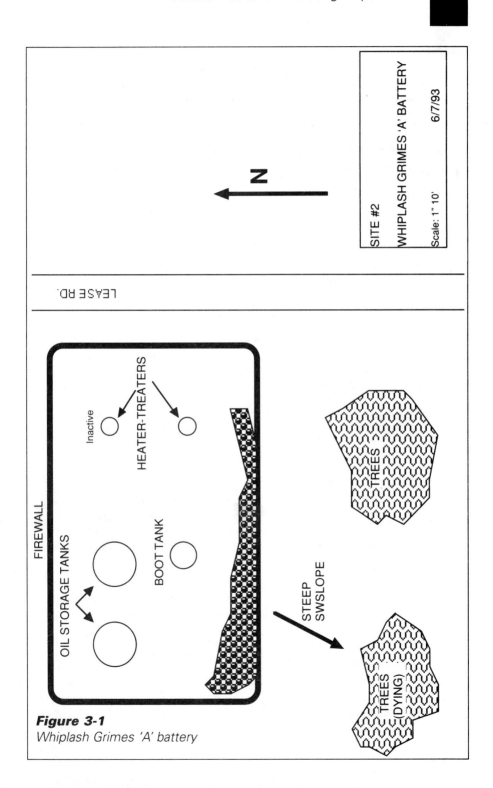

Figure 3-1
Whiplash Grimes 'A' battery

EXAMPLE B: PHASE TWO AUDIT

After seeing the Phase One report on the property, Little Nell, being the chaste and pure (but shrewd) operator that it is, delayed the closing date and commissioned a Phase Two study of the Whiplash Grimes 'A' Tank Battery. A portion of what that report might look like is included below.

SITE #2
WHIPLASH GRIMES 'A' TANK BATTERY
SITE/WORK DESCRIPTION
LOCATION

The facilities at this location sit topographically, on a slope where the ground surface gradient is about 6% to the south and southwest.

SOIL

Speculation concerning the soil conditions (noted in the Phase One Report) proved to be accurate. The soil exhibits a very low CEC of 1-2 meq./100g. indicating that this system is very weakly buffered.

VEGETATION

Once again, the ground vegetation appeared to be reasonably healthy, but the trees, shown in Figure 3-1 as being southwest of the tank battery, are stressed and dying (in contrast with the other trees in the vicinity).

SOIL BORINGS

Four 10 ft. soil borings were drilled and sampled: three from downgradient of the facility and one from upgradient. (Figure 3-2). The sampling was done by compositing 2 ft. intervals. The results of the lab analysis are shown in Table 3-1.

PROBLEM ANALYSIS

Based on sample analysis results, it appears that the Whiplash Grimes 'A' Tank Battery is acting as a point source for a contamination plume (consisting of crude oil and brine) that has spread through the soil toward the southwest. The weak buffering of the soil system has allowed a wider diffusion of the contamination than might otherwise have been possible.

The plume itself has migrated downgradient at a higher angle than the land surface. This explains the healthy appearance of the shallow rooted ground vegetation in contrast with the deep rooted vegetation.

The important thing to glean from this highly oversimplified discussion, is that the operator, landowner, working interest partner, or whoever becomes involved with an audit of a property should be aware of the likely issues and plan an orderly program of investigation that will address those concerns. Rather than drown in a sea of terminology invented by government bureaucrats and environmental consultants (to add to the smoke and mirrors), you should understand simply that oil

Table 3-1
Whiplash Grimes "A" battery sample results

0-2' DEPTH

	SAMPLE LOCATION			
PARAMETER	B-1	B-2	B-3	B-4
Oil & Grease (%)	0.06	0.87	.78	.65
EC (mmhos/cm)	1.2	2.9	1.9	2.1
CEC (meq/100 gm)	1.33	2.01	2.39	1.78

2-4' DEPTH

	SAMPLE LOCATION			
PARAMETER	B-1	B-2	B-3	B-4
Oil & Grease (%)	0.13	0.93	.81	.73
EC (mmhos/cm)	1.1	6.8	5.7	6.1
CEC (meq/100 gm)	2.56	3.94	4.62	4.09

4-6' DEPTH

	SAMPLE LOCATION			
PARAMETER	B-1	B-2	B-3	B-4
Oil & Grease (%)	0.07	2.07	1.93	1.87
EC (mmhos/cm)	1.3	12.4	10.6	11.0
CEC (meq/100 gm)	2.59	4.04	4.57	4.98

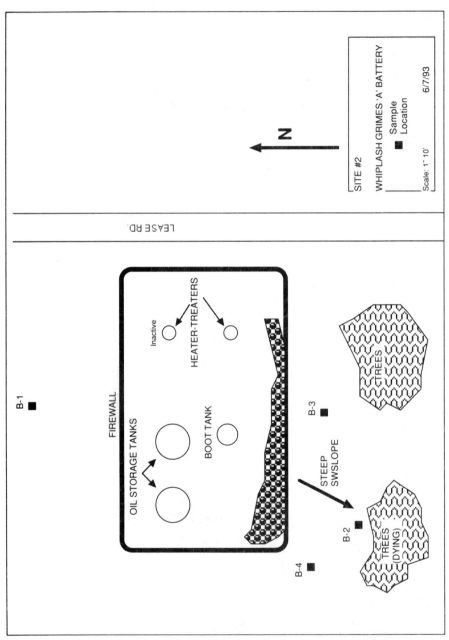

Figure 3-2
Whiplash Grimes "A" battery sample locations

and gas production gives rise to specific concerns and those concerns need to be addressed effectively.

Ideally, the Phase One Audit should provide a reconnaissance of the property and catalog likely concerns. The Phase Two Audit begins to define the nature of the problem somewhat more quantitatively. Frankly, it has been my experience that in conducting Property Transfer Audits, there is usually insufficient time to thoroughly quantify the level and extent of the contamination. To really nail down the volumes and costs with a high degree of accuracy, further study will be needed as was discussed above. However, a good consultant can usually give reasonable estimates of remediation costs after a Phase Two Audit.

When a property changes hands, the bottom line for the buyer is "What will it cost me to clean it up if I accept it?" and "Might I, realistically, have to clean it up?" These issues can be very difficult, given the usual short time constraint and the Machiavellian nature of the negotiation process. Typically, a company buying a property will want to have those answers in black and white. Realistically, however, anything which involves the regulatory world will, from time to time, be more grey than black and white. The buyer will usually be faced with a decision in which, after getting a best approximation of the cleanup cost, must make a risked decision. At that point, the risk aversion characteristics of the buyer will determine where and if the deal proceeds.

PHASE ONE PROCEDURE

It would be useful to discuss some of the aspects of doing the Phase One Audit and some of its ingredients and for that purpose, it would be good to spend some time looking at the checklist. The checklist can be found in many different forms and can be a help. More often than not, it is used to cover up an expertise deficit. I have had occasion to review a number of Phase One Audit reports. One gets the impression that some environmental consulting firms are sending underqualified people into the field with a checklist with the hope that it will overcome his knowledge and experience deficit. It will not.

The above is not to say that using a checklist is always bad, but that it can be. Simply put, the environmental condition of a property is not a collection of items on a check list: it is a functioning system. The soil, water, and air become linked to and interwoven with production facilities (which are themselves a system). When one becomes focused on checking items off a list, he can fail to see cause and effect. If one does not understand the natural and industrial processes at hand, he will not adequately report the condition of the property. A checklist is not a good substitute for technical background and good powers of observation.

I have generated more than one checklist, for the purpose of jogging the memory to ask the right questions. A portion of one such list is provided as an example in Figure 3-3.

FIELD: _____   **LOC.** _____

WELL: _____   **API #** _____

TYPE: _____

1) Where are the flow lines buried and how deep? Map available?

2) Cement comments.

3) Evidence of high resistivity sands in the surface hole?

4) Was surface CSG shoe tested?   Jug?   Leakoff?
   Evidence of having to squeeze cmt. @ surface csg shoe?
   Available test data and general comments.

5) Dates.
Drill date_____   Completion Date _____

Recomplete Dates _____   Plugging date _____

Plugging Report? _____   Completion Report?_____

General comments.

6) What completion/workover fluids were used?

7) What materials left in hole when plugged (if applicable)?

8) Channeling behind pipe?

9) Blowouts?

10) Pressures
Wellhead Pressure_____   Flowline Pressure_____

Gas lift? _____   Pressure readings _____

11) General appearance of wellhead. _____
_____
_____
_____

12) Associated Facilities. (Also, see checklist.)

13) NORM readings.

14) General Site Description.

Figure 3-3
Field checklist for environmental project managers

The checklist shown in Figure 3-3 relates, obviously, only to one small portion of the audit. Wellheads are not the only type of equipment in the oil patch, although they are intrusive and important. Actually, there are even different kinds of wells, including salt water disposal wells, producers, fresh water supply, etc. It is worth noting that someone who is not industry trained in being able to understand information within a well file has little or no chance of comprehending its significance. A Pressure Integrity Test and a "Jug Test," for instance, are two items that, though similar, have distinct differences, but someone with no operations background is unlikely to be able to comprehend those differences. Furthermore, the oil industry tends to use its own system of jargon and abbreviations. This can make the reading of certain documents like deciphering a dead language.

There are many other activities within the oil patch which are of concern environmentally. There are flowlines, separators, free-water knockouts, stock tanks, heater-treaters, pits, glycol dehydrators, glycol reboilers, amine towers, etc. It is important to understand the processes that are occurring at facilities in order to know what type of waste one might expect to find. Sometimes, in order to find a problem, you need to be looking for it. In addition, it is not always certain that all wastes are going to enjoy the oilfield RCRA exemption.

Other aspects of the Phase One Audit include looking for indicators such as faunal diversity or stressed vegetation (Photo 3-1), stained and discolored soil, as well as water. Certain types of pines, for instance, can show a higher resistance to elevated salinity. Others are more indicative as litmus tests. Additionally, it is sometimes advisable to turn up a spade full of soil from beneath that shell/gravel material.

COMMON OILFIELD FACILITIES AND THEIR RELATED ENVIRONMENTAL CONCERNS

In the following discussion, different types of equipment will be noted, and some very general information will be given concerning the items one might look for in an audit.

WELLHEADS. A number of possible types of contamination associated with producing wellheads can occur, both on the surface and in the subsurface. The well history data file is extremely important in trying to pin down potential problems in the subsurface. However, visual inspection of the wellhead area can reveal problems. One might look for the presence of paraffin, spilled oil, produced salt water, or contaminated soils. Likewise, gear box lubrication may be present or spilled. These things might indicate the need for a sampling program.

FLOW LINES. These things are everywhere in old fields; burie,; unburied, submerged, or any state in between. Rarely, will there be a facilities map that will show the location of flow lines. One of the necessary qualities of an auditor is the ability to reconstruct old operations so that it is possible to tell where to look for certain things. Flow line spills can be large. Sometimes, infrared aerial photos can be useful in locating large historic spills in remote locations. There might also be paraffin build-up on the connections and scale.

SEPARATORS. Tank bottoms from these vessels can yield produced sand and scale. Washout can leave soil NORM.

FREE WATER KNOCKOUTS (FWKO). Here you can find oil emulsions, produced waters, solids, and bottom sludges drained from tanks. In an old facility of this sort, a large volume of contaminant waste may have gone onto the ground.

OIL STOCK TANKS. They have leaked (Photo 3-2). Assume that they are guilty until proven innocent (if you are the buyer, anyway). The question is, "How much has been spilled and what is under that shell/gravel material?" How much bottom sludge is in it and is it NORM? How often do tank bottoms have to be severed from these tanks and where did it all go? Yes, what we have here is, indeed, a riddle. If you are the seller, of course, all of the above must be nonsense, right?

DISCHARGE PITS. This requires an entire treatment by itself and will be handled in detail in a subsequent chapter. Suffice to say that unlined pits are a potential source for groundwater contamination. In one horror story I know of, a small blowdown pit near a gas plant had contamination to a depth of 187 ft. when the problem was found. Out of site is not out of mind. It may be in Farmer Brown's agricultural well. Here, NORM rears its ugly head in its most ferocious form. Pits are not always easy to recognize. They should be carefully identified and noted (Photos 3-3, 3-4).

HEATER-TREATERS. They have leaked. They may have bottom sludge and NORM that may amount to a significant quantity in the case of some of the larger units.

COMPRESSORS. These little jewels are really hot and noisy. They have crankcase oil and cooling water everywhere. In addition, the older models can crank out some impressive air quality pollutant tons per year.

Is that it? Nope, the items listed in this chapter are simply a sampling of the what might be taken into account in a Property Transfer Audit. A thorough audit is an intensive process and adds new emphasis to the word "diligence." There are some broad categories of tasks that are normally a part of the audit process.

- Proprietary File Search: Investigation of materials that are disclosed in data rooms, including any environmental information, well files, facility files, etc.

- Public File Search:Review of state and federal agency files such as RCRA Notifiers, CERCLIS, RRC (in Texas), DEQ (in Louisiana), etc.

- Field Work: Photographic documentation, site mapping, inspection of facilities, soil sampling, water sampling, monitor well drilling, NORM surveying, etc.

INDUSTRY STANDARDIZATION

After many years of discussion within the environmental industry concerning standardization of environmental audits, the American Society for Testing and Materials (ASTM) has published "Standard Practice for Environmental Site Assessments: Phase 1 Environmental Site Assessment Process." This standard was published in May 1993 under the fixed designation E 1527-93. It is issued under the jurisdiction of the Committee on Environmental Site Assessment but is specifically the responsibility of the Subcommittee on Commercial Real Estate Transactions.

It should be carefully noted that the development of this ASTM standard is apparently highly derived from commercial real estate transfers and as such will reflect some differences with the realities of oil and gas property transfers. However, there is creditable work here in defining many of the terms and issues that become important in the environmental audit process. It is intended to clarify and establish what constitutes "appropriate inquiry" for purposes of CERCLA's "innocent landowner defense" and the stated intent is that it is to be used on a "voluntary basis."

By way of clarification, the EPA has broad authority to investigate and order cleanups of sites under CERCLA. There are any number of horror stories of individuals and companies being pulled into Superfund sites, or even sites that were moved to the National Priorities List (NPL). In response to questions about the unfairness of innocent landowners (who purchased properties in good faith) being pulled into the liability for cleanup of these properties, there is an "innocent landowner defense" is provided in CERCLA 42 USC § 9601(35) and § 9607(b)(3). One of the requirements for this defense is that the party in question (the buyer) must have made "all appropriate inquiry into the previous ownership of the property consistent with good commercial or customary practice." What does that mean? Well, most environmental consultants sought to design their audit process to fulfill this requirement in one way or the other, but there has been no real standardization of the terms and practices involved. Therefore, ASTM Standard E 1527 has been developed.

E 1527 identifies four major components of a Phase 1 Environmental Site Assessment: records review, site reconnaissance, interviews, and the report. The standard describes the type of records that should be reviewed and the extent to which verification efforts should be made. Likewise, details such as the types of individuals to be interviewed and the general format of the report are discussed.

Not everything in ASTM Standard E 1527 is directly applicable to transfer of oil and gas properties, but it will probably begin to be a question in any number of court cases where the question of "appropriate inquiry" arises. Much of it is adaptable to oil and gas practice and, to the extent to which that is practically possible, it would be a good idea to begin to keep these guidelines in mind.

In the final analysis, property transfer audits are technical/scientific projects that should be undertaken by qualified people with technical/scientific backgrounds who understand the production processes and the natural processes. Suit yourself; it is your future.

Soil Analysis: A Primer

Decision making must be based on good data. That is simple to the point of being cliched, but there must be understanding of the data in order to effectively utilize it. Preceding that, the data must be gathered in such a way as to be meaningful and valid. Soil sampling is integral to the environmental analytical process, but what parameters should one look at? What are those numbers on that sheet of paper really telling you? What the heck is "CEC," anyway? What is the difference between "TPH GC" and "TPH IR" and why bother? The ensuing discussion should serve to help the reader understand what is being examined and what is being accomplished by soil sampling.

SOIL DEVELOPMENT

Soil is a product of weathering. Subaerially exposed rocks are subjected to the chemical and mechanical processes that result from contact with the atmosphere. These processes create a layer of loose rock debris, called a regolith in geologic terms. The word is derived from the Greek "rego" (blanket) and "lithos" (rock) signifying a blanket of loose rock material that covers the solid bedrock.

Regoliths can be divided into two types. Residual regoliths are formed in place, but transported regoliths are composed of weathered debris that has been removed from its source and located elsewhere by processes such as fluvial, aeolian, glacial, etc. Soil is the upper portion of the regolith, whether transported or residual.

Since soil has great significance economically and is widely distributed geographically, it should come as no surprise that there are a number of definitions for it. One might define it as the unconsolidated mineral matter on the immediate surface of the earth, which serves as a natural medium for growth of land plants. A second, more detailed definition would describe soil as the unconsolidated mineral matter on the earth's surface, which has been subjected to and influenced by genetic and environmental agents such as parent materials, micro and macroorganisms, climate, etc.[1]

In addition to the mineral material, soils will contain varying amounts of organic matter and will vary in thickness. In general, soils in arid and arctic climates will be thin and contain minimal organic matter. In more humid climates, where chemical processes are accelerated, soils can be quite thick and contain significantly more organic matter.

While development of soils may vary, a mature soil profile usually will have three horizons (Figure 4-1). These zones are consistently and widely found in soils regardless of the geographic location. Horizon A is topsoil which itself can frequently be divided into three zones. The uppermost surface is characterized by leaf mould and the like, particularly in forest settings. Below the leaf mould layer is a humus rich layer. A third, more bleached layer is located at the bottom of Horizon A.[2]

Horizon B is composed of colloidal materials and clays washed down from Horizon A. Finally, Horizon C is a zone of broken and partially weathered bedrock material.

Soil serves two major purposes that will be considered in this book. First, it is a source of plant life, which has direct economic implications. Crops depend on soil quality. Likewise, vegetation binds the soil and inhibits topsoil erosion. This purpose is pretty obvious.

Perhaps less obvious is the fact that the soil acts as a buffer system that protects the groundwater resources. If the soil is damaged and the buffer system is overloaded, drinking water and agricultural water sources can be compromised. For this reason, it is often useful to sample not only for contaminant levels but also to look at parameters that reveal the inherent soil characteristics.

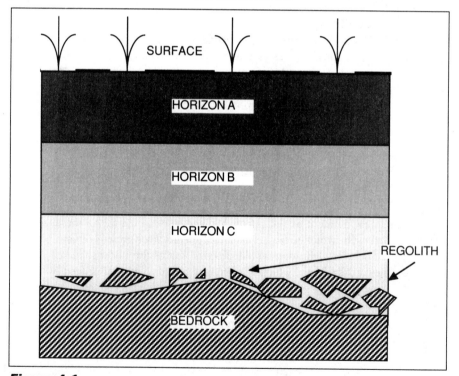

Figure 4-1
Idealized cross section showing
general aspects of three horizon soil development

SOIL STRUCTURING

E&P wastes tend to affect the structuring of the soil, which in turn damages the soil's ability to perform its design functions. It is appropriate to review soil structuring briefly so as to understand what happens to a soil subjected to production wastes. Most people look at soil as dirt. "What's all the fuss about a bunch of dirt?" one might ask. Well, it isn't just dirt. To a soil scientist (which I am not), soil is a wonderland of chemical and bacteriological and mechanical processes delicately interwoven into a delightful fabric that shimmers brightly (albeit brownly) before the discerning eye. To the soil aficionado, there are few things more lovely than a muck soil.

Facetiousness aside, soil is more than meets the naked eye. It can be described in terms such as "aggregation," "field capacity," "bulk density,". and "porosity." Structuring of soils allows the movement of air and water through the soil profile. A well-aerated soil will have a soil air composition similar to the atmospheric composition. On the other hand, poorly aerated soil will have a lower oxygen content.

AGGREGATION

Aggregation is an important aspect of soil structuring. It is not desirable that soil be texturally homogeneous. Adhesion of particles within the soil produces aggregates. A higher percentage of water-stable aggregates in the soil is desirable. This condition will increase the percentage of macropores, and that is good because macropores allow a free flow of air and water. Micropores, by contrast, being much smaller, cause a more tortuous flow path for fluids. Suffice to say that the more the flow of air and water is impeded, the more deleterious the effect.

SOIL AGGREGATION STRUCTURE TYPES

Granular	Prismatic	Massive
	Blocky	Platy

Water Movement Fast ————————————————▶ Slow

Aggregate %Higher ◀———————————————— Lower

Table 4-1

Relationship of soil aggregation structure type to water movement

As can be seen in Table 4-1, water movement is relatively faster through soil types with higher levels of aggregation. Massive soils would, for instance, be roughly equivalent to good liner material for an earthen pit. That should give some indication of the porosity present at that end of the spectrum.

What agents cause aggregation in soils? Structural components such as microbial gums and oxides contribute to aggregation. However, isomorphous substitution in the tetrahedral (or silica) layer of clays can be the "Achilles heel" of soils. Soils that contain abundant montmorillonite clays have this substitution process particularly accentuated.

Readers with a minerology background will remember that clays are phyllosilicates (or sheet silicates). These sheet silicates wherein isomorphous substitution in the silica layer has occurred can have clay layers with unsatisfied surface valences or, in other words, negative charges waiting to capture the odd passing cation. Some clays do have anionic capture potential, but those instances are not sufficiently significant to figure into this discussion. While there are other ways to balance the charge potential in the clay, adsorption of cations onto the surface of individual clay layers is common.[1]

Why discuss this at all? What does a bunch of inorganic geochemistry have to do with anything. Hang on? There is method to this madness.

Aggregation is important, right? The more the better, right? Well, aggregation (along with bulk density) is one of the major aspects of soil quality attacked by brine contamination, which is a major pollution source in the E&P realm.[1] Without going into all the details, a divalent cation such as calcium, when adsorbed onto the clay surface, tends to increase aggregation in soil. The adsorption of monovalent cations such as sodium tends to increase clay dispersion which in turn causes disaggregation. Brine is reeking with sodium, and soil attacked by brines, particularly on a long term basis, can be seriously damaged. Figure 4-2 is a highly simplified diagram that depicts cations adsorbed by unsatisfied surface charges.

When clays become disaggregated, the packing coefficient is changed for the soil and the bulk density (defined as the mass of dry soil per unit bulk volume) will tend to change and the soil macroporosity will decrease. In other words, add a little brine and a little heat, and you can make a great brick. If you are in the brick-making business that may be good, but if you are in the oil business, it is less than desirable, especially since the soil belongs to Farmer Bob, your surface owner.

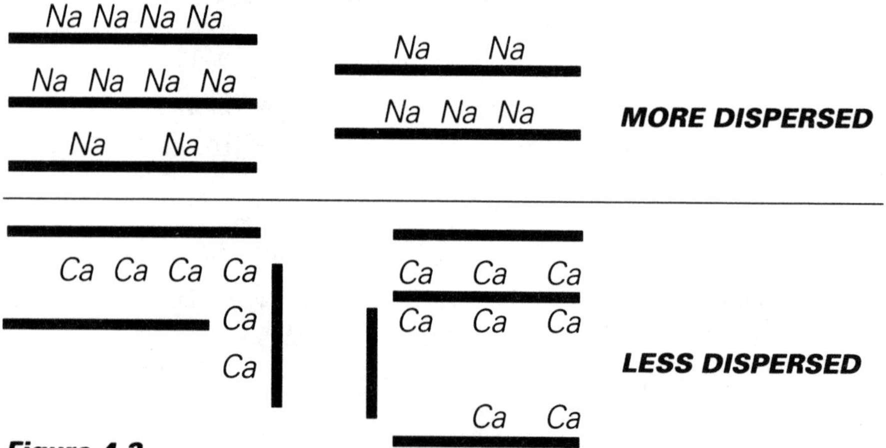

Figure 4-2
Idealized diagram illustrating adsorption of cations onto the surface of clay layers (dark black lines) in soil. In the upper portion of the diagram, monovalent sodium (Na) cations promote dispersion of the clays, whereas the calcium (Ca) cations are divalent (have a charge of +2) and promote aggregation.

BULK DENSITY (ρ)

In addition to aggregation, a related soil characteristic affected by production waste is bulk density. This is a measure of compaction. As a rule of thumb, it can be considered that the higher the compaction, the greater the ρ. Likewise, the greater the ρ, the lower the effective porosity will be. Porosity (ø) is defined by the equation:

$$ø = 100 - ρ \times 100/\text{particle density}$$

Table 4-3
Relationship of certain soil types to average bulk density and porosity

Soil Type	ρ	ø
Sand	1.55	42
Sandy Loam	1.4	48
Fine Sandy Loam	1.3	51
Loam	1.2	55
Silty Loam	1.15	58
Clay Loam	1.1	59
Clay	1.05	60

At first blush, upon looking at Table 4-3, it would appear to the discerning reader that the preceding discussion of aggregation is contradictory to the data in the table. In the aggregation discussion the conclusion one would reach is that an increase in bulk density is not necessarily good. However, the table shows that the increase in bulk density carries a corresponding increase in porosity. The resolution of the conundrum lies in the fact that, as the progression is made toward the clay end of the soil spectrum, an increasing percentage of the total porosity is microporosity.

As a matter of note, a higher soil clay content will tend to decrease the macroporosity and increase the Cation Exchange Capacity (CEC), which increases the effectiveness of the soil buffer, but at the same time tends to make soil remediation more difficult. For risk assessments where groundwater pollution is a concern, it may be useful in many cases to have more data on the soil itself such as clay content and ratios, CEC, bulk density, etc. Often, sample analysis of a contaminant is undertaken with little understanding of the soil system itself. More discussion of CEC and other sampling parameters will be covered in the rest of this section.

SAMPLE PARAMETERS (NON-ORGANIC)

There are numerous sampling parameters used in soil sampling around oil and gas sites. Of course, each one has its own abbreviation (to make it even more obscure and to get it to fit more neatly onto the sample analysis results data sheet Figure 4-3). A brief description of the more common sample parameters and their uses follows.

CATION EXCHANGE CAPACITY (CEC). This parameter defines the total amount (per unit volume) of exchangeable cations (calcium, sodium, magnesium, etc.) that a soil is able to absorb. It gives an indication of the amount of buffering which a soil can provide for the groundwater. CEC is affected by soil texture, clay percentage and type, and to some degree, pH. A rough CEC range for various soil types is provided in Table 4-4.

Table 4-4

Showing ranges of cation exchange capacity (CEC) for various soil types

Soil Type	CEC (MEQ/100 GM)
Sandy	1 - 5
Fine Sandy Loams	5 - 10
Loams/Silty Loams	5 - 15
Clay Loams	15 - 30
Clays	>30

In the event of a brine spill, where a risk analysis is in view, this parameter would be useful in getting some appreciation for the threat to groundwater. Other procedures such as clay analysis may be used in conjunction with this parameter to assess the natural quality of the soil. Several clays could be listed showing their individual CECs. Illite, for instance has a range of 20-40 meq/100 gm, while kaolinite rates only 2-15 meq/100 gm. It can be seen that the clay types and ratios do make a difference in the CEC of a given soil.

SODIUM ADSORPTION RATIO (SAR). The SAR is a soil parameter that has been empirically related to defective characteristics of soil and to plant toxicities. It describes the ratio of sodium to calcium and magnesium and is defined by the equation:

$$SAR = Na/\sqrt{(Ca + Mg/2)}.$$

SAR is usually used in conjunction with CEC and ESP as a salt damage indicator in soils. It is a required parameter for post-closure pit samples under Louisiana Statewide Order 29-B, as are CEC and ESP. One study indicates that more than 65% of the mud pits studied had SARs in excess of 12.[1] As the SAR goes higher, the condition of the soil for plant growth can be assumed to be worse.

EXCHANGEABLE SODIUM PERCENTAGE (ESP). ESP represents the percentage of the total CEC of the soil that is taken up with sodium. As with SAR, extremely high values here are not good news. This parameter will be reported, of course, as a percentage.

ELECTRICAL CONDUCTIVITY (EC). EC is a common way to indirectly quantify salinity in soil. It is measured directly in units of resistivity, and then the reciprocal is reported in millimhos per centimeter. Actually, EC indirectly measures Total Dissolved Solids (TDS) which, in oilfield waste are apt to be mostly sodium chloride. The most effective method is arguably the saturated paste method.

This parameter, along with direct chloride measurement, can be deceptive in areas of older historic spills, though. I have seen areas with heavily damaged soils and yet chlorides and ECs that were not that remarkably high.

CHLORIDES. Direct measurement of chloride content in parts per million (ppm) can be made both in soil and water and is required in some states with pit closures and spill sampling. Chlorides can be a good indicator in groundwater of many types of contamination. Chlorides are a more direct measurement of salt concentration than EC or SAR but do not address the condition of the soil itself.

PH. Many state agencies set regulatory limits for pH. The parameter itself describes the acidity or alkalinity of a substance. Most commonly, drilling muds have a very high pH indicating that they are alkaline. However, other oil field fluids, such as hydrochloric acid (used in stimulation jobs), will have a very low pH. I have seen few pits that fall outside the normal 6-9 standard units s.u. limits. However, a small amount of acid dumped or spilled onto a weakly buffered soil can produce some startlingly low pH values.

In one instance, I sampled an area that had sustained what was probably a very small quantity acid spill, and yet the soil pH was <2. It is important to understand the characteristics of the soil system with which one is dealing. Regulatory limits can be stupid things in and of themselves. They can utterly fail to address the problem or the reality of the situation. There may on occasion be good reason to seek a variance from certain regulatory limitations, but one needs reliable data, correctly interpreted, in order to approach regulators with such a request.

TOTAL METALS. There are any number of circumstances that might require one to get a handle on metals contamination. Metals contamination within soil involves highly complex chemistry and is perhaps less well understood than many believe. Some specialists believe that Total Metals Analyses provides the only measurable index for the assessment of E&P wastes relative to environmental impact, due to fluctuating environmental conditions.[1]

Fate and transport analysis of metals in soil can be difficult due to the fact that there are a number of processes that affect it. Solvation, complexing, and cation exchange processes are included among the processes that affect metal mobility as well as bioavailability. Heavy metals can be taken up by plant life under the right circumstances.

Metal contamination in soils can result in heavy metals being held in various forms, including oxides, carbonates, and even organics. The greatest environmental concern, however, is for those heavy metals that are: in water soluble form, exchangeable, and/or proven to be organically bound fractions. In other words, can it migrate into the groundwater or be taken up by plant material and thus get into the water supply or the food chain? Again, there is some divergence of opinion on whether E&P wastes represent a significant threat in this way. Some workers believe that E&P wastes contain little or no water soluble or exchangeable heavy metals and therefore constitute minimal risk.

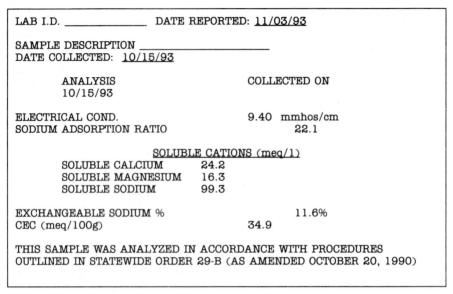

LAB I.D. _____ DATE REPORTED: **11/03/93**

SAMPLE DESCRIPTION _____
DATE COLLECTED: **10/15/93**

ANALYSIS   COLLECTED ON
10/15/93

ELECTRICAL COND.   9.40 mmhos/cm
SODIUM ADSORPTION RATIO   22.1

SOLUBLE CATIONS (meq/1)
SOLUBLE CALCIUM   24.2
SOLUBLE MAGNESIUM   16.3
SOLUBLE SODIUM   99.3

EXCHANGEABLE SODIUM %   11.6%
CEC (meq/100g)   34.9

THIS SAMPLE WAS ANALYZED IN ACCORDANCE WITH PROCEDURES
OUTLINED IN STATEWIDE ORDER 29-B (AS AMENDED OCTOBER 20, 1990)

Figure 4-3
An example of a sample analysis data sheet reporting "salt parameters for a given sample

The EPA's E&P SW-846 Method 3050 protocol has proven to be an effective method for all the metals with which we are concerned in the E&P world, except barite. Generally, a "true total barium" run using the Louisiana Dept. of Natural Resources (DNR) protocol will be more effective.

Total metals will be reported in parts per million and should be distinguished from the Toxicity Characteristic Leachate Procedure (TCLP), which will be discussed later. A total metals analysis simply gives one a raw number showing how much of each metal is included in the sample (Figure 4-4). It makes no attempt to determine how much might be soluble or movable.

Generally, environmental work concerns itself with eight metals because of the discussion found in 40 CFR §261.24 concerning toxicity characteristic. Those are: arsenic, barium, cadmium, chromium, lead, mercury, selenium, and silver. A ninth metal, zinc, is added under Louisiana Statewide Order 29-B. Zinc is not a metal regulated under RCRA, but it can be detrimental to plant life and is quite common in E&P wastes.

Mercury contamination is becoming an issue in areas where old mercury gas meters were in use. In North Louisiana, fish with elevated mercury levels have been found in recent years. This has lead to scrutiny of the gas meters.

```
LAB I.D. _____  DATE REPORTED: 08/25/93

SAMPLE DESCRIPTION _____
DATE COLLECTED: 08/05/93

        SLUDGE COMPOSITE COLLECTED ON 8/05/93
        @ 1115

        PERCENT MOISTURE                    49.16%
        OIL & GREASE  (% dry weight)        17.31%

                TOTAL METAL CONTENT (ppm)

ARSENIC    6.07    CHROMIUM  24.3    SELENIUM  0.054
BARIUM     8152    LEAD     <5.00    SILVER   <0.700
CADMIUM  <0.300    MERCURY  0.188    ZINC        335

        TRUE TOTAL BARIUM                   19102

        pH MEASUREMENT                       5.98 S.U.
        ELECTRICAL COND.              99.0 mmhos/cm
        SODIUM ADSORPTION RATIO            379.38

                SOLUBLE CATIONS (meq/l)
        SOLUBLE CALCIUM         98.85
        SOLUBLE MAGNESIUM       63.53
        SOLUBLE SODIUM          3418


PASTE SATURATION %                         57.6%
EXCHANGEABLE SODIUM %                      >100%
CEC (meq/100g)                             6.37

THIS SAMPLE WAS ANALYZED IN ACCORDANCE WITH PROCEDURES
OUTLINED IN STATEWIDE ORDER 29-B (AS AMENDED OCTOBER 20, 1990)
```

Figure 4-4
*Sample analysis results data sheet showing how metals and pH are report-
ed. Note that the "True Total Barium" differs from the barium reported with
the other eight metals in the above section of the data sheet*

With the possible exception of cadmium, all of the metals just discussed occur
in soils naturally on a widespread basis. Cadmium is particularly nasty and at even
very low levels in soil, can affect plant growth. It can occur as an oxide, sulfide,
carbonate, or oxidate.

A listing of the natural concentration ranges of the other E&P metals
(depending on geographic location and variations) is listed in Table 4-5.

Table 4-5
Showing E&P Metals and Their Natural Occurence in Soil

METAL	NATURAL OCCURRENCE RANGE (PPM)
Arsenic	1-40[1]
Barium	100-3,000[1]
Chromium	5-3000[1]
Mercury	<0.2[1]
Lead	≈15[1]
Selenium	1-7[1]
Zinc	10-300[1]
Silver	<1[3]

The informed reader will note that there are some natural occurrences shown in the Table 4-5 that are above established regulatory limits in certain states. This underscores the need to understand the soil as a system that fits into a regional picture. If your sample is showing 39 ppm arsenic and the soil in the area is generally comparable, then you may be a candidate for exemption from the regulation. You may not have a problem. However, if your comparison occurrence is from a hydrothermal alteration halo 2,000 miles away, you are unlikely to command respect from the regulatory community.

TOXICITY CHARACTERISTIC LEACHING PROCEDURE (TCLP). As was mentioned in the chapter on industry regulation, many operators are leaning heavily on the RCRA exemption. However, this exemption may prove to be a "bruised reed" in the future and in fact something that one may want to avoid leaning his total weight upon even now. I have has seen instances where TCLP can be helpful or even necessary.

Simply put, wastes can be "characteristically hazardous" if they exceed the levels established in 40 CFR §261.24 after being subjected to TCLP. The TCLP process subjects the sample to leaching by an acetic acid solution and then measuring the concentrations of the eight RCRA metals and 32 other organic substances in the resulting extract.

This procedure differs from the total metals protocol in that the TCLP values for the metals will be lower than total metals. As was discussed, the main concern with heavy metals is related to those metals that are in states that can ultimately find their way into the food chain or water supply. TCLP is a regulatory approach to measuring that potential.

SAMPLE PARAMETERS (ORGANIC)

Well, since we deal with petroleum, petroleum fractions, and petroleum products, there is apt to be a good deal of it lying around. Try as we might to minimize the possibility (oil on the ground is lost revenue), it will happen from time to time.

There are several approaches to analysis of soil contaminated by petroleum, petroleum products, and petroleum fractions that will now be discussed.

TOTAL PETROLEUM HYDROCARBONS (TPH). This type analysis may be used to determine levels of hydrocarbons in soil that are related strictly to petroleum contributions. TPH samples may be analyzed using one of two methods: infrared spectroscopy (IR) or gas chromatograph (GC). Depending on what you are wanting to accomplish, one or the other may be used. For instance, if you are using it to track the effectiveness of your remediation project, GC may in some cases be the more useful method.[1]

TPH will be sometimes be reported in parts per million, but most often it will be reported in milligrams per kilogram (mg/kg) in solids or milligrams per liter (mg/l) in liquids.

OIL & GREASE. This method has the same purpose as TPH, i.e., isolating the petroleum contribution to the soil. However, this method uses gravimetric assay in its protocol. Oil & Grease results will be reported as a percent of dry weight value.

Most states base their regulatory threshold on either Oil & Grease or TPH. Louisiana, for instance, uses Oil & Grease for its 29-B analysis, but has TPH limits established for soil contamination that does not qualify as NOW.

TOTAL ORGANIC CARBON (TOC). TOC is another approach that has value as an inexpensive and fast turn-around screening technique. The drawback is that the results are not limited strictly to petroleum, but any organic carbon in the soil will contribute to the result. This may tend to exaggerate the contamination levels in soils that have high natural organic content. However, TOC results will generally be comparable to Oil & Grease results.[1] TOC will be reported as a percentage (Figure 4-5).

BENZENE, TOLUENE, ETHYLBENZENE, XYLENES (BTEX). We would be doing a lot more of this if not for the RCRA oilfield exemption. But there are cases where it becomes necessary even now. This type of sample is designed as a tripwire. It will be reported in ppm (except when reported as mg/l in liquids or mg/kg in solids), and the rule of thumb is that, if you are above detection limits, you should consider that you might have a problem (Figure 4-6). This is especially true with benzene.

VOLATILE ORGANIC ANALYSIS (VOA). This is the big dragnet approach to soil sampling.

I have stood on more than one occasion looking at a site and scratching my head. It was not just the poison ivy. There was real uncertainty. Despite a keen eye for detail and diligent auditing technique, I did not have clue what I was looking at. "What had this facility been? What had they dumped here?

What the…? What did I step in?"

There are times you just do not know, and that is the time for VOA. It scans 44 volatile, regulated substances, including BTEX (Figure 4-7). Results generally will be in ppm and if you are above detection, sit up and take notice.

REPORTING REQUIREMENTS

One of the things that must be mentioned is that several of the parameters cited carry with them reporting requirements. State regulatory thresholds are sometimes called "regulatory limits" and sometimes "action levels." Regulatory limits often require immediate remedial action. Exceeding action levels, on the other hand, does not necessarily mean that you are snared in cleanup liability, but you are required to report the results to the appropriate agency and may be required to (at least) do further study of the problem.

SOIL SAMPLING

The following discussion is very generalized and not intended to make anyone expert in the soil sampling aspect of site characterization. The formality and detail of your sampling plan will vary with purpose. It is far beyond the scope of this book to present a sampling plan that covers even most of the circumstances that would require sampling of the soil for contaminants. It is more profitable at this juncture to introduce the main issues.

SAMPLING PLAN

It is of primary importance to understand why you are sampling and what you are trying to accomplish. For a property transfer audit, given the limited time available, it may be most useful to have a less formal grid and do some compositing. Likewise, it might be useful to sample obvious hotspots.

If one is trying to sample a pit or an area of soil NORM, or to define the limits of a spill, then the program will need to be designed to be representative of the area in question. Delineation sampling prior to remedial action may require a grid that is statistically meaningful.

Ignoring these reporting requirements may be understandable, but it is not advisable. Hell hath no fury like an underpaid public servant scorned.

Common to all these sampling circumstances are four aspects. First, there must be a selection of the sample location or locations. In some cases these may need to be surveyed and premarked.

Second, there must be a selection of parameters and number of samples to be taken. Do they need to be split? Composited? Are depth interval samples needed?

Third, one must be familiar with the minimum sample volume needed for each relevant protocol and the type of container prescribed.

Fourth, safety is a major consideration. Sometimes sampling can bring someone into contact with hazardous substances. At the risk of violating the code of silence, NOW can contain things that you, the reader would not want to ingest. Also, while I do not advocate terror of NORM, there is no use being an idiot. It doesn't take

| Company: |
| Submitted by: |
| Project Name: |
| Received: |
| Reference #: |
| Report Date: |

Parameter	S6-1S	S6-20	S6-3ST	Tech	Date	Regulatory Threshold
Moisture, %	4.3	3.0	3.6	BW	08/25	– –
SP Moisture, %	21.3	– –	21.5	LF	09/05	– –
pH	7.2	– –	6.5	SBC	09/02	6.09.0+
SP EC, mmhos/cm	1.6	– –	1.1	SBC	09/02	4.0+
Chloride, ppm	102	– –	85	KM	09/07	3,000++
Soluble Cations, meq 1						
Sodium	1.0	– –	1.7	ALB	09/08	– –
Calcium	3.1	– –	0.4	ALB	09/08	– –
Magnesium	0.2	– –	3.2	ALB	09/08	– –
SAR	0.8	– –	3.2		Calculation	12.0+
CEC, meq/100g	1.7	– –	0.7	ALB	09/08	– –
Exchangable Cations, meq/100g						
Sodium	<0.1	– –	<0.1	AJA	09/08	– –
Calcium	4.4	– –	0.5	AJA	09/08	– –
Magnesium	<0.1	– –	<0.1	AJA	09/08	– –
ESP, %	<0.1	– –	2.3		Calculation	15.0+
Total Metals, ppm						
Arsenic	3.5	– –	3.6	AJA	09/09	10+
Barium	35.1	– –	26.4	AJA	09/08	40,000+
True Total Ba	453.7	– –	441.5	AJA	09/08	40,000+
Cadmium	1.4	– –	<1.0	AJA	09/08	10+
Chromium	<5.0	– –	<5.0	AJA	09/08	500+
Lead	4.8	– –	1.5	AJA	09/08	500+
Mercury	0.2	– –	<.1	AJA	09/09	10+
Selenium	0.3	– –	0.3	AJA	09/09	10+
Silver	<5.0	– –	<5.0	AJA	09/08	200+
Zinc	10.6	– –	6.5	AJA	09/08	500+
TOC, %	0.3	– –	<0.1	KM	09/08	– –
TPH by IR, mg/kg	49.58	55,158	22.15	KO	08/31	10,000+
PCB's mg/kg	<1.0	<1.0	<1.0	CAW	09/01	– –

* Analysis Methods are from Laboratory Procedures for Analysis of Oilfield
  Waste Louisiana DNR, August, 1988
+ Louisiana 29-B Regulatory Threshold
++ Texas Rule 8 Regulatory Threshold

Figure 4-5
*Sample analysis results data sheet showing reporting of TOC values for soil
as well as TPH IR values for soil and groundwater (at bottom)*

```
LAB I.D. _____  DATE REPORTED: 09/02/93

SAMPLE DESCRIPTION _____
DATE COLLECTED: 08/11/93

                 ANALYSIS   DATE        REFERENCE    DETECTION    CONCENTRATION
ANALYTE          INITIALS   COMPLETED   METHOD       LIMIT        mg/l (ppm)

TOTAL XYLENEs    SF         08/13/93    SW846-8020   0.002 ppm    0.003
BENZENE          SF         08/13/93    SW846-8020   0.002 ppm    BDL
ETHYL BENZENE    SF         08/13/93    SW846-8020   0.002 ppm    BDL
TOLUENE          SF         08/13/93    SW846-8020   0.002 ppm    BDL

TPH - DIESEL     SF         08/16/93    SW846-8015   10.0 ppm     32.0
```

Figure 4-6
Typical BTEX analysis reporting as seen along with TPH soil value

long to put on a pair of rubber gloves. Likewise, the conditions at the time of sampling can cause real concern. Working in a 100° sun can result in heat stroke, particularly if protective suits are required.

SAMPLE EQUIPMENT

There is a fair amount of pre-field planning required in sample acquisition. This may sound ridiculously obvious, but it is important to have the right equipment on hand to do the job (Photo 4-1). It would be unfortunate indeed to drive two hours to a site with your split spoon auger only to find out that your problem was a pit or to take a PVC sample tube to a location outside Tulsa to find an ancient pit that has been baked into brick. Has it been done?

Whatever is needed, be it the correct type sample jars, a spade, a hand auger, a sample probe, a Shelby (core), or whatever, it is best to follow the Boy Scout motto. "Lids…where are the lids? Didn't you bring the Lids? Oh, they're in the boat…which is where?"

SAMPLE COLLECTION

Most sampling procedures are variants on the theme of "scoop it up and put it in the jar." There are issues that complicate it, however, such as sampling practices and equipment decontamination practices designed to minimize cross contamination.

Sampling sludge solids can be accomplished by using a PVC sampling tube. The tube can be designed with a rubber stopper on one end or a twist valve, either of which is intended to create a suction to allow the mushy sample to be extracted. For soils, a spade or "sharpshooter" can be used to collect surface samples, but a soil probe or auger may be needed for depth interval sampling.

Blending for compositing will most often need to be done in the field. Depending on the purpose for sampling, it may be useful to composite an area based upon depth interval. As an example, the area inside a firewall for a tank battery might

LAB I.D. _____ DATE REPORTED: 09/02/93

SAMPLE DESCRIPTION _____
DATE COLLECTED: 08/11/93

ANALYSIS Date Analyzed 08/20/93 Method KPA 624/8240-GC/MS Volatiles

COMPOUND	RESULT	COMPOUND	RESULT
acetone	BDL	cis-1, 3-dichloropropylene	BDL
acrolein	BDL	trans-1, 3-dichloropropylene	BDL
acrylonitrile	BDL	ethylbenzene	0.96
benzene	BDL	fluorotrichloromethane	BDL
bis (chloromethyl) ether	BDL	2-hexanone	BDL
bromodicholromethane	BDL	methylene chloride	BDL
bromoform	BDL	methyl-isobuytl-ketone	BDL
bromomethane	BDL	methyl-ethyl-ketone	BDL
carbon disulfide	BDL	paraldehyde	BDL
arbon tetrachloride	BDL	styrene	BDL
chlorobenzene	BDL	1, 1, 2, 2-tetrachloroethane	BDL
chlorodibromomethane	BDL	tetrachloroethylene	BDL
chloroethane	BDL	toluene	BDL
2-chloroethylvinyl ether	BDL	1, 1, 1-trichloroethane	BDL
chloroform	BDL	1, 1, 2-trichloroethane	BDL
chloromethane	BDL	tr ichloroethylene	BDL
dichlorodiflluoromethane	BDL	vinyl acetate	BDL
vinyl chloride	BDL	o-xylene	
1,1-dichloroethane	BDL	m-xylene TOTAL	8.0
1,2-dichloroethane	BDL	p-xylene	
1,1-dichloroethylene	BDL	1, 2 dichlorobenzene	BDL
1,2-trans-dichloroethylene	BDL	1, 3 dichlorobenzene	BDL
1,2-dichloropopane	BDL	1, 4 dichlorobenzene	BDL

All results reported in **ppm** unless otherwise specified.
ND = not detected at detection limit **0.50 ppm**

ND** = not detected at 50 ppb
ND* = not detected at 50 ppb

SURROGATE RECOVERIES	(%)
1, 2 DICHLOROETHANE-D4	100
TOLUENE-D8	98

Figure 4-7
Typical BTEX analysis reporting as seen along with TPH soil value

need to be divided into four equal areas and each area sampled on a grid. Then all of the 0-1' samples for each area would be blended as would all the 1-3' samples. The resulting mixed samples might then be transported to the laboratory where a representative sample split would be taken.

Ideally, samples should be composited on a weight to weight or a volume to volume basis, and the blending would be done under controlled conditions. Before analyzing any composite sample, care should be taken to thoroughly homogenize the material. In fact, homogenization should be done before a final sample is pulled for analysis.

Compositing frequently results in a partial loss of volatile constituents, so the sample results may tend to understate volatiles. That fact should be kept in mind when reviewing data in composite samples. In fact, compositing tends to have the effect of minimizing all parameter values because of dilution. In general the tighter and more detailed the sample grid becomes, the higher the individual sample values become.

SAMPLE HANDLING & SHIPPING

Some diligent recordkeeping is worth its weight in lawsuits and regulatory penalties. Samples, once collected, must be correctly labeled and protected from tampering. A field notebook should be used to record sample information. Sometimes some descriptive phrases can be written in the notebook for jogging your memory at a later date. Something like, "Cloudburst at 2 pm at the Grimes Jolly Rodger #21 Tank Battery." That might sound silly, but it can be handy. We tend to forget details of a job with the passing of time.

Keeping a complete chain of custody record is essential and, if you are actually ordering the sample analysis, it is good to fill out a formal sample analysis request sheet.

These samples must reach the lab somehow, and that is not always an easy task. Some protocols require that samples be kept cool. As general procedure, organics need to be kept on ice. Samples can be bulky and may not fit into the trunk of your rental Geo Prizm. Glass jars can be broken. If you are outside the country, try explaining to customs why you need to ship containers of hazardous waste *into* the United States.

Most of these transportation problems are solvable, but again require some forethought. If one is outside the country, for instance, it might be most time and cost-effective to send the samples by one of the express delivery services that will take charge and walk the samples through customs for you. Likewise you can express deliver or air freight samples to your favorite lab from a remote location. These days, air freighting might require the services of a professional freight forwarder, however.

---

1   Lloyd E. Deuel, Jr., Ph.D and George H. Holliday, Ph.D, Soil Remediation for Petroleum Extraction Industry, (unpublished training course materials, 1993)

2   W. Kenneth Hamblin, The Earth's Dynamic Systems, (Minneapolis, Minnesota: Burgess Publishing Co., 1975).

3   Conrad B. Krauskopf, Introduction to Geochemistry, (New York: McGraw-Hill Book Co.

Groundwater 5
Considerations

One of the more feared skeletons in the E&P closet is groundwater contamination. Oil and gas production activities are intrusive by nature. Large quantities of E&P wastes have been brought to the surface and then reinfiltrated into the soil or leaked through casing directly into the groundwater. This is not to say that every oil field has significantly contributed to contamination of a drinking water supply, but it has happened in all oil producing states to some degree. Remediation of damaged aquifers is very difficult and expensive, as will be discussed further, and the expenditure for one cleanup could ruin a small company financially.

BACKGROUND

Most of the time, the attention of those in the oil patch is directed past the groundwater to deeper horizons and the "surface hole" is afforded, of necessity, less time and attention. Therefore, it might be good to review some of the basics of groundwater in order to make the ensuing discussion more meaningful to the reader.

Groundwater refers to the subsurface water from which about half of the population of the United States derives its drinking water. Most often, it is limited in application to the zone below the water table where soils and/or geologic formations are fully saturated with water. Immediately above the water table one frequently, but not always, finds a zone of capillary action which is in turn overlain by an unsaturated zone. In this unsaturated zone, the pore spaces are partially filled with air.[1] Figure 5-1 illustrates this relationship. Groundwater is commonly held in a geologic unit defined as an aquifer.

This water in the ground is not usually static unless limited as is the case with a "perched aquifer." A perched aquifer is a shallow aquifer of limited areal extent that mainly seems to function to prevent people's toilets from flushing properly. It should be distinguished from a true regional aquifer, which carries drinking and agricultural quality water and has dynamic flow characteristics. Figure 5-2 illustrates these groundwater systems and the difference between them.

Most regional groundwater flow systems have local variations and complexities that are outside the scope of this work, but they have two major components in common. The first is a recharge area where meteoric water infiltrates down to re-plenish the groundwater, which is moving downgradient. The second component is the discharge point, which may be into a lake or river. It is significantly important to

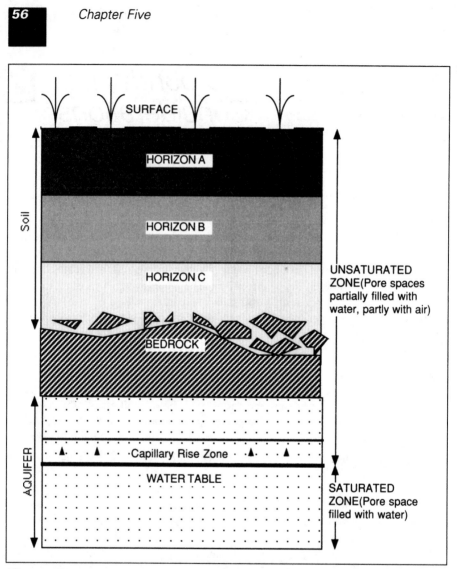

Figure 5-1
Idealized cross section showing the progression from the ground surface to the water table

note that one should be careful to distinguish between groundwater and aquifers. The two words are not synonymous and the distinction can be important from a regulatory standpoint. For instance, your underground storage tank may have contaminated groundwater but not a regional aquifer. In that case, your problem may not be nearly as serious.

Oil and gas production can harm these aquifers in several ways. (Photo 5-1) Contaminants introduced into the aquifer by E&P operations can include salt water, heavy metals, crude oil, and radium. There are other contaminants that are less significant in volume such as solvents, refined petroleum products, and natural gas.

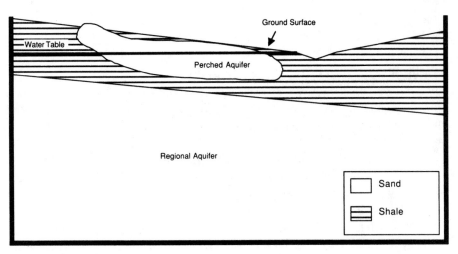

Figure 5-2
Idealized cross section showing the relationship between perched and regional aquifers.

When these contaminants enter groundwater, they each behave somewhat differently. Crude oil that carries significant volatile fractions, for instance, may move in ways difficult to predict. It may float on top of the water table or travel in a diffused fashion in the water. The volatile fraction may segregate and derivative gases move up into the unsaturated zone. Once in the unsaturated zone, the gas may move completely independently of the contaminant plume. Heavy metals may combine with chlorides and diffuse down at a gradient steeper than the regional or local gradient.

In 1974, when Congress passed the Safe Drinking Water Act, the first step in a growing concern for the safety of the country's drinking water was taken. The body of regulations established under this act is growing and has been delegated to the state level in many cases.

OIL FIELD CONTAMINATION SOURCES AND INDICATORS

Infiltration of E&P wastes from the surface is a possibility associated with production or exploration activities, but oil and gas operations differ from many industries in that the activities are intentionally intrusive. In other words, a hole has been opened to the aquifer through drilling which can, under certain circumstances, result in a conduit for contaminants to reach the fresh water aquifer in the surface hole of the well.

While the detailing of these possibilities may be elementary for some, the contamination sources will be detailed in order to help the reader understand the potential for groundwater impact that his operations may carry. In this treatment, potential contamination sources will be divided into surface infiltration problems and subsurface contamination problems. The discussion will be kept general and is not intended to be all-inclusive but only to examine major points of concern. In an orderly and ideal universe, the potential contaminant sources discussed below would be systematically examined in a Phase 1 Audit. Soil sampling might then be conducted in a second phase that would be used in a groundwater risk assessment.

SUBSURFACE CONTAMINATION PROBLEMS

Several different types of wellbore usage are common to the production process including secondary recovery (waterflood), salt water disposal, and production. Of these, the most troublesome are the salt water disposal wells, followed by the secondary recovery wells.

SALT WATER DISPOSAL. Actually, the salt water disposal well system represents a double threat to the groundwater in that there is surface storage of brine as well as underground injection. Figure 5-3 shows a sketch of the components of an SWD system.

The well itself is frequently a converted producer well that no longer has utility or, in some cases, may have been drilled especially for the purpose of salt water injection. Whereas the waterflood well is injecting into a producing horizon, the SWD well is most frequently being injected into a convenient zone in the shallow subsurface below the USDW.

Converted producers that are used for SWD are scary because they were not designed and drilled for that purpose (Photo 5-2). Most production wells are designed with the idea in mind that most of the activity would be in the lower one-third of the hole. Therefore, what grade casing is in the surface hole? What did the cement program look like? Did they get cement returns to the surface and could there be channeling behind pipe? Did they run a PIT on the casing shoe? Frequently, these are not big considerations in a production well.

The most frequent offender in the SWD well is a casing leak. Salt water is corrosive and is being injected in large quantities under pressure. If the surface pipe is compromised, brine can be injected directly into the fresh water aquifer. It is happening somewhere right now. Most oil producing states require periodic testing in the form of Mechanical Integrity Tests (MIT), but the periodicity (3-5 yr. depending on where you operate) does not preclude leakage. MITs can take the form of tracer surveys or pressure tests.

WATERFLOOD WELLS. While waterflood wells are individually perhaps somewhat less problematic than SWD wells, they weigh heavily in terms of well population density. A single pattern waterflood project can involve the use of a large number of wellbores. The demand for such a large number of wells within a field may result in a bad wellbore or two being selected, and a large amount of brine and surfactant may find its way into the shallow subsurface.

PRODUCTION WELLS. It may sound cynical, but one of the reasons that active producers are less of a problem in terms of groundwater contamination is that there is real tangible short term incentive to prevent casing leaks. Tubing and casing leaks cost money in the form of lost production revenue. The main problem is with unplugged inactive or improperly plugged wells. In Texas, RRC has taken a very

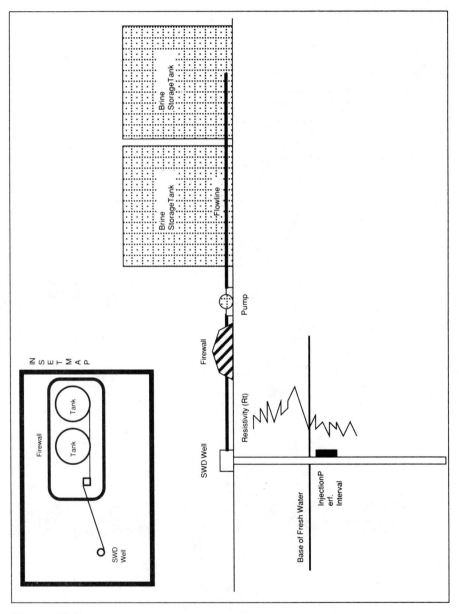

Figure 5-3
Idealized cross section and inset map showing major components of a salt water disposal system

aggressive approach to seeking to eliminate the thousands of wells in their jurisdiction that fall in this category.

The problem here is that the fluid levels in these wells can rise to shallow depths where they can contaminate the fresh water in the aquifer as the surface casing deteriorates. Likewise, older plugging techniques sometimes utilized materials that would not stop the upward movement of fluids. For instance, bentonite might have simply been dumped in the annulus and perforations may not have been squeezed. Figure 5-4 illustrates the potential adverse affect of an ineffective plug and abandonment (P&A) job.

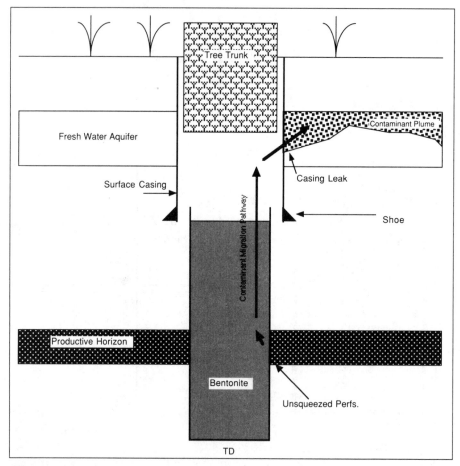

Figure 5-4
Wellbore Sketch Showing how Improper Plugging of a Well can Produce Groundwater Contamination with Little or no Surface Indication.

I have seen numerous horror stories where surface casing was set in such a way as to save money by failing to cover the fresh water in the shallow subsurface. Here, the problem can be extreme in that a casing leak anywhere in the production string can result in fluids moving from the productive formation to behind pipe and thus, into the aquifer. It would be rare for non-channeled cement to exist behind the production casing all the way from total depth (TD) to the surface casing shoe.

Blowouts are usually related to the actual initial drilling of the well, but they also can contaminate the aquifer if the surface casing shoe fails and the blowout is behind pipe and underground. In the case of a blowout, the shallow horizons can be "charged" by higher pressure fluids coming from depth. This has happened in the past, and one large scale example can be found in Harris County, Texas, where a 1940s vintage underground blowout in the north part of the county has rendered the shallow aquifers largely unusable over a significant area.

SURFACE INFILTRATION PROBLEMS

Of the several scenarios that could be cited here, three items will be considered: production pits, oil and brine storage tanks, and chemical drum storage areas. Other oil field related emplacements, such as flowlines should not be overlooked, however. One of the largest and ugliest spills I have seen was a flowline leak.

PITS. There was a time in the oil patch when wastes were commonly disposed into earthen pits, and the effects of that activity linger today. During the 1970s though, underground injection began to be the mandated waste disposal option. It is not, however, sufficient to say that closing all the pits on a property will take care of the groundwater concern. First, past closure standards have been quite lenient. True, closing the pit will stop the active disposal of wastes, but it does not account for the past. Out of sight is not out of mind in all cases. When buying a property or managing an existing one, this should be kept in mind.

By virtue of the fact that the soil has been excavated to create the impoundment, some portion of the buffering capability of the soil has been removed. Discharge of produced waters into these pits has caused infiltration of crude oil, brine, heavy metals, and NORM into the soil and, in some cases, into the groundwater. There is some disagreement as to the solubility and mobility of E&P metals, but I would strongly caution that the safest course of action should be taken by operators.

A very large area of intense soil contamination can result from pit discharge and the result can be that the soil acts as a groundwater contamination source. Frequently, pits and old pit locations can be located by discolored soil or highly stressed vegetation, but that is not always the case. There are times (particularly in old or "historical" sites) when the salts may have migrated into the soil profile below the rooting zone of shallow rooted vegetation or a covering of fill material may belie deeper contamination. Often, shallow rooted plants will flourish as the salt moves deeper into the soil profile. This is due to the fact that salt is highly mobile and may concentrate in discrete layers below the shallow rooting zone. Therefore, while grass might grow on it, a deeper rooted plant such as a tree would shrivel up quickly. Brine has several effects on soil, one of which is to change the osmotic potential to the extent that the plant can not overcome the salt in order to get water. Without going into great detail on the art of pit finding, suffice to say that it is important to know where pits have been as well as where they are known to be.

Also, it should be noted that things other than NOW have been dumped into some of these pits. I have seen some pretty strange things dredged up from production pits. An old, poorly closed pit may act as an active hazardous waste threat to the groundwater. Call this a word to the wise: an open pit is a nearly irresistible temptation to trash dumpers and some "midnight run" waste haulers. If your name is on the title deed, it does not matter whether you or someone else, dumped inappropriate materials into the pit. EPA's Mixture Rule could work against you to say that you have thousands of barrels of hazardous substance in a pit that is contaminating groundwater.

OIL & BRINE STORAGE TANKS. "Marler's Axiom of Purchasing Stock Tanks on a Property" states: "They have leaked." Memorizing and acting on this axiom will save heartache and money. Most stock tanks will have handled tens if not hundreds of thousands of barrels of produced fluids. Even a persistent small leak will add up over the years.

Most tank batteries will be enclosed with a berm or firewall, but it should be clearly understood that the function of the firewall is to contain spills and fires. It does not, unless lined, prevent the downward movement of fluids through the soil to the groundwater. Any old and/or large tank battery should be carefully examined. It is difficult to use stressed vegetation as an indicator in these cases, because the use of herbicide is common around this type of facility. Exactly what is under all that tidy fresh shell or gravel material? Hmmmm?

CHEMICAL STORAGE FACILITIES. E&P operations require the use of substances such as surfactants, solvents, and refined petroleum products that are not covered by the E&P RCRA exemption. Careful attention should be paid to the location and storage method of these substances. Proper management is imperative. Frequently, although not always, these substances will be found in drums. Aboveground storage tanks are also widely used.

Old drum storage areas are prime areas for groundwater contamination problems to begin. There are cases where a spill of one or two barrels of certain solvents can produce a groundwater contamination plume more than 1,000 ft long and 100 ft thick. A little can go a long way. SARA Title III requires that a facility inventory be kept of regulated substances and be available. This can be invaluable in determining what types of contamination might exist at the site, but it is not foolproof. Before the SARA Title III regulations were enacted, there may have been other chemicals in use on the site that are no longer present or inventoried.

Cost is a major factor with these wastes. If the contaminated soil must be handled as hazardous waste, then the cost will escalate three to five times the cost to handle them as NOW materials. Likewise, if the aquifer is compromised with these substances, the regulatory stress meter will be pegged in the red-line area. Appropriate onsite management of waste is terribly important, and here is an area where failure can cost the operator about a gazillion dollars (preliminary estimate).

EVALUATION AND RISK ANALYSIS

The above items are part of a larger system that may need to be evaluated for any one of several reasons. Whether the property is being audited for transfer of ownership or whether it is part of ongoing surveillance or whatever, the object here is: (1) to evaluate the potential risk to the groundwater and (2) to decide on the most prudent action path.

Determining whether a problem exists with the types of facilities and install-ations just listed is complex and requires specialized knowledge and skills. For instance, a casing leak will not normally be observed at the surface. Well, OK, there was one case where the author's attention was called to salt water gushing up out of the ground around the wellhead, but that did not require Aristotelian deduction. More often the answer will lie in the well history files. To benefit from such files, an investigator will need to be technical and oil industry-trained. For historical casing leaks, the old workover reports are invaluable. Production/pressure histories can be indicators of current casing/tubing leaks.

In other cases, NORM surveying has been used to confirm the presence of old pits, and infrared satellite data has been used to indicate old areas of soil contamination by flowline breaks.

Keen observation, sufficient E&P background to understand present operations (or reconstruct old ones), and good data are all essential ingredients in a risk assessment. Also, baseline groundwater data such as depth to groundwater, groundwater velocity, groundwater gradient, and soil characteristics are important. When confronted with evidence of a past spill or in dealing with effects of a present spill, it makes a great deal of difference whether the regional aquifer is at 50 ft with a soil CEC of 5 meq/100gm or whether it is at 200 ft with a thick soil profile having a CEC of 45 meq/100gm.

Topographic maps can be extremely useful in risk analysis as a preliminary means of assessing groundwater gradients. This kind of information would be good to have on file in report form for any property that you are operating. Additionally, it is good to be aware of operations in the vicinity of your property that might represent an aquifer threat. If a regulatory action occurs, you may not be the responsible party at all. The source of the contaminant plume may be some other facility than yours, and the sooner you can get lawyers and regulators looking away from you, the sooner you can get back to business. Sure, this is finger-pointing, but if it's good enough for the White House, it should be good enough for you.

Gathering baseline data requires some expenditure of time and money, but it can be useful in ultimately saving you money. You can't drill monitor wells every time you spill brine, so you have to have data by which you can assess the risk of a spill.

Having gathered baseline data on the groundwater and soil in the area of operation, then a model for groundwater risk will require information regarding the size of the spill, the type of materials spilled, and the time of the spill. Frequently, when purchasing a property, this data will not be available because many historic spill instances were simply not recorded. Also, a problem may be cumulative in that the contamination may result from numerous small spills and leaks during a period of years that would not have been recorded. In such cases, there will be less certainty in the risk assessment.

Salinity of the brine is an issue as well as solubility of any heavy metals. A "fate and transport" analysis of the spill materials will look at the chemistry of the spill contents. Most frequently, in the oil patch, the spill materials will be crude and/or brine, in which case, the more concentrated and larger volume spills will obviously present the greatest risk. However, if the spill materials contain heavy metals in soluble form or listed solvents or other hazardous materials, then the behavior of the spill in the soil profile may vary widely depending on the substance and the conditions prevailing in the soil itself.

GROUNDWATER SAMPLING

Let us assume for a moment that you have analyzed a historic spill on a property you are considering buying and have determined that there is sufficient reason to be concerned about risk to groundwater. What do you do first? Well, first (and most importantly) you curse the miserable wretch of a consultant who has found the problem and is messing up your business deal. I would suggest that you restrict this stage of the process to a 24 hr period, because it can result in uncontrollable twitching on the part of everyone involved, if prolonged. However, after having completed that stage of the investigation, you are going to have to get a groundwater sample. It is the only way you are going to know for sure. Just as a good prospect can only be proven by turning the bit to the right, a risk assessment is a best guess until samples are taken and analyzed. Even then, there may be uncertainty as to whether there is contamination.

Let's get something straight. What we are talking about here is not engineering in the sense of building a bridge. We are talking about earth science that does not submit itself well to the test tube. In the geologic realm, precision is less than perfect. When a great deal of money is at stake, everyone wants every answer to be correct to the Nth degree. That is, unfortunately, not likely to happen. Anyone who wants to imply to you that "risk analysis" and "fate and transport analysis" is an exact process or even that groundwater sampling is infallible should be hosting one of those 3 a.m. infomercials. Without going into details, the very process of sample collection can render the results somewhat skewed. Likewise, the dynamic and sometimes vague state of the existing regulations makes it uncertain whether action is required.

All this talk about inherent uncertainty is meant to help balance the reader's perception. It makes sense right now. It will not when you have millions of dollars at risk and a looming closing date. You will want absolute certainty and it will frequently not be available. When buying a property for which there is significant uncertainty

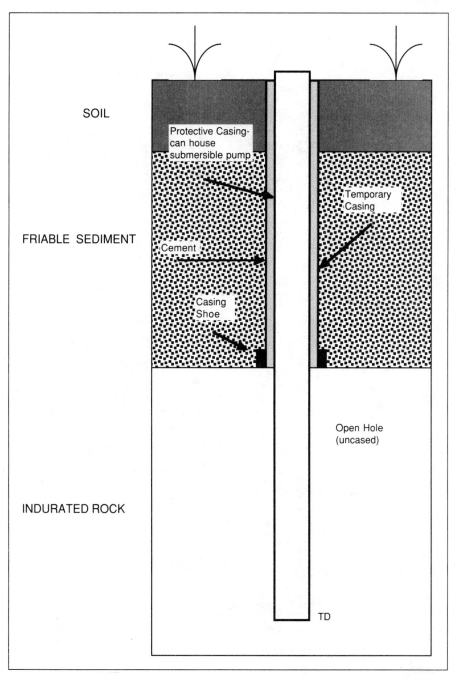

Figure 5-5
Monitoring well design frequently used in areas where the aquifer is composed of indurated rock but overlain by friable material

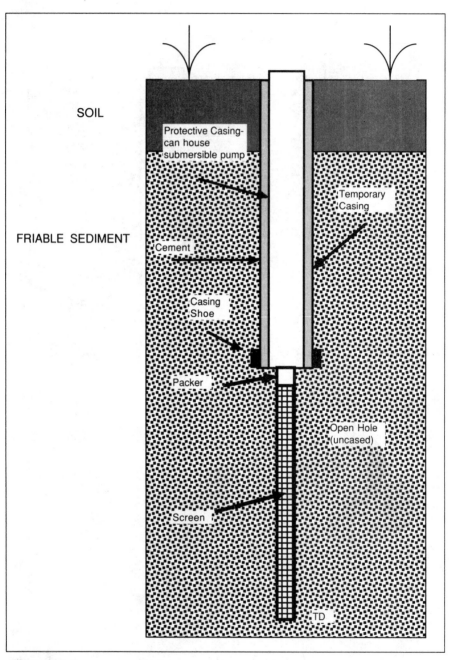

SOIL

FRIABLE SEDIMENT

Protective Casing-
can house
submersible pump

Temporary
Casing

Cement

Casing
Shoe

Packer

Open Hole
(uncased)

Screen

TD

Figure 5-6
*Monitoring well design frequently used in areas where the aquifer is and
bounding geologic formations are composed of friable material*

Photo 2-1

This is a colossally bad idea. Potentially hazardous substances stored inside a NOW pit. If leakage occurred, the entire pit contents could be ruled hazardous. Does the reader have any idea what it would cost to dispose of 10,000 BBL of hazardous waste? This little jewel would probably cost about $6 million.

Photo 3-1

Extreme case of stressed vegetation. In this case these trees have been killed by discharge of production waste. Seller's Phase One for this property stated that there was no stressed vegetation on the property. Frequently, stressed vegetation is more subtle and on a smaller scale.

Photo 3-2
Oil stock tanks shown here at an inland location. Note the firewall around the tanks and remember that this serves only to limit the areal extent of a potential spill. It does not prevent groundwater and soil contamination unless it is lined.

Photo 3-3
What is this? It might not look like it, but it is an ancient production pit.

Photo 3-4
A typical lined production discharge pit.

Photo 4-1
Sampling for hydrocarbons using a standard soil probe.

Photo 5-1
The inside of this tank battery firewall has received a surface spill of crude oil and brine that could infiltrate into the groundwater system.

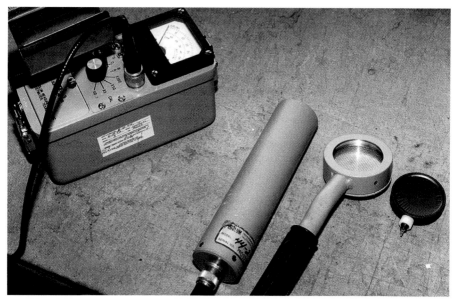

Photo 6-1
Some of the equipment used for NORM surveying including a Pancake G-M (left) and a scintillation detector (right). A typical meter is in the center.

Photo 6-2
Surveying for NORM using a Ludlum Model 3 Meter with a 44-2 detector.

Photo 6-3
These vessels and tubulars are all potential NORM accumulations. Sludge in the stock tanks and scale in the heaters are not uncommon.

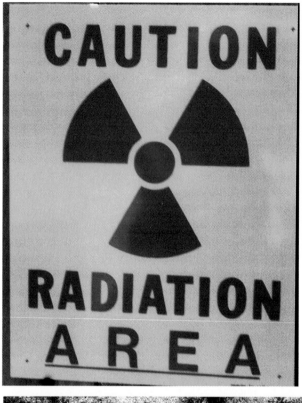

Photo 6-4
Tri-Foil Symbol to be used in the posting of restricted areas, labeling of drums, warning notices, etc. Additional information can be be added to the symbol as appropriate, such as "Restricted Area" or "Radioactive Material."

Photo 7-1
Production pit in use as a discharge pit to receive produced brines. Note the oil staining the levee. Yellow material is sulfur.

Photo 7-2
Pit sampling using PVC sampling equipment inside pit complex. The selection of sampling parameters and protocols is an important aspect of pit analysis.

Photo 7-3
Pit in foreground is the primary discharge pit and shows obvious oil and grease content while pit in background is the secondary and is markedly less contaminated.

Photo 8-1
Pits prior to remediation.

Photo 8-2
Pits after remediation.

Photo 9-1
View of Site 1 area as seen looking NE from Tank Battery 1, which is located on the south side of the east-west elongated area.

Photo 9-2
View of the Site 1 Area as seen looking NW from the #1 Tank Battery. Deforestation is extensive. Lilies seen in the photo are not rooted and therefore not affected by the soil conditions.

Photo 9-3
Deforested Site 1 as seen looking NW from Tank Battery #2. More stumps are still standing on the east end of the site.

Photo 9-4
Lily pads (center of the photo) mark the location of the closed Tank Battery #2 Pit, north of the #2 Tank Battery and within the Site 1 Area.

Photo 9-5
Tank Battery #1 and its associated heater-treater platform as seen from the SW. The Site 1 Area is on the far side of the platforms.

Photo 9-6
Both concrete and steel grating decks in use on the heater-treater platform for Tank Battery #1.

Photo 9-7
Oil staining on the wooden deck of Tank Battery #1. The containment system observed consisted of individual drain pans around each tank, as seen in photo.

Photo 9-8
Salt Water Disposal Facility west of Tank Battery #1 showing Site 1 in the background.

Photo 9-9
Tank Battery #2 and its associated separator platform as seen from the SW.

Photo 9-10
Heater-treater platform for Tank Battery #2 as seen from the SW.

Photo 9-11
Steel grate decking at the heater platform for Tank Battery #2 .

Photo 9-12
Wooden platform deck in use on Tank Battery #2 heater platform.

Photo 9-13
Wooden platform deck and individual drain pans in use on Tank Battery #2.

Photo 9-14
Unidentified active oil producer as seen from the west. Note canal in background. Edge of site is about 30 ft from the canal. Yellow drum is a demulsifier unit.

Photo 9-15
Site #1 as viewed from the southeast. Bog area, rimmed by stressed and dead vegetation and dark staining, is in foreground. Water may be brine.

Photo 9-16
Additional view of Site #1 from the southeast showing the contaminated area and the dead vegetation.

Photo 9-17
Closeup of flowline on south edge of site showing elbow where line goes underground. Note oil staining and cloudy water.

Photo 9-18
Vandalized demulsifier drums in bottom of canal as seen from the north edge of Site #1.

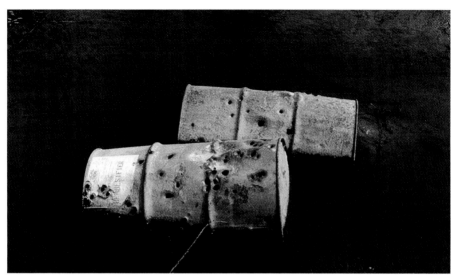

Photo 9-19
Closeup of demulsifier drums in the bottom of the canal north of Site #1. It is unknown whether the drums were full when perforated.

Photo 9-20
Winger #1 Tank battery, as viewed from the southeast. Note meter in foreground and chain link fence surrounding the installation. Inside the chain link is an older post and cable barrier. Three heater-treaters are in the foreground. Three stock tanks are in the background.

Photo 9-21
View of three storage tanks within their subdivided firewall area. Note the height of the oil stain on the far firewall.

Photo 9-22
Closer view of south side of easternmost storage tank showing evidence of recent overflow. Note oil staining on the side.

Photo 9-23
Free oil and water standing behind the tank battery inside firewall. View is looking east toward the heater-treaters along the north side of the facility.

Photo 9-24
View from the south of the Winger #1 facility showing free oil and water standing inside the heater-treater firewall subdivision. Note height of oil stain on storage tank firewall in lower left foreground.

Photo 9-25
Northeast corner of heater-treater installation showing free oil and water standing inside the firewall. The heater-treater is an old unit that was observed to be leaking at a flowline junction near the flange.

Photo 9-26
View of the Winger #1 production pit from the east. Note flow line extending into the pit in the foreground. Flow line appears to be an overflow line from inside the heater-treater firewall area.

Photo 9-27
View of water-filled production pit looking south toward the Winger #1 Tank Battery. Water level is very high.

Photo 9-28
Valves and oil staining on ground on west side of tank battery showing dead vegetation/saplings. Area is on eastern edge of contaminated, barren, boggy area.

Photo 9-29
Closeup of valves and oil staining and dead vegetation on the west side of
the tank battery.

Photo 9-30
Barren, boggy area as viewed from northeast near the backside of the
Bender #1 Tank Battery. Note cloudy water and dead vegetation and pine
tree (far right).

Photo 9-31
View of bog area as viewed from the southeast. Note dead pine tree in the foreground and dead ground vegetation. Water (probably brine) is pooled in background.

Photo 9-32
Barren soil showing oil staining around flowlines on the north side of the Bender #1 facility site.

Photo 9-33
Closeup of rusted flowline on north edge of site showing oil staining and cloudy water. Note dead ground vegetation.

Photo 9-34
Apparent shipping terminal on south side of tank battery. Photo shows 4" flowline dripping oil into a partially buried drum. Both drum and standpipe (upper right) are oil filled. Note slight patina of oil on the ground surface.

after groundwater sampling, it may be useful to risk your probable financial exposure in the same way that you would run risked economics for a drilling prospect. By the way, do not forget to run your economics on a Before Federal Income Tax (BFIT) and After Federal Income Tax (AFIT) basis, because the IRS has recently reversed its ruling and will now allow capitalization of environmental expenditures such as for constructing a groundwater remediation facility/network.

With this newly balanced perspective in mind, what is possible and what do you do? Well, there are several ways of gathering groundwater data. First, the obvious method of drilling groundwater monitoring wells is available for a wide range of costs depending on what type of well is needed and its depth. Different geologic conditions will allow or mandate different types of wells. Figures 5-5 and 5-6 illustrate different types of monitoring wells that might be used under different circumstances. Where unconsolidated sediment is the host for the groundwater, some sort of screen will need to be in place. If the aquifer being sampled and monitored is indurated sandstone, however, the screen may not be necessary. There are other variations that could be described, but the idea is that different situations require different solutions. A deeper monitoring well with more frills can cost more than a shallow well with no frills.

When drilling monitoring wells and analyzing groundwater samples one usually has a set of state regulatory action or threshold levels in mind against which the results will be compared. However, it is important to remember to compare results with local background levels (naturally occurring metals and compounds that would be typical for uncontaminated water in the aquifer in the area). It can be in local instances that the background is near or above the regulatory limits, although that is not likely. In such a case, you may not have a contamination incident at all. Conversely, the risk with such an analysis is that the local background levels are very far below the regulatory limits and, even though your samples are below the limits, you may nevertheless be contaminating the aquifer.

In the past several years effort has been expended by regulatory agencies, both state and federal, to establish regulatory limits for contaminants in drinking water. MCLs have long been established under the SDWA and can be found in 40 CFR 141. The groundwater quality standards stewarded by individual states are generally based, to one degree or another, upon these MCLs.

More recently, in recent years, the EPA has sought to establish water quality standards under the auspices of the RCRA. Specifically, these threshold limits are intended for use in RCRA TSD (Treatment-Storage-Disposal) Facilities and would be included in 40 CFR 264-265 as "Subpart S." These regulations were proposed in the July 1990 *Federal Register* and were scheduled to become final in December 1993, but have not been finalized at this writing. A brief rundown of the proposed Subpart S levels is included in Table 5-1.

Table 5-1
Subpart S groundwater action levels*

PARAMETER	LEVEL	COMMENTS
Benzene	5 ppb	
Toluene	1 ppm	
Ethylbenzene	700 ppb	
Xylenes	10 ppm	
Chlorides	250 mg/l	Secondary
As (Arsenic)	50 ppb	Note: Louisiana 29-B Metal
Ba (Barium)	2 ppm	Note: Louisiana 29-B Metal
Cd (Cadmium)	5 ppb	Note: Louisiana 29-B Metal
Cr (Chromium	100 ppb	Note: Louisiana 29-B Metal
Hg (Mercury)	2 ppb	Note: Louisiana 29-B Metal
Pb (Lead)	15 ppb	Note: Louisiana 29-B Metal
Ra (Radium)	5 pCi/l	Gross a & ß = 15
Volatile Scan		If not natural, anything above detection level must be reported.

*As proposed under RCRA in the July 1990 Federal Register by the EPA

While it is a fact that the Subpart S regulatory limits have not been finalized as yet, at least one regulatory agency in the oil patch is considering their usage in a broader context than RCRA TSD Facilities.

In addition to sampling the groundwater with a view to regulatory guidelines, there are also established protocols and sampling procedures that must be observed. A monitoring well, for instance, will need to be bailed (purged) prior to sampling, and some sample analyses (such as BTEX) require zero headspace on sample jars. The collection technique for other kinds of samples is less critical. Valves may need to be flushed prior to sample collection. EPA has established certain laboratory procedures for analysis, and the laboratory should be aware of the necessary protocol as it relates to your purpose in sampling.

There are two other sources that may need to be considered when investigating possible groundwater contamination. First surface waters in the area that are likely to be affected by groundwater pollution can be sampled. Also, it might be useful to sample residential and agricultural wells that are in harm's way.

All right…Let's summarize where we are. We have looked at your property in terms of doing a groundwater risk assessment. Some of the ingredients of a good risk assessment that have been discussed are as follows:

- Equipment in use
- Types of processes
- Soil characteristics
- Type of spill materials
- Quantity of spill materials
- Groundwater depth
- Groundwater gradient
- Groundwater velocity
- Historical file data

Likewise, we have talked about groundwater sampling and seen that there are several aspects of the sampling and analysis process that must be kept in mind including:

- Source of sample (monitoring well, lake water, etc.)
- Appropriate monitoring well construction
- Regulatory action levels (state and federal)
- Background levels
- Appropriate container
- Proper laboratory protocol

In all this do not forget that you can tailor your sampling parameters much more effectively if you know what was spilled. Sampling for arsenic is simply a waste of time and money if arsenic was never spilled in the location in question. Figure 5-7 shows an example of a BTEX sample analysis data sheet and Figure 5-8 shows a metals analysis data sheet for groundwater. In some cases, the contents of the spill will not be known and a broad "net" approach to sampling will need to be used that will have the effect of increasing the laboratory analysis cost for the project. However, once your initial sampling determines the type of contaminants, the parameters can be shrunk to zero in on the known problem.

Likewise, the reason these wells are called "monitoring" wells is that there is an implied need in the name. "Monitoring" carries the connotation of ongoing surveillance. Often, depending on the purpose at hand, sampling must be repeated over a period of time (say, 6 months or even a year) in order to understand the scope and magnitude of the problem. Computer modeling of the plume may be helpful or necessary in order to understand its fate and transport factors.

```
LAB I.D. _____    DATE REPORTED: 11/02/93

SAMPLE DESCRIPTION _____
DATE COLLECTED:  10/19/93  12:00
```

ANALYTE	ANALYSIS INITIALS	DATE COMPLETED	REFERENCE METHOD	DETECTION LIMIT	CONCENTRATION mg/l (ppm)
TOTAL XYLENEs	SF	10/26/93	SW846-8020	0.002 ppm	0.075
BENZENE	SF	10/26/93	SW846-8020	0.002 ppm	0.106
ETHYL BENZENE	SF	10/26/93	SW846-8020	0.002 ppm	0.016
TOLUENE	SF	10/26/93	SW846-8020	0.002 ppm	BDL
TOTAL PETROLEUM HYDROCARBON	TG	10/28/93	EPA 418.1	10 ppm	BDL

Figure 5-7
BTEX sample analysis data sheet

```
LAB I.D. _____    DATE REPORTED: 11/02/93

SAMPLE DESCRIPTION _____
DATE COLLECTED:  10/19/93  12:00
```

ANALYTE	ANALYSIS INITIALS	DATE COMPLETED	REFERENCE METHOD	DETECTION LIMIT	CONCENTRATION mg/l (ppm)
ARSENIC	TS	10/25/93	EPA 206.3	0.0004 ppm	0.0372
BARIUM	TS	10/22/93	EPA 200.7	0.0004 ppm	13.1
CADMIUM	TS	10/22/93	EPA 200.7	0.0003 ppm	BDL
CHLORIDE	MF	10/28/93 14:00	EPA 325.3	2.0 ppm	7,020
CHROMIUM	TS	10/22/93	EPA 200.7	0.007 ppm	0.219
MERCURY	TS	10/20/93	EPA 245.1	0.00002 ppm	0.00048
LEAD	TS	10/22/93	EPA 200.7	0.050 ppm	BDL
pH	NP	10/20/93 10:55	EPA 150.1	0.1 s.u.	6.77 s.u.

Figure 5-8
Metals analysis data sheet

MONITORING WELL NETWORK DESIGN

We have to back up a step at this point and talk about the strategy for drilling sample collection points. Where and how many monitoring wells are needed will depend upon several factors:

- Economics. How much money do you have to spend or how much are you willing to spend?

- Your purpose. If you are merely trying to confirm groundwater contamination in order to flee a potential purchase, then one well, located as close as practicable to the contaminant source and downgradient, might be sufficient. If you suspect that you have been severely damaged by someone else's operation, you may want to do a very thorough study before unleashing the "dogs of law."

- The size of the area affected. This is fairly self-explanatory. If you have 100 acres of contaminated soil that changes from a loam to a sandy loam with 12 separate potential groundwater gradients, one well will simply not suffice.

- Groundwater characteristics. There is often uncertainty as to the exact gradient and the velocity of the groundwater, so how far has a plume moved and where is it?

The most traditional method for monitoring well placement is the "one up - two down" or "one up - three down." In other words, one well is placed upgradient of the point source. The point source is the leaking tank, or pit, or whatever has been identified as a probable origin of the contaminant plume. Upgradient of that point, the water should not be contaminated, so having a well in this location allows several things to be determined. First, if the groundwater is uncontaminated, it can be analyzed for background levels of the substances being investigated. Second, it allows confirmation of the preliminary groundwater gradient assessment. Third, if the water upgradient proves to be contaminated, either the assumed gradient is wrong or the wrong facility has been identified as a point source or more than one contaminant source is present.

The two or three downgradient wells are arrayed in such a way so as to intercept the contaminant plume and allow assessment of its size as well as the level of contamination present. Placement position of the downgradient wells will be dependent upon the groundwater velocity and the time interval between the spill and the investigation. Also, the number of required wells will vary with variances in the impact area and time factors.

By way of background, it should be noted that flow in an aquifer will not be turbulent but laminar. As a result, little mixing of the contaminants will occur because the contaminants will tend to move with the groundwater along the path dictated by hydraulic gradients. Flow rates for the groundwater that are under consideration here are not exactly clipping along at Warp Factor Three. Depending on the hydraulic conductivity of the aquifer, the movement rates of the plume may vary from a few inches to several feet per day.

It should be noted again, however, that different substances will behave somewhat differently in response to a given hydraulic gradient. Volatile organics are very mobile, and their physical characteristics will cause them to respond differently than metals. Therefore, there are other factors that must be considered in the establishment of a monitoring well network besides location. It is a three-dimensional problem (actually four, counting time). Figure 5-9 illustrates how a monitoring well can be properly placed and yet fail to give a true picture. The depth of the well and the length of the screened interval in the well must be appropriate to the type of contaminant in question.

HOW BIG IS BIG?

What you would like to have at this point (after having done your risk assessment and establishing your monitoring well network) is a clear understanding of whether you actually have an environmental or regulatory problem. Beyond that, if a problem exists, are you obligated to further action? What is that action? What will this cost you? Do you transfer your remaining funds to a bank in Brazil?

Nothing in this discussion represents good news to the operator. It is a question of bad or worse news. Hopefully, you are purchasing and can simply walk away, but you have already spent money on the issue. If you are the owner, you are likely to spend tens and possibly hundreds of thousands of dollars to prove that you are not liable, if that is even possible. If you *are* the responsible party, you are looking at a potentially disastrous expenditure on a pump and treat. We are not talking about silver linings to clouds here. With all due apologies to the Japanese, crisis does not necessarily imply opportunity. What we are talking here is a process of delaying (within the bounds of decency and ethics) and minimizing expenditures and finding a way to survive.

A larger independent or a major can sustain more of this kind of setback, but a small independent is highly jeopardized. It would be strongly advisable to look hard before you leap. Buying someone else's mess is risky business. if you already own the problem, there may be good reason to argue against the dictates of the plain brown vanilla wrapper regulation (i.e., "We've got a limit and you are over it"). A well-reasoned argument based on facts may establish a minimization of your expenditure and it may be worth a try.

---

1   R. Allen Freeze and John A. Cherry, Groundwater (Englewood Cliffs, New Jersey, Prentice-Hall, Inc., 1979.

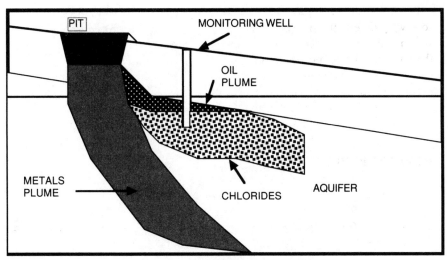

IDEALIZED CROSS SECTION OVER PIT AND MONITORING WELL.

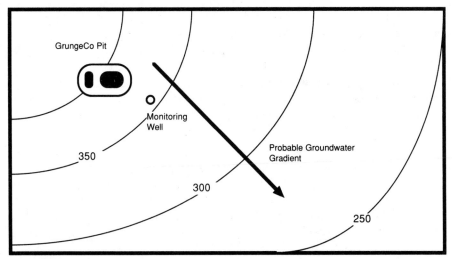

IDEALIZED TOPO MAP SHOWING PIT AND MONITORING WELL LOCATION.

Figure 5-9

Idealized topo map and cross section showing typical case for monitor well placement and groundwater sampling. Note in cross section that the well,

Naturally Occuring **6**
Radioactive Materials
(NORM)

Naturally Occurring Radioactive Material (NORM) is a relatively recent arrival on the oil and gas regulatory scene. In the last several years, it has come to center stage, particularly in Louisiana, as a widespread and expensive regulatory problem. NORM will probably continue to constitute a problem for producers, so it will be important to understand the basics.

The production process itself tends to concentrate radium (Ra) isotopes in the form of mineral scale and can over time build up to levels that will affect the operating cost of the producer. Most of the problem, with exception of some specific health and safety issues, is tied up with disposal, storage, and abandonment costs.

Initially, most NORM discussion concerned the existence and disposition of NORM contained in tubulars and production related vessels such as heater-treaters and storage tanks. However, it has become obvious that NORM is not limited to the interior of vessels. Soil has in many instances also been affected. Discharge pits have been found to contain significantly elevated concentrations of Ra226/Ra228. When one begins to consider the volumes of materials contained in these pits, the cost of closure and remediation can be staggering.

THE PROBLEM

NORM is not an exposure problem. The level of energy emission from NORM is simply not likely to induce measurable tissue damage. Standing next to a vessel generating gamma radiation from NORM materials is not a high-risk activity. The problem with NORM is ingestion of alpha particles, which can take up residence in the bone structure and cause lingering damage. Therefore, the concern is to prevent the ingestion of these alpha particles by workers and others who come in contact with it. Additionally, it becomes important to keep it out of the food chain.

BACKGROUND

Radiation can be defined as the spontaneous emission of particles or electromagnetic waves that are given off by an unstable atom. NORM consists of three different types of radiation.[1] They are: alpha particles, beta particles, and gamma radiation.

Gamma radiation has no mass or electrical charge. It is not particulate in nature and is similar to x-rays. It has high penetrating ability and can penetrate the entire human body. When a NORM meter (Scintillation detector or otherwise) is used to measure emissions of radiation from inside a steel tank, gamma radiation primarily is the activity that is being measured. This is because of the nature of the other two forms of NORM radiation.

Both alpha and beta particles have mass and electrical charge. They are particulate, alpha particles having the largest mass. While these particles, particularly the alphas, are the primary concern due to their propensity to cause biological damage, they have very low penetration ability. In fact, a thin sheet of plastic will screen out the beta particle and a dead layer of skin is sufficient to prevent penetration by the alpha (Table 6-1). This is why measurement of NORM from outside a vessel by a meter is measuring gamma radiation.

Table 6-1
Comparing penetration by radiation type

RADIATION	MASS	CHARGE	PENETRATION UNIT	COMMENTS
gamma	none	none	Whole body	photons from nucleus
beta	1/1836	+ or -	Thin plastic sheet	mass = electron
alpha	4	2	Skin layer	2 protons + 2 neutrons

*Adapted from Radiation Technical Services.[1]

Therefore, the great objective with NORM is to deal with the problem in such a way so as to prevent its ingestion. Exposure levels due to gamma radiation are relatively low. Relative health risk from exposure to the levels of gamma radiation generated by NORM is low.

A detailed study of the health physics of NORM radiation is outside the scope of this book. However, contamination by NORM can lead to ingestion of alpha particles. In dusty conditions, airborne particulate matter can be inhaled. Carelessness and ignorance can result in contaminated material being transferred from hand to mouth, perhaps during eating. Once the alpha particles get inside the body, a portion of them will be absorbed and the radiation will be emitted within the body for an extended time.

For instance, the biological half life of radium (the time it takes the body to eliminate half the atoms through normal bodily processes) is about 45 years. The effective half life calculates to just less than 44 years.

Obviously, this must be considered a more or less permanent condition on a scale of human lifespan. Certainly, the effects of internally emitted radiation abate with time, but that is small comfort to someone who at age 30 ingests a substantial quantity of alpha particles. Therefore, it is important that employees receive proper training in the handling of these materials and proper application of "time, distance, and shielding" for NORM related work.

UNITS

There remains a great deal of confusion in the industry about the units involved in describing NORM. People are bewildered by the use of terms such as Rad, Rem, Roentgen, Curie, DPM, CPM, etc. A brief discussion of these terms should help, and the reader will see that in dealing with NORM most people will be confronted mainly with two of the above terms.

Roentgen is, in radiation parlance, a unit of exposure. It is the amount of x-ray or gamma radiation that will produce one electrostatic unit of charge in 1 cm³ of dry air at standard conditions. Given the relatively low levels of NORM radiation, exposure is denoted by the term microRoentgens per hour or µR/hr. This means that the meter is measuring 10^{-6} Roentgens/hr. NORM meters are, therefore, measuring exposure to gamma radiation. This term is distinct from the Rad and Rem, but is frequently confused.

Rad, is a unit of dosage. It is an acronym for "Radiation Absorbed Dose" and represents the amount of radiation that will deposit 100 ergs of energy per gram of material. Rem (or Roentgen Equivalent Man) is a unit of biological damage. Both Rad and Rem are less frequently used terms, but it is important to understand their distinction from Roentgen.

The second commonly used term is Curie, which is a measure of the *rate* of radioactive decay. It describes the disintegrations that are occurring per second in any radioactive material. A Curie is defined as the amount of any radioactive material that will disintegrate at a rate of $3.7 * 10^{10}$ disintegrations per second. Again, because of the relatively low activity levels that exist in NORM materials, a modifier of this term (Curie) is used. NORM activities are expressed in picoCuries per gram or pCi/gm. This means that NORM activities are being measured in trillionths of a Curie or 10^{-12} Curies. When soil samples are taken for NORM the lab results will be reported in pCi/gm.

In summary, the two most common units to be encountered in NORM work are µR/hr and pCi/gm. MicroRoentgens per hour is the unit of exposure while picoCuries/gm is a unit of activity. There are, occasionally, times when it would be desirable to be able to convert µR/hr to the equivalent pCi/gm. Such will be discussed in a following section.

NORM SURVEYING & TESTING EQUIPMENT

There are a number of instances where it would be a good idea to be aware of the quantity of and location of NORM on a property. You might want to have an estimate (for planning purposes) of the amount of additional NORM related expenses that you will have to add to your abandonment costs. Likewise, you might need to have the same information available to figure into your economics for the purchase of a property. Equipment and soil NORM has been accumulating as a result of the seller's production process. Why should you bear the full cost of disposal of accumulations from which you did not profit? That disposal cost could prove to be disastrous.

Finally, you might simply need to survey in order to fulfill regulatory requirements. In Louisiana, for instance, you have a choice to either register the entire field as a NORM facility or to survey site by site and only register those parts that are NORM contaminated above the regulatory threshold.

There are several types of equipment available that are used to measure NORM exposure levels, but the most commonly used types of equipment utilize either scintillation or ionization as the mechanism. Two general classes of detection instruments are used in working with NORM: gas filled detectors and solid state detectors (Photo 6-1). The gas filled detectors utilize ionization while the solid state detectors most often used in NORM work are scintillation counters. In both types of detectors, the radiation is measured indirectly by measuring its effect in the material in the detection chamber.

NORM survey equipment, either ionization or scintillation, has three basic parts in common: a detector chamber, a power supply and amplification component, and a measuring device/meter.

Because of its high sensitivity to low radiation levels, the Geiger-Mueller tube is commonly used in NORM surveying. It is an ionization type detector. A variation on the theme is the "pancake G-M (Geiger Mueller)," which is often used for decontamination station checks of workers. However, the Geiger-Mueller device is not able to distinguish between different types and energies of radiation as are other types of gas filled detectors such as the ion chamber and the proportional counter. Therefore, it is not possible to directly discriminate between alpha and gamma with the Geiger-Mueller, although there are techniques that will allow a calculation of the approximate proportions under some circumstances.

In the case of the scintillation detector, the operative reaction being measured is the excitation of certain materials by the gamma photons to produce light. The light is measured and the amount of radiation exposure is calculated.

Different materials are used to detect different types of radiation. For instance, a thin sheet of zinc sulfite is commonly used to detect alpha radiation, while another instrument might use sodium iodide thallium crystals as an agent in detecting gamma radiation.

SURVEYING & TESTING

Any number of circumstances or situations might require a NORM survey and many terms might be applied to these various occasions, such as baseline (property transfer), release, periodic, etc. The important thing is to recognize the nature of the NORM issue and to know why and when it might be necessary. If you are rattling pipe or are in an environment where employees may be exposed to loose contamination, you will be very concerned with the health and safety aspect of NORM and will need periodic testing and monitoring. If you are operating a well with NORM contaminated facilities, you will be concerned with being within regulatory guidelines. If you are buying a producing property or a former NORM storage facility, you will be (or had better be) keenly interested in the magnitude of the problem you are inheriting.

The nature of your problem will define the degree of detail needed and the scope of your survey. For instance, if you are releasing a producing property in Louisiana for unrestricted use, you will need to be very detailed in your surveying and sampling program, because you are attempting to demonstrate that the property is within regulatory tolerance and needs no cleanup. Everything from your pre- and post-survey calibration check to your surveying technique is important. On the other hand, if you are checking the NORM situation on a potential purchase, you will be interested in the "meat" of the matter. How much is there, and what will it cost you to close and abandon?

Whatever the cause, there are three components to the survey: the pre-survey operational check, the survey itself, and a post-survey operational check.

PRE-SURVEY Before a NORM survey, it is important to know the regulatory environment of the state in which you are working. Different states have different regulatory threshold limits for NORM contamination (Table 6-1). Is the limit 50 µR/hr including background or 50 µR/hr above background or is it 25 µR/hr? The meter must be within proper calibration limits. Background radiation levels should be properly checked, and the meter should be given an operational check. Low batteries can make a property look pretty good. It is helpful to have a check source such as Cs137 to compare before and after the survey. Pre-survey actions should be recorded.

SURVEY. Someone trained in NORM surveying will be familiar with the methodologies involved, but that is really outside the scope of this book. Therefore, this chapter will concentrate on ingredients of an effective NORM survey (Photo 6-2).

I have found that a picture is worth a thousand words. This was discovered through many instances of trying to make sense of NORM survey sheets and relating them to facility sites and vessels. A surveyor may well know where he took readings and what he surveyed, but memory will eventually fail and someone reading the report may have little or no idea what is being communicated. Site sketches (intelligible) and maps can be invaluable, particularly where soil is a concern.

Obvious areas where NORM contamination may exist would include just about any vessels handling (or formerly handling) produced fluids (Photo 6-3). A partial list of potential NORM vessels would include: stock tanks, salt water storage tanks, heater treaters, free water knockouts, tubulars/flowlines, and pits.

This list is far from complete. It simply does not take a rocket scientist to stick a probe on these items and record the readings. However, there are some NORM measurements that require more thought. For instance, soil contamination might require grid surveying and soil sampling.

In Louisiana, a release survey is required before a licensed NORM facility can be released for unrestricted use. Louisiana's release survey regulations require that the grid spacing for NORM readings be no more than 10 m (3 m in known contamination areas). This grid then will be used to determine the need for and design of a confirmatory sampling program. Readings of more than twice background levels are

Table 6-2
NORM regulatory summary table for Louisiana, Mississippi and Texas

State	NORM Limit: Equipment	NORM Limit: Soils - For Release		Restricted Area Boundary
		Ra Emanation rates <20pCi/M^2/sec.	Ra Emanation rates >20pCi/M^2/sec.	
LA	25 µR/hr >Backgrd	30 pCi/gm Ra226 or Ra228 Ave. over 100 m^2 or 150pCi/gm of any NORM radionuclide	5 pCi/gm (1rst 15 cm in depth), 15 pCi/gm successive 15 cm depth intervals	600 µR/hr
MS	25 µR/hr >Backgrd	30 pCi/gm Ra 226 or Ra228 ave. over 100 m^2 for 1rst 15 cm of depth	5 pCi/gm (1rst 15 cm in depth), 15 pCi/gm successive 15 cm depth intervals	600 µR/hr
TX	50 µR/hr incl. Backgrd.	30 pCi/gm Ra 226 or Ra228 ave. over 100 m^2 for 1rst cm of Depth	5 pCi/gm (1rst 15 cm in depth), 15 pCi/gm successive 15 cm depths	600 µR/hr

Note: Both Mississippi and Texas have Airborne Radioactivity Area posting requirement set at 25% of one DAC Value. Also, both Mississippi and Texas have a loose surface contamination limit of 200 dpm/100 cm^2 averaged for alpha emitters.

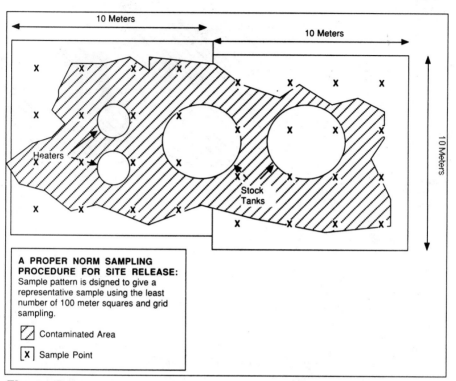

Figure 6-1

Example of a proper survey grid for release of facility site with NORM contamination potential

to be marked as possible sampling sites. Post release values should not exceed 30 pCi/gm averaged over 100 square meters if the radon emanation rate is less than 20 pCi/m2/sec. If the emanation rate is more than 20 pCi/m2/sec, the limit is 5 pCi/gm averaged over the upper 15 cm of soil and 15 pCi/gm for the next 15 cm down. Texas has similar numbers.

These regulations can be confusing and require some thought in planning the survey and sampling program. Furthermore, for release survey purposes, it is intended that the sampling program be unbiased. Figure 6-1 is an example of one way to arrive at a representative sample using a grid system. The number of samples taken from within the contaminated area must balance with those taken outside (but within the 100 square meters area) in order to give an accurate representation of the average values. The intent of the regulations seems to be to preclude the possibility of subdividing a contaminated area in such a way as to avoid cleanup liability. Figure 6-2 shows a sampling grid that clearly would fail to accurately represent the condition of the soil at the site.

Historical issues enter into the picture when buying a producing property. Are all the facilities where they used to be? Are there old facility sites that might have

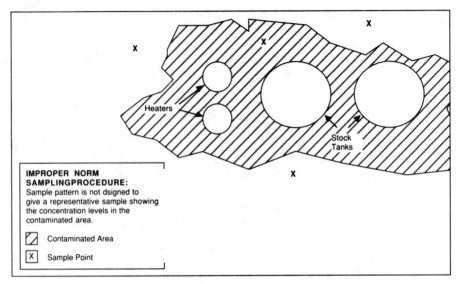

Figure 6-2
Improper NORM sampling procedure

contamination of soil and materials that are not obvious? One needs to be able to look at base maps and records and reconstruct relic operations. Frequently, I have found "overprint" of successive generations of facilities within very old fields. Contamination may exist where there is no existing facility site.

Finally, one of the most alarming aspects of NORM is the existence of contaminated pits. The sheer volume of material found in these pits makes them a potential financial disaster. As has been stated before, pit analysis is complex and will be treated as a subject by itself in a subsequent chapter.

NEW EPA DEVELOPMENTS

The Environmental Protection Agency is in the process of developing regulations for cleanup levels for sites that are radionucleide contaminated. The EPA issued an Announcement of Notice of Proposed Rulemaking, 58 Federal Register 54474, on October 21, 1993, and several NORM questions were raised. The question of whether NORM should be included in the cleanup standards for the general category of radionucleide contaminated sites was raised.

This is somewhat different than the the usual regulation path of development. Historically, the primary driving force has been federal regulations that are then mandated to the state level. However, in the case of NORM, oil producing states appear to have taken the lead.

Other questions raised by the EPA include:

- The current extent and nature of NORM contamination at Superfund sites and federal facilities.
- Whether future federal regulations would be useful.
- The impact of federal NORM regulations on existing state regulations.

It is difficult to assess at this point what the affect of federal NORM regulations would be. That possibility tends to muddy the waters somewhat.

In addition, regulations at the state level must also be regarded to be somewhat dynamic. Louisiana, which has created one of the more difficult regulatory situations for NORM, may be about to propose some changes in its regulatory regime. Proposed changes include (to name a few):

- Adding a 60 pCi/gm "hotspot" threshold amendment to the soil contamination exemption.
- Raising the equipment NORM limit to 50 µR/hr.
- Establishment of a non-soil contamination limit of 30 pCi/gm for NOW that is sent to a 29-B NOW landfill.
- Addition of 29-B site disposal for NOW containing exempt NORM. NOW that contains non-exempt NORM could be sent to a permitted 29-B facility.

At the time of this writing, the above amendments have not been proposed in the Louisiana Register. It is not known when or if the changes will be made.

DISPOSAL OPTIONS

While a multitude of NORM reduction technologies have been heralded, none of them as yet have gained widespread approval in the regulatory community. Additionally, most of these processes have proven to be of a high cost-low efficiency nature. Therefore, it might be good to discuss the existing viable options.

- The first option is simply to avoid the problem by storing the waste until you get a better idea. This does not really get rid of the problem, but it can delay expenditure. In Texas, for instance, there is not as yet any time limit on storage. However, that is not the case for Louisiana, where a general licensee can store NORM wastes on site for as long as 90 days. For storage more than 90 days, the materials must be moved to a licensed storage facility. Such licensed sites are few and far between and the last cost figure I saw was $2-3/55 gal. drum/day.
- Annular disposal is an option for low volumes of NORM material. This option does not involve injection of material into the geologic formation, but rather makes use of space in wells that are being plugged and abandoned. With this option, PVC pipe or well tubulars are filled with material and placed in the well to be P&Ad. The material is then cemented in place. The last cost figure I saw on this option was about $1,500/55 gal./drum/day.

- NORM treatment and disposal facilities are another common option. There are treatment and disposal facilities in Louisiana, Washington, and Utah. There are pros and cons that probably could be found for each of these facilities depending on the exigencies of the particular job itself, but there is good reason to become familiar with all these operations. Cost of disposal has ranged $400-800/55 gal. drum using this option.

- Injection into the formation has been viewed by many as the most logical way to deal with the problem and was intuitively believed to be the low cost option. This has not yet proven to be the case. Louisiana, for instance, does not allow injection. The Minerals Management Service (MMS) has allowed injection on the offshore continental shelf but does not allow wastes generated onshore to be injected offshore. One or two instances of special permission to do so have made history, but the cost, both in time and in money, has been prohibitive. This method has generated disposal costs ranging $900-1,400/55 gal. drum.

Any way you slice it, slurry it, inject it, or whatever, NORM is an expensive and maddening problem and it is probably here to stay as a regulatory issue.

PERSONNEL TRAINING

While detailed training information is outside the scope of this work, some basic principles of worker safety and the regulation thereof are in order. Since NORM is primarily an ingestion problem, the exposure to the radiation field itself is perhaps less applicable than in a nuclear reactor. However, it is important to understand the applicability of the basic health and safety principles.

Even now, there is still no equation that allows health physicists to predict flawlessly the extent and type of biological damage a person would sustain if exposed to a given level of ionizing radiation. As a result of this uncertainty concerning what constitutes a "safe dose," the As Low As Reasonably Achievable (ALARA) principle was formulated by the Atomic Energy Commission in 1971. In 1973, the International Committee of Radiation Protection concluded that, in view of the serious potential consequences of exposure to ionizing radiation, exposure should be kept to the lowest possible level.

Therefore, much regulation has been brought forth based on this ALARA Principle. NORM regulation also is derived from that principle.

Several definitions were put forth by the federal government in 10 CFR, Part 20 that pertain to ALARA. They are:

- Restricted area. Any area, access to which is controlled by the licensee for purposes of protection of individuals from exposure to radiation and radioactive materials. "Restricted area" shall not include any areas used as residential quarters, although a separate room or rooms in a building may be set apart as a restricted area.

- Unrestricted area. Any area, access to which is not controlled by the licensee for purposes of protection of individuals from exposure to radiation and radioactive materials and any area used for residential quarters.

- Radiation area. Any area, accessible to personnel, in which there exists radiation, originating in whole or in part within a licensed material, at such levels that a major portion of the whole body could receive in any one hour a dose in excess of 5 millirems.

Identification and posting is required for restricted and radiation areas. Several states have adopted labeling requirements for NORM areas, and their regulations are generally derived from or related to the preceeding definitions.

Another ALARA-related principle worth noting is that of "Time, Distance, and Shielding." As far as exposure goes, the worker's dose is directly related to the time spent in the radiation field. Actually, it is directly proportional. Therefore, by reducing time spent in the pathway of the gamma radiation, the dosage can be reduced. Distance is also important. The intensity of the radiation field becomes less as distance increases. Therefore, at 3 ft, the worker is absorbing less radiation than at 6 in. Likewise, he is getting less intensely bombarded at 10 ft than at three. Finally, shielding reduces exposure by absorbing or otherwise interfering with the radiation path. Placing a lead or steel shielding between oneself and a source can greatly reduce the amount of radiation reaching the body.

More detailed discussion is necessary to truly train workers, but these principles are mentioned briefly to show a need for proper posting and labeling and proper training of workers. If workers are aware of restricted or radiation areas and practice "Time, Distance, and Shielding," NORM related health risks can be practically eliminated.

However, a more serious concern for NORM contaminated areas relates to the ingestion problem. Areas of loose surface contamination and/or airborne contamination are serious problems and should be treated so.

LOOSE CONTAMINATION

Any number of activities can expose a worker to loose contamination. Cleaning out tank bottoms, rattling pipe, changing filters, etc. are all processes that can lead to ingestion of alpha particles. There are numerous incidents of workers eating with unwashed hands after handling NORM materials. One incident I know of involves a worker going out to get pizza with unwashed hands and work clothing. A trail of NORM was followed into several places, including his vehicle. Workers have tracked the material home onto carpets and furniture. Loose contamination areas should be identified and posted. Protective clothing should be worn to prevent the loose contamination from coming into contact with the worker's skin. Rubber gloves, disposable coveralls, boot covers, etc., are items of protective clothing. The type of clothing used should be in keeping with the type of work.

It is advisable to have a decontamination station with a pancake G-M (for detecting contamination on clothing) on hand for workers leaving restricted areas.

Mild soap and water are still the best decontamination materials available.

Bottom line: having trained personnel involved in your work process is important. Health problems, real, imagined, or contrived, are almost certainly going to result in an avalanche of lawsuits in the future. Abiding by the regulations and the health and safety principles of NORM not only serves to protect the health of your employees, but may blunt the edge of future litigation against you.

AIRBORNE NORM CONTAMINATION

As with loose contamination, airborne contamination can result from any number of work activities such as, grinding, welding, sandblasting, etc. Once airborne, the alpha particles can be ingested through respiration. Areas where the threshold level of 25% of the Derived Air Concentration (DAC) established by the newly updated 10 CFR Part 20 is exceeded must be posted as an "Airborne Radioactive Material Area." The DAC is defined as the concentration of a given radionuclide in air that, if breathed by the reference man for a working year of 2,000 hr under conditions of light work, results in the intake of 1 ALI (Annual Limit on Intake). An ALI is defined as the smaller value of intake of a given radionuclide in a year by the reference man that would result in a committed effective dose equivalent to 5 rem or a committed effective dose of 50 rem to any individual organ or tissue.

Generally, if an area is posted as an airborne radiation area, then proper respiratory gear should be worn. It should be noted that not all filters and respirators are appropriate and effective for this purpose. Depending on the level and type of airborne contamination present, a respirator with higher protection factor might be needed. By the way, failure to post and label appropriately in general is the number one source of NORM-related fines.

Air samples are needed to determine the level of airborne radioactivity. The sampling determines which radioisotopes are present, which allows a selection of DAC. Since all radioisotopes have different DACs, the types of radionucleides present must be determined in order to select the proper DAC.

SUMMARY

Most operators feel that NORM is a pain in certain parts of their corporate anatomy. It has proven expensive and complex. It has added to the already mushrooming burden of environmental regulations to which they are now subject. It will probably not go away.

Therefore, operators are going to have to find ways (hopefully legal) to deal with the situation. The author would counsel the following.

- NORM avoidance. Before you take possession of that property, you had better know the money value of the NORM on that property. Once you take possession, it is yours, friend. You may very well be the last owner of record of the property and the cleanup burden will fall on you. It is tempting to fall in love with a property and lose all perspective. The author has seen this over and over. To salivate over revenue without

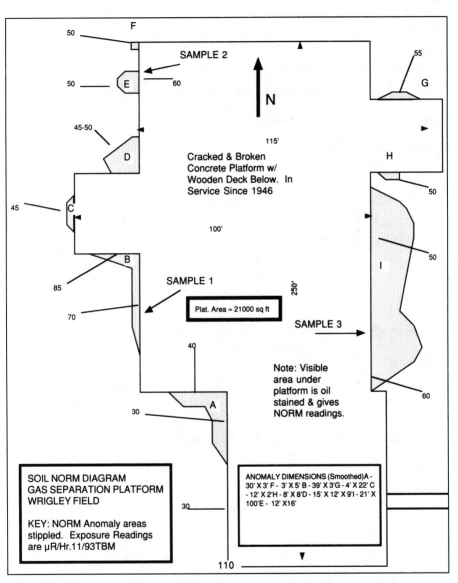

Figure 6-3
Soil NORM diagram

```
Page 2                        Report          Work Order #
Received: 10/20 93     10/30/93  10:10:52

VIGILANT ENVIRONMENTAL

Analysis of GAS PLATFORM #1 SAMPLE 1 - UNDER CEMENT SLAB collected
on 10/19/93 at 1100 and received at lab on 10/20/93 at 0800. Sample was
assigned No. and analyzed for Radioactivity as follows:

TEST DESCRIPTION                              RESULT (pCi/g)
Radium 226                                        78.15
Radium 228                                        21.83

COMMENTS: EPA Method 9315A, 9310, 9320.
```

Figure 6-4
NORM analysis sheet

```
Page 3                        Report          Work Order #
Received: 10/20 93     10/30/93  10:10:52     Continued From Above

VIGILANT ENVIRONMENTAL

Analysis of GAS PLATFORM #1 SAMPLE 2 collected on 10/19/93 at 1100 and
received at lab on 10/20/93 at 0800. Sample was assigned No. and analyzed
for Radioactivity as follows:

TEST DESCRIPTION                              RESULT (pCi/g)
Radium 226                                        15.37
Radium 228                                        1.072

COMMENTS: EPA Method 9315A, 9310, 9320.
```

Figure 6-5
NORM analysis sheet

```
Page 4                        Report          Work Order #
Received: 10/20 93     10/30/93  10:10:52     Continued From Above

VIGILANT ENVIRONMENTAL

Analysis of GAS PLATFORM #1 SAMPLE 3 collected on 10/19/93 at 1500 and
received at lab on 10/20/93 at 0800. Sample was assigned No. and analyzed
for Radioactivity as follows:

TEST DESCRIPTION                              RESULT (pCi/g)
Radium 226                                        40.68
Radium 228                                        8.791

COMMENTS: EPA Method 9315A, 9310, 9320.
```

Figure 6-6
NORM analysis sheet

considering the liability is not wise. Negotiate something you can live with.

- Have a strategy that minimizes NORM disposal expenditure and spreads it out over a period of time. When the pumps finally shut down is not a good time to begin looking at options. Identify your problems and systematically attack them.

- Invest in training and abide by the safety and health principles. This can save you both fines and litigation. It can keep a lot of things off your conscience. Treat your workers like you would wish to be treated.

PROBLEM ANALYSIS EXAMPLE

GAS SEPARATION PLATFORM (WRIGLEY FIELD) SOIL NORM

This vignette was taken from a transfer audit of a producing property where a very old separation facility was located. The separation equipment was located on a concrete deck (Figure 6-3) that had been built over an older wooden stucture. The overall construction was such that it was not possible to get underneath, although you could look underneath in places.

Readings of the soil around the platform indicated several areas of NORM ringing the platform. Based on the construction of the platform, the cracked and broken nature of the upper concrete deck, and NORM readings under the platform (where possible) the soil NORM was thought to possibly be pervasive under most or all of the platform.

Three confirmatory composite soil samples showed significantly elevated values for Ra 226. Figures 6-4, 6-5, and 6-6 are sample analysis sheets that show the NORM activity levels for the site. The result of this work was to realize that there is a good possibility of increased abandonment costs at the time of the release of the property. Potential cost figures for this possible NORM remediation were calculated and provided to the purchaser.

That's the Pits **7**

There are uncounted production pits present throughout the oil producing states – more than anyone knows or is willing to admit if they do know. They come in all manner of sizes, shapes, and construction. There are discharge pits, fresh water makeup pits, reserve pits, and so on and so on. Analyzing these pits to determine closure requirements can be complex. In this chapter several aspects of pit analysis will be considered.

The problem with these pits is not just what has been legally placed into them, but what has been unintentionally or surreptitiously placed into them. An open pit has, in the past, been an open invitation beckoning to all "come, dump here." That siren song has been heeded perhaps more frequently than we would care to consider.

By its nature, a pit is a hole in the ground. That means that if the pit was dug 15 ft deep, then 15 ft of soil buffering between the waste and the groundwater has been removed. Often, this 15 ft would be the main portion of the soil profile capable of buffering the contaminants. We are talking about oil, salt water, NORM, solvents, metals, drilling mud (sometimes in large quantities), and the like being dumped into these holes in the ground. Very few of these pits were constructed as lined pits.

Without panic or running to hug the nearest tree, it must be admitted that there has been some effect on soil and groundwater from the use of these pits. The idea in this book is to be able to analyze and to ascertain within reason what is the extent of the damage. God has created a natural order that is remarkably resilient and capable of taking care of itself. In some instances, it is probably useful to step in, however, and lend a hand, if risk analysis indicates a need. In other cases we simply have no technology to fix what is broken. Many times, the physical reality of the situation is made moot by regulatory fiat. When that happens, common sense no longer applies, and it doesn't matter whether the problem constitutes a threat to human health or industy, or not. Your wallet assumes center stage.

Pits represent a threat to surface water as well as to groundwater. If not properly maintained, a pit can contribute pollution to wetlands, lakes, streams, etc. Some are concerned about birds and migratory water fowl being affected as well. In Texas, pits must be netted to prevent birds from getting into the sludge and water.

While most of the discussion of this chapter involves instrument and laboratory work, there are some things that can be noted visually. Frequently oil staining can be seen going up and over the outer walls of the pits. This is a pretty good indication of fluid levels being up and over the pit walls. If so, then that means spillage. How much? How often? Sometimes, what you see is fresh gravel material or shell material. Why?

The fact of the matter is that most companies are driven by a single motivation: fear. No one wants to be the bearer of bad tidings, particularly if he is the cause. Oh, I know we see quality programs that *talk* about "driving out fear," but the average employee is not dumb enough to fooled by that. Therefore, blunders and violations continue to be covered up. So, it pays to be be nosy, particularly if you are buying someone else's problems.

Many people do not believe that they have pits on their properties. Such is rarely the case, but the mistake is usually an honest one. In 1986, the oil industry was stricken with amnesia. When oil prices fell to $9/bbl, older employees who remembered the historic development of the fields retired from companies in droves, leaving younger workers who postdated most of the operation to work the fields – usually shorthanded at that. In essence, most companies do not have a really full accounting of what is on their properties and have been (perhaps understandably) less than anxious to aquire said accounting.

I have rarely been on a property where I did not find pits.

GETTING STARTED

Ok, where does one start? We will look at three aspects of pit analysis apart from regulatory considerations (for the moment). We will perform:

- Visual inspection and site analysis.
- Sampling for various oil field contaminants.
- NORM analysis.

VISUAL INSPECTION AND SITE ANALYSIS.

In addition to looking at the items mentioned, such as extensive oil staining, there are other details that can be helpful. First, what volume of fluids has the pit received historically? Was it receiving a large volume of salt water? Dead vegetation can be a "dead giveaway." If the vegetation appears white, for instance, it could be an indication of high zinc levels.

Is the pit actively receiving fluids? Is it inactive? These questions bear on whether any existing problem is growing or is strictly historic in nature. If there is evidence of spillage or washover, what is the drainage gradient like in the area of the pit (Figure 7-1)? Where is the spillage draining? Is the receptor state waters or a farm pond?

The fact that a pit is not active does not neutralize it as a pollution source. Existing contaminated soil can act as a source of groundwater pollution. The fact that shallow rooted vegetation appears to be healthy around the vicinity of the pit also is not a de facto clean bill of health. Out of sight is not out of site, so to speak.

Another peculiar occurrence I have observed is the apparent malleability of definition of the word "pit." On several occasions, where older pits have been found, weathering has removed most or all of the levees leaving only the pit bottom and material. Sellers seem to find all sorts of noncommittal names for these features. This is, perhaps understandable but if you are buying it and it is a problem, it is still a pit whether it looks like one or is called one. A rose by any other name...

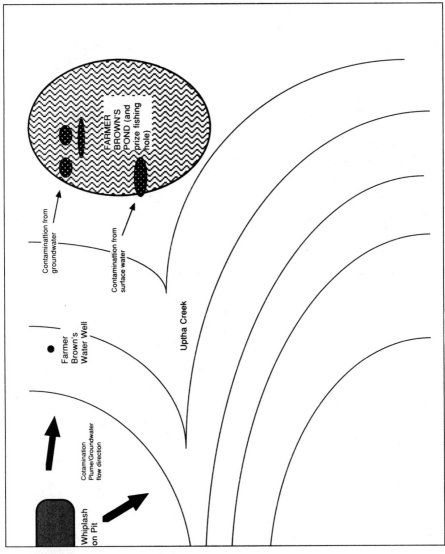

Figure 7-1

Idealized topo map showing relation of production pit to surface drainage. Note that both the domestic water well and the state waters are affected by the pit

SAMPLING FOR OIL FIELD CONTAMINANTS

Pit sampling is a bit complicated, and endless discussion could be generated concerning statistically valid sampling plans. There are instances where the appropriate regulators are more than happy to give "guidance" on what they believe to be a valid sampling plan. In other cases, such as a property transfer, it is simply a matter of trying to adequately determine a picture of the real scope of the problem and the liability exposure inherent in the pit for negotiation purposes.

A sampling plan must be designed which fits the purpose of the analysis, whether pre-closure, post-closure, property purchase or sale, etc. Whatever the case, the objective is to come up with a representative sampling procedure that will result in an average value for the pit contents and levees.

The following is a brief description of the pleasantries of a pit sampling. It is mid-afternoon in July. A hot sun is beating down on you to the tune of about 95°F. The pit is full of salt water with a skim of oil and the levees are black with oil staining to the top. This staining has absorbed light and is radiating heat like crazy. You drag your small flat bottom boat into the pit water and step in, trying desperately to keep your balance while loading sampling equipment and NORM metering equipment. Once in the boat you begin to notice several things. First, your black rubber boots are broiling your feet. Second, the pit walls that are now above and all around you have cut off what little breeze you once enjoyed and your throat is burning from the benzene fumes you are breathing. It occurs to you that you really are not charging enough to do this sort of work. Again, you are desperately anxious not to fall in. The pit is, after all, highly NORM contaminated, and you can almost see little glowing alpha particles settling comfortably into your bones.

Well, at this point, while you are extracting samples, someone's H_2S detector goes off, and you have to don protective clothing and emergency breathing apparatus. You do not really know what the temperature is inside the Tivek, but you do know that you have been drinking constantly for several hours and have had no inkling of a need to use the "little consultant's room."

The purpose of this little vignette is not to whine (well, not too much anyway), but to illustrate the fact that analyzing a production pit can be physically challenging as well as technically complex. It is best to have some kind of sampling plan going in because, under the circumstances just described, it will be difficult to think as clearly as one might suppose.

While on the subject, however, it is also needful to point out some specific health and safety issues. For instance, if the pit walls are higher than the height of someone standing or operating within the pit, then the pit should be considered a "confined space." Based on that, confined space entry procedures should be adhered to as closely as possible. Likewise, air monitoring for contaminants (known or suspected) should be undertaken. Benzene levels, for instance, could be elevated to such an extent that personal protection equipment may need to be added or upgraded. A written health and safety plan should be part of such a sampling plan.

People used to fairly wallow in these pit materials, but we now find ourselves loathe to come in contact with them at all. Things have changed.

Sampling of the pit levees can be conducted using a standard soil probe, but if the pit is filled with water, sampling the bottom sludge probably will require a PVC sampling implement. These can be made from PVC material or purchased, but they use a vacuum principle to extract bottom sediments that would simply slide out of a standard soil probe. These PVC sampling tubes can serve two purposes: They extract the desired sample and, they can be used to plumb the depth of the sludge for volumetric calculation purposes. *WARNING:* The contamination does not stop at the bottom of the sludge. The soil beneath it is also contaminated. Therefore, whatever volume you generate from the sludge material in your calculations is a minimum volume.

Depending on the size and type of pit in question, the sampling program might be designed somewhat differently. Samples might need to be taken and analyzed as individual samples or to be composited in different ways. Your pre-closure sampling plan might tend to be most detailed since it will influence your closure method and the amount of materials you might have to excavate and remove. In larger pits you might have to isolate "hot spots" within the pit for special handling. More detailed sampling allows better definition.

The selection of sampling parameters and protocols is an important aspect of pit sampling. Frankly, what one samples for can be highly dependent on where the pit is located geographically. If one is in Texas, sampling for oil and grease and chlorides may be all that is required. If one is in Louisiana, he will find himself under the auspices of Statewide Order 29-B, which specifies several sampling parameters.

Perhaps a word about regulatory requirements is in order here. Depending on the reader's perspective, the following statements may or may not be happily received. The fact is that being able to meet regulatory post-closure guidelines does not mean that no environmental damage has occurred. In fact, it may still be occurring even though post-closure requirements are met. Let me give some examples.

When the State of Louisiana issued emergency orders mandating pit closure, a number of pits were closed hastily and within 29-B limits (hopefully). However, NORM was yet to become an issue. Many of these pits were not sampled for NORM. Many were closed in situ. What if you went back now and sampled these pit sites for Ra226 and found them hot? Has it happened? Hmmmm?

As another example, chlorides tend to be a short term indicator. I have sampled historical contamination incidents and found chloride levels to be normal, yet the vegetation and the other salt parameters showed quite a different story. There is a good reason for this. Chlorides tend to pass on through the soil profile downgradient, but sodium cations tend to be adsorbed onto clay in the soil and remain long term.

These are only two of many illustrations I could cite. Yes, you may be within guidelines and be actively polluting. "Who cares?" you ask. "We have the oil field exemption from RCRA. Why worry as long as we are within the regs?" Go back and reread Chapter 2. That exemption covers you as long as the materials lie undisturbed in tank bottoms. If the plume from that pit, however, reaches a regional aquifer, then you may find yourself under the auspices of the SDWA, which does not recognize the RCRA exemption.

In this book, Louisiana Statewide Order 29-B will be considered as a standard and used in the discussion, because it represents the broadest range of required parameters for production pit analysis that I know of. LAC Title 43: Part XIX.Sec. 129.B.6 & 7 requires post-closure analysis for five categories of sample parameter. They are: pH; total metals content (nine metals); oil and grease; Soluble salts and cationic distributions; and Radioisotopes.

An example of a 29-B sample analysis is shown in Figure 7-2. Various laboratories have different presentations of the data and there is no required presentation format. Additionally, the protocol for 29-B samples is (by the way) very lenient in regard to chain of custody, storage, transportation, and time limits. As a friend of the author puts it, "You could put 29-B samples in your underwear if you wanted to." The author does not recommend this as a sample transport method, however.

pH. Normal range for the pH for pits should be 6-9. In almost every case, where I have sampled or reviewed sample data, the pH is well within the normal range. It has not been a big offender in oil and gas production pits. One study indicates that, of more than 1,200 pits sampled, 61.4% of the pits were in the normal pH range and averaged 7.9 s.u.[1]

Drilling muds tend to have initially a rather high pH due to alkaline additives, but exposure to the elements tends to mitigate this, which would explain the large percentage of normal pHs found in the above study.

METALS. Of the nine metals tested by 29-B protocol (arsenic, barium, cadmium, chromium, lead, mercury, selenium, silver, and zinc), I have most often encountered problems with arsenic, lead, and zinc. In personal experience, cadmium, selenium, and silver seem to crop up the least of the metals. It should be noted that this metals analysis suite is *total metals* and not TCLP.

There is much discussion about the risk associated with high metal content in pits. Opinions range from one end of the spectrum to the other. Some researchers believe that there is "zero risk" associated with metals generated by E&P wastes, except for chromates. Other specialists of my aquaintance are less certain.

OIL AND GREASE. Obviously, an oil and grease content of more than 1% (dry weight) for discharge pit samples is not uncommon. Not surprisingly, in a cascade system or pit complex, the first pit in the sequence normally will have the highest oil and grease content.

Oil and grease is a pretty broad category. Without the oil field RCRA exemption, producers probably would be dealing with TPH and BTEX analysis of the samples. Under certain circumstances, such as a groundwater enforcement action, that might still be the case. However, in general, it is not common practice.

Definition and uses of BTEX and TPH parameters are discussed in detail in Chapter 4. While not commonly used in the oil patch, these parameters have a definite place.

```
LAB I.D. _____   DATE REPORTED: 08/25/93

SAMPLE DESCRIPTION _____
DATE COLLECTED: 08/05/93

        SLUDGE COMPOSITE COLLECTED ON 8/05/93
        @ 1115 BY

        PERCENT MOISTURE                49.16%
        OIL & GREASE   (% dry weight)    17.31%

                    TOTAL METAL CONTENT (ppm)

ARSENIC    6.07    CHROMIUM  24.3    SELENIUM 0.054
BARIUM     8152    LEAD      <5.00   SILVER   <0.700
CADMIUM <0.300     MERCURY   0.188   ZINC        335

        TRUE TOTAL BARIUM                  19102

        pH MEASUREMENT                    5.98 S.U.
        ELECTRICAL COND.           99.0 mmhos/cm
        SODIUM ADSORPTION RATIO         379.38

                    SOLUBLE CATIONS (meq/1)
        SOLUBLE CALCIUM        98.85
        SOLUBLE MAGNESIUM      63.53
        SOLUBLE SODIUM         3418


PASTE SATURATION %                       57.6%
EXCHANGEABLE SODIUM %                     >100%
CEC (meq/100g)                           6.37

THIS SAMPLE WAS ANALYZED IN ACCORDANCE WITH PROCEDURES
OUTLINED IN STATEWIDE ORDER 29-B (AS AMENDED OCTOBER 20, 1990)
```

Figure 7-2
An example of a 29-B sample analysis presentation.

RADIOISOTOPES. The fourth item covered by Louisiana Statewide Order 29-B has raised a number of questions and presents a potentially crushing financial liability. NORM has been found in many production pits. Depending on the regulatory body of the individual state, pit NORM might be a devastating problem or of very little concern.

Where the regulation of pit NORM does create a financial problem for the operator, such as in Louisiana, the core of the problem is volume. Pits can contain literally thousands of barrels of NORM contaminated material, which must be specially handled, stored, transported, and disposed of. It *ain't* cheap.

Right now, some states will allow in situ closure of pits by blending processes that dilute the radium content of the pit materials. Louisiana regulations, on the other hand, specifically prohibit dilution of NORM. Special permission has been afforded by Louisiana to one or two companies to allow them to dilute NORM, but I am unaware of any guarantee that this privilege will be extended to operators in general.

The message is: "caveat emptor." As I said, I have yet to look at a property (in an area where discharge pits have been historically used) where I failed to find pits. In fact, I have found production pits on virtually every property I have examined. What is in those pits? How does one evaluate them?

An operator had better pay attention to the regulations pertaining to soil and material NORM in the state where he operates. Before you buy that property, you had better be able to evaluate the condition and closure cost potential of that pit that "does not exist" before you sign that "as-is-where-is" contract. Oh, the stories I could tell you... This may come as a shock to the reader, but people will tell you things that are not true in order to sell you things. The Biblical doctrine of the depravity of man has few starker manifestations than in the transfer of producing properties. Properties have been sold with the avoidance of expensive pit closures in mind. Suit yourself, believe your consultant or believe the guy in the orange blazer and striped pants who is trying to sell you something.

PIT EVALUATION

OK, so how do you know if you have a problem? There are ways to analyze a pit that will give you an approximation of the average value of the Ra226 and Ra228 present in the pit. First, it is frequently possible to get an indication of trouble by a simple NORM survey of the pit levee and the periphery of the sludge. Elevated values on the levee surface are probably indicative of the need for further investigation. A lack of significantly elevated values on the surface of the inside of the levee is *not* proof that a NORM problem does not exist within the pit, however.

A little background of the pit itself is in order. The sludge is being deposited over time in conjunction with the waters that move through the pit. During the life of that pit, the discharge from the separation facilities into the pit may ultimately derive from different geological horizons as the field develops and matures. Recompletion and workovers occur. New wells are drilled. Things change. The fact is that not all geological horizons produce the same amount of NORM. It is possible that, buried in the ancient sludges of the pit, NORM lies lurking from an older period in the life of the field. A meter survey of the levee may not find it, and you may experience an unpleasant surprise in the future. NOW landfills can accept only up to 30 pCi/gm materials. The unsuspecting operator, upon closing a pit, could find his material turned away at the gate. This pretty severely limits one's options.

FIELD: LUMINOUS **Date of Survey:** 6/94

Pit Name PIT1 **Surveyer's Name:** TBM (VEC)

RADIOMETRIC Data

TYPE	[X]	2" PVC – in situ	k =	
	[ ]	2" heavywall PVC	k =	
OF	[ ]	Bucket – 5 gal., 2" PVC	k =	RA 226 =
	[ ]	Mason Jar	k =	RA total =
SAMPLE	[ ]	Surface reading, large mass	k =	RA background =

	SAMPLE DEPTH											
	1	pCi/g	2	pCi/g	3	pCi/g	4	pCi/g	5	pCi/g	6	pCi/g
A			250	37.5	180	27	150	22.5	100	15	100	15
B			42	6.3	300	45	230	34.5	80	12	25	3.75
C	100	15	330	49.5	480	72	380	57	280	42	110	16.5
D	320	48	420	63	315	47.3	310	46.5	205	30.8	200	30
E	110	16.5	210	31.5	1050	158	190	28.5				
LOC. 1	160	24	230	34.5	200	30	500	75	500	75		
LOC. 2	260	39	500	75	400	60	250	37.5				
LOC. 3			220	33	250	37.5			300	45		
LOC. 4					400	60	350	52.5			250	37.5

Figure 7-3

Spreadsheet showing average NORM values in a pit by converting μR/hr to pCi/gm.

However, there are ways to get a handle on the potential for NORM. It is possible to design a statistically valid sampling program, but the difficulty lies in the fact that the contamination tends to be neither horizontally continuous nor contiguous. Likewise, the vertical profile is not terribly predictable. This problem is exacerbated by the fluid nature of the pit bottom material itself.

I use a combination of techniques to arrive at an assessment. First, a sampling grid is laid out commensurate with the size of the pit in order to extract representative samples that are subsequently composited. Next, a shielded NORM meter is used to obtain foot by foot incremental readings of the bottom sludge material. This method somewhat changes the geometry of the gamma ray emission being detected by the instrument but has usually yielded reasonable results.

The results of the sample analysis are then used to convert the the meter readings from μR/hr to pCi/gm. A spreadsheet routine I developed CAN THEN BE utilized to produce an average value for the Ra226 and Ra228 in the pit. Volumetric analysis is completed for the pit, and a closure cost estimate is made. An example of a spreadsheet showing the average value of the pit is shown in Figure 7-3.

There are probably other methodologies out there some readers may be aware of, but the described methodology has proven effective. There may be skepticism about the effectiveness of this technique, but a defense of the methodology is really outside the scope of the book. It merely is introduced in here for the purpose of illustrating that some care should be exercised in analyzing pits.

A further caveat should be noted that may be obvious to most, but warrants saying anyway. Contamination in a production pit is not likely to stop at the base of the sludge. The soil below may be deeply and extensively contaminated, and excavation may be far more extensive than any pre-closure estimate could accurately predict. Suffice to say, there are several real life experiences to bear this out. Likewise, just as "murder will out," pits that are not remediated to depth can come back to haunt the unsuspecting operator and the surface owner. Has this happened? Have pits passed post-closure sample analysis and later been found to be contaminated? Yup.

---

1 Lloyd E. Deuel, Jr., Ph.D and George H. Holliday, Ph.D, Soil Remediation for Petroleum Extraction Industry, (unpublished training course materials, 1993).

Remediation Options

So you have a mess. It happens. When your business is that of bringing fluids to the surface, you are going to spill some. Also, for crying out loud, when you built that discharge pit 23 years ago, who thought of it as a problem? Back then, NORM was the guy you bowled with on Thursday nights. Who would have thought it could have come to this?

Yep, there are a number of things that have to be cleaned up that no one ever imagined. Frankly, in many cases, if left to their own devices, natural systems would take care of the problem better than you could. However, that really does not matter anymore. These are the 90s, when the earth has been granted human qualities and consciousness. More sensitive folks than you can hear Mother Gaia's cries of pain and outrage over the mistreatment she has received at the hands of those who brutally pillage the environment.

Once again the author waxes sarcastic, but, on the balance side of the equation, there are sound reasons (apart from environmental wackos) for taking action to ameliorate damage that could imperil human health and safety. Likewise, the law is the law, and we have an obligation (so long as those laws are not immoral and/or unconstitutional) to abide by them. In truth, the earth has yielded a great deal of money in the oil patch for those who were willing to take the risk. There has been a high side, but just as a certain amount of work needs to be done at field abandonment, there are unpleasant tasks left at this time of "industry abandonment."

Three paragraphs is probably sufficient space for moralizing. The thrust of this chapter is practical. Where there are problems, what are the options available to the operator? In this chapter we will attempt to systematize the available options according to problem types, whether the source of the concern is a pit, a brine leak, or NORM. In any case, the treatment options are almost all going to fall into one of the following categories:

- In situ treatment. Here, something is going to be added to or done with the material on site without moving it very far. Landfarming and bioremediation would be examples of this type of treatment.

- Underground injection. This is putting it back to whence it came. The applicability is highly dependent upon what you intend to inject. Some materials can not be injected but still can be placed in the annulus of P&A wells for disposal. Others simply can not go down Class II wells.

- Incineration, the "up in smoke option". This technique is required for some substances, but it can be a problem with large volumes of material.

- Off-site disposal, "the scoop it and haul it option." This is frequently the most expensive and most available option. The contaminated materials must be excavated according to regulations, transported according to regulations, and stored at an appropriate treatment, storage, and disposal (TSD) facility. There are hazardous waste facilities, solid waste facilities, and NOW facilities.

In this chapter we will discuss various remediation options for soil, pit closure, NORM, and groundwater contamination. The information will be general and will not be intended to be a technical treatise so much as an introduction to various accepted methods of remediation.

GROUNDWATER REMEDIATION

The very phrase "groundwater remediation" strikes fear into the heart of the PRP and for good reason. Groundwater remediation projects are wildly expensive and frequently unsuccessful. Bringing a badly damaged aquifer back to a usable state for drinking is not often successfully accomplished. It is not at all uncommon for a hydrogeologic investigation of groundwater contamination to cost $500,000. In most cases, the best that can be accomplished is to limit the extent of the damage. Worse yet, many oil field operations exist in areas where no use is made of the aquifer anyway.

This is a formula for "insult to injury." An operator can spend a great deal of money on groundwater remediation in a place where no one is really damaged by the contamination and have the remediation prove to be ineffective to boot. Groundwater cleanups are more apt to total in the millions of dollars than in the hundreds of thousands. For this reason, it is good policy to practice waste management in such a way as to minimize the possibility of affecting groundwater. Also, it is advisable to walk away from buying properties with groundwater problems.

However, regrets aside, let's assume you have a groundwater problem. You were minding your own business and tying some new flies for that trip to the mountains. In your mind you had already poured the Tabasco sauce on that sizzling pan-broiled brookie. It was at this point that your field superintendent came in with a report about ol' Jed who lives on the ridge above that old pit you had been meaning to close. "You remember Jed?" he asks. "Oh yeah," you reply, "the poor mountaineer that barely kept his family fed." "Well," your Supe says, "yesterday he was shootin' at some food, when up from the ground came a bubblin' crude – oil that is."

Well, Jed took a sample of the oil and it was green 35° API oil just like you were producing. Then he spent some time hunkered over his topo sheet, stroked his chin and said to no one in particular, "Californee is the place I ought to be..."

From that point on the whole thing was a matter of lawyers, geometries, and gradients (Oh yeah, and money).

As mentioned, it is unlikely that you will be able to restore the aquifer to its original pristine condition. Your options are limited and the most likely action for you is to "contain" the problem. In other words, you need to limit the ability of the contaminants to do further damage and spread farther areally.

As was alluded to in the chapter on groundwater, E&P contaminants can be difficult to delineate in an aquifer. Petroleum products may not follow the gradient you expect. Metals can concentrate in the lower aquifer.

Before any groundwater treatment is going to have a chance of success, the source of the contaminants must be eliminated. In the preceding example, the pit would have to go. When one begins to consider remediation from a groundwater standpoint, it is imperative to see the interrelationship of the natural system. In the case of a surface discharge, for instance, if the soil is saturated with contaminants, then it is not just contaminated soil. It is itself a contaminant source. Therefore, it often happens that a groundwater remediation project must concurrently be a soil remediation exercise.

In general, groundwater remediation involves a spectrum of approaches that ranges from pure containment/immobilization of the plume to containment/ withdrawal to pump and treat methods. Some possibilities are most effective in shallow aquifer situations, and some are more effective for specific contaminant types. The right medicine is needed to address the specific disease. Some avenues of groundwater remediation would include the following:

INTRODUCTION OF A PHYSICAL SUBSURFACE BARRIER TO IMPOUND THE PLUME (PHYSICAL CONTAINMENT). With this option, you might put in slurry walls around the plume by injecting cement into the shallow subsurface and impounding the water. However, this method, in addition to requiring a shallow aquifer, requires a confined aquifer that is underlain by an aquitard (impermeable layer) to prevent communication with deeper aquifers. Recovery wells would have to be used in this scenario because no amount of impoundment design will create a total permeability barrier. To control infiltration, some water will have to be withdrawn, but at a low rate, thus reducing disposal costs.

INJECTION OF CHEMICALS AND/OR BIOLOGICAL STIMULANTS TO ALTER THE CHEMISTRY OF THE CONTAMINANT PLUME IN ORDER TO DEGRADE IT, NEUTRALIZE IT OR POSSIBLY TO IMMOBILIZE THE CONTAMINANTS. To successfully use this method, the anti-contaminant substance and quantity must be selected and used for the specific contaminant type and the chemical conditions existing within the plume. Bioremediation enters the picture here. Within the aquifer, organisms exist that break down organic contaminants. By injecting nutrients and oxygen, it is thought that the degradation of the plume can be accelerated. Likewise, by injecting chemicals (such as sulfides) the amount of soluble metals can be reduced. Soluble metals are the main problem in metals contamination and create one of the more difficult groundwater remediation scenarios. There is no large scale pumping of groundwater with this method. Ideally, everything is fixed right out of sight. The problem with this method from the standpoint of the producer is easily stated: It frequently doesn't work.

CONTAINMENT OF THE PLUME BY DRILLING A NETWORK OF INTERCEPTOR/RECOVERY WELLS THAT AFFECT THE GROUNDWATER SYSTEM HYDRAULICALLY AND CAPTURE THE CONTAMINANT PLUME. After being brought to the surface, the contaminated water can be hauled off site for disposal or perhaps reinjected into a Class I or Class II injection well onsite. It seems pretty obvious that this type of containment by hydraulic methods is cheaper to put in place than the physical barrier containment, but here is the rub: disposal costs. Generally, in order to remove the plume or at least get the contaminant production from the recovery wells asymptotic, a great deal of water has to be withdrawn. Transport and disposal costs can be high. A variation on this method is called the "pump and treat."

PUMP AND TREAT. The pump and treat option is like the preceding option, but with a twist. Rather than pay expensive transportation and disposal costs, the water withdrawn by the recovery wells is treated on the site and then reinjected into the same aquifer or discharged on the surface. It has become a very popular option. Well actually, it is sort of like hemorrhoids: No one likes them, but a lot of people have them. At any rate, depending on the exact situation, this frequently is the most cost effective option.

PIT REMEDIATION

Many pits have been closed in the oil patch since 1988. Some of them were even closed correctly. There are also pits that were properly closed by the regulatory standard of the day, but that would not pass muster today. This is a very ticklish area deserving mention. The fact that the closure method for those pits met the regulatory standards in place then does not mean that they are neutralized as an environmental hazard. In some cases the contaminated soil was not remediated to the base of the contamination, and/or fill dirt was simply used to cover the problem.

As was said in the discussion of goundwater, the soil can be a groundwater contamination source. The buyer had better beware. Even if the seller has documentation of the appropriate regulatory body having signed off, there are other issues raised by the condition of that pit. It is very important to know where pits are and evaluate even the closed ones. It might be chock full of NORM.

At this time there is quite a bit of experience out there concerning closure methodologies and costs. Many people have been visited by the service companies and heard their share of the horror stories, so this book will cut directly to the chase and give a brief discussion of various types of pit closure.

Louisiana Statewide Order 29-B alludes to several pit closure options including onsite land treatment, offsite transport of materials, burial, and solidification. It is one of the most detailed regulatory bodies within the oil patch that deals exclusively with production pits, and it has set a standard. The parameters cited by 29-B as post-closure requirements for land farming closures are shown in Table 8-1.

Table 8-1
29-B Post-closure Requirements

REQUIRED PARAMETER	THRESHOLD VALUE
Oil & Grease	≤1% (dry weight)
Total Metals	
Arsenic	10 ppm
Barium	
submerged wetland	20,000 ppm
elevated wetland	20,000 ppm
upland	40,000 ppm
Cadmium	10 ppm
Chromium	500 ppm
Lead	500 ppm
Mercury	10 ppm
Selenium	10 ppm
Silver	200 ppm
Zinc	500 ppm
Electrical conductivity (EC)	
Wetland	<8 mmhos/cm
Upland	<4 mmhos/cm
Sodium Absorption Ratio (SAR)	
Wetland	<14
Upland	<12
Exchangeable Sodium Percentage (ESP)	
Wetland	<25%
Upland	<15%
pH	6-9 s.u.

In Texas, the Railroad Commission's Statewide Rule 8 deals with groundwater protection and in the process addresses pit closure standards. Its closure requirements are less specific and far less rigorous than 29-B. In fact, Rule 8 does not list specific parameters but focuses on time limits for closures. In §3.8.(d)(4)(G), Rule 8 requires closure of pits having a chloride concentration of 6,100 mg/l or less within one year of activity cessation. Those pits with greater than 6,100 mg/l must be closed in 30 days or less.

State Rule 91, however, is about to become final and will deal with spills of crude oil onto soils. The final soil loading rate used in this rule will require a final cleanup level of 1% TPH, and it may be advisable for operators to utilize this level in post-closure analysis of pits.

The OCC's regulations pertaining to commercial and noncommercial pits are highly detailed in regard to operation of these pits, but, like Texas, its post-closure sample parameters are less detailed and rigorous (Table 8-2).

Table 8-2
Oklahoma Post-closure Parameters

REQUIRED PARAMETER	THRESHOLD VALUE
Chlorides	3,500 mg/l
Total Dissolved Solids (TDS)	7,000 mg/l
Metals	
Arsenic	20 mg/l
Chromium	10 mg/l
pH	6 - 9.5 s.u.

New Mexico is somewhat interesting in that it takes a different approach. Rather than use the oil and grease percentage and salt-related parameters of the previously mentioned states, it cites TPH and BTEX levels and couches the post-closure limits in those terms. In the oil patch, TPH and BTEX are not normally encountered as regulatory parameters due to the oil field RCRA exemption. Additionally, New Mexico directly requires a groundwater investigation and remediation (if necessary) as part of its closure requirements. Table 8-3 parameters apply to the unsaturated contaminated soil associated with the pit.

Table 8-3
New Mexico Post-closure Parameters

REQUIRED PARAMETER	THRESHOLD VALUE
TPH	100 mg/kg
BTEX	50 mg/kg
Benzene	10 mg/kg

Of the cited states, only Louisiana considers NORM as part of its pit closure requirements as far as I am aware. Though not cited above, the 29-B regulations require compliance with all Louisiana Title 33, Part XV, Chapter 14 NORM regulations. The fact that the other states do not specificallyaddress pit NORM creates, in my opinion, a very dangerous situation for purchasers of producing properties in those states. NORM regulations are in flux and will probably grow more restrictive. The concern is that a purchaser may take possession of a property in good faith that is in com-pliance only to get ensnared with pit NORM problems down the road.

PIT CLOSURE OPTIONS

First off, it is needful to note that pits are the trash heaps of yesteryear. I have seen some pretty bizarre things dredged up by a backhoe from some of these old pits. Regulation of pits was a great deal less stringent in the 40s and 50s and things were done that would make the hair stand up on a consultant's head today. Hopefully, you readers are practicing sound waste disposal techniques with your pit. (Please say that you didn't dump those drums of solvent in the discharge pit). The problem is, however, that that gaping hole is an open invitation to every passerby with trash. In South Louisiana, shrimp boats can pull right up alongside the pit and dump their gunk. Has it happened?

Supposing that you do not have a hazardous waste stream due to hazardous materials being dumped into your NOW, we will proceed with discussion of various closure techniques. The techniques to be described are: Commercial facility (offsite) disposal, land farming, road spreading, dilution burial, solidification.

It should be understood that the decision to utilize any one of the above methods is a function of one or more of the following considerations:

- The limiting constituent parameters contained in the regulations of the state in which you are working.
- The contents of the pit in terms of contaminants and their concentrations.
- The physical characteristics of the local soil.
- The logistical and the operational limitations of the location.
- State prohibitions on certain types of closure.

COMMERCIAL FACILITY (OFFSITE DISPOSAL)

This is the "scoop and haul" method. It is usually an available option. It is almost always the most expensive option. When one begins to excavate contaminated soil, things are going to get expensive.

Frequently, the logistics of the situation determine this option for you. When the pit is in the marsh, for instance, you are usually not going to dig a hole anywhere to bury anything. Furthermore, spreading this material at sea level is an open invitation to a CWA violation. In one instance I know of, a company had to build about a mile of board road across a marsh to haul out pit solids and haul in fill material, and the cost was in the immediate neighborhood of $2 million.

In this option, after analyzing the pit for its contents, equipment is moved in and the material is excavated and transported to a licensed NOW facility. It can be that the exact situation may require a long distance transport to the nearest facility and a closer hazardous waste facility can be the most cost-effective option (careful with that one). There will be excavation costs, transportation costs and gate fees/disposal costs.

LAND FARMING

The term "land farming" is a picturesque way of saying that waste is mixed with soil at the location to dilute contaminants to below the regulatory limits. It can be spread out (subject to the loading characteristics of the material), and various bioremediation options and soil amendments may be used to render the waste-blended land useful for its future intended use..

Also, ultraviolet radiation from the solar insolation can assist in breaking down hydrocarbon constituents that are exposed to the surface. Was it mentioned that a small amount of heavy fraction hydrocarbons can actually be beneficial to soils in some cases by raising the cation exchange capacity?

Under the 1984 RCRA amendments, a series of prohibitions and limitations on land disposal methods began to be phased in. Generally, these statutes affect hazardous waste disposal and the term "land disposal" is very broadly defined. For instance the term would be applied to placement of a hazardous waste in a hazardous waste landfill, waste pile, injection well, or underground mine. Other waste disposal location types are affected by the 1984 amendments, but these are mentioned to show just how broad the land disposal definition has become.

Here is an area where the RCRA exemption is of great benefit to the industry. Because most pit contents are classified as non-hazardous oilfield waste, the land farming techniques are still in use.

The general procedure for land farming includes:

• Pit constituent/contaminant analysis.

• Pit is dewatered by any of several options such as evaporation, flocculation, underground injection, etc.

• Solid materials from the pit will be mixed with levee material and/or fill dirt to dilute the contaminants. This alone may get the pit solids below the prescribed regulatory limit.

• The material can also then be spread over the adjacent land surface and disked into the soil using farming equipment.

• The disked waste-soil mixture can then be treated with chemicals (soil amendments) or bioremediation agents to take care of specific problem constituents such as salt or oil.

• Monitoring of the progress of the soil amendment or bioremediation can be accomplished through soil sampling.

The post-closure testing requirements for land farming under Louisiana Statewide Order 29-B are listed in Table 8-1. In states where parameters such as SAR, ESP, and metals are not expressly addressed, it is still useful, as a matter of prudent operatorship, to manage these parameters in accordance with the intended future land use. Having 5 acres of land, intended for use as forest or agricultural land that is covered with soil with an electrical conductivity of 12 is going to expose the operator to lawsuits (and possibly other kinds of environmental liability) whether he is within the oil and gas regulatory limit or not.

As a word of caution, one should be very careful about the specific site selected for this type of closure. Highly saline pit solids may require intensive and long term remediation work. If the operator is not prepared for that eventuality, another option should be considered.

ROAD SPREADING

This is a popular option in some parts of the oil patch with oil spills, but salt content is the limiting factor. Some pits could qualify for this process. The best candidate for road spreading will be a waste with a high oil and grease content but a relatively low salt content.[1] Such a waste would be blended directly with road oil and spread onto the roads. Not much needs to be done except to blend it directly into the building materials for the road bed.

This can lead to some peculiar questions such as why one can spread this material on a road and it is OK, but to spill it alongside the road is a violation. Well, ours is not to reason why...

Another consideration for this option is the volatile content of the oil in question. Due to the RCRA exemption, the industry usually does not normally deal with ignitability characteristics, but here is a place where it becomes important. Materials with a low flash point can result in a fire hazard in the road spreading process. Therefore, weathered crude (due to the low volatile content) is an ideal candidate for this option provided that the final road spreading mixture can achieve a low enough salt content. Best yet, sometimes people will actually buy this material from you.

DILUTION BURIAL

Dilution burial could be expanded to "dilution of the waste with native soil followed by burial of the waste-soil mixture onsite." This is a fairly popular option in agricultural areas due to the relaxed salt parameter requirements.

In essence, the pit solids are mixed with native soil to specific concentration levels. A trench or hole is then excavated, and the mixture is buried out of sight out of mind (hopefully). This burial cell is dug deeply enough to get the top of the soil-waste mixture below the the plant rooting zone. The cell is then covered with native soil. In agriculture, the plants in question are usually relatively shallow rooted s   o 5 ft is usually sufficient. If the land use, however, is for pulpwood tree farming, this option could create a problem.

Likewise, in areas of shallow groundwater, this could be trouble. In wetlands areas, it is frequently impossible because the ground surface is the top of the groundwater. The state of Louisiana requires that the base of the cell be a minimum of 5 ft above groundwater (and that is being pretty lenient). While many do not believe E&P metals to be a problem in terms of solubility, the old adage "better safe than sorry" may apply here.

Table 8-4 shows the closure requirements and post closure limit on dilution burial established by LSO 29-B. A comparison of the parameters with the landfarming parameters listed above will show this option to be less rigorous in terms of waste treatment.

Table 8-4
LSO 29-B Dilution Burial Requirements

REQUIRED PARAMETER	THRESHOLD VALUE
Oil & Grease	<3% (dry weight)
Total Metals	
Arsenic	10 ppm
Barium	
submerged wetland	20,000 ppm
elevated wetland	20,000 ppm
upland	40,000 ppm
Cadmium	10 ppm
Chromium	500 ppm
Lead	500 ppm
Mercury	10 ppm
Selenium	10 ppm
Silver	200 ppm
Zinc	500 ppm
Electrical conductivity (EC)	<12 mmhos/cm
pH	6-9 s.u.
Moisture content	<50% (by weight)

It can be seen that such parameters as SAR and ESP drop out, the assumption being that the waste is buried below the the rooting zone and is of no danger to plant life. In these preceding options, one idea that should be emerging in the mind of the reader is that the operator has more plentiful and less expensive options available to him now than he will have if the RCRA exemption is lost. The author is frankly surprised that the exemption has not at least been partially removed already

SOLIDIFICATION/STABILIZATION

The last pit remediation option to be discussed in this chapter will be solidification, which can be accomplished in situ. In solidification/stabilization, the strategy is to contain and immobilize the waste somewhat like the containment strategy in groundwater remediation. Like dilution burial, the treated materials can then be buried on site. Unlike dilution burial, the materials are not mixed with native soil, but are encapsulated in solid materials and/or chemically or physically altered to produce a solid or stabilized body. Stabilization and solidification are not perfectly synonymous terms or processes but are designed to effect the same end and therefore are discussed together here.

Pit materials are pretty "smooshie" as my daughters would say, but stabilization limits or eliminates the mobility of the *contaminants*, thus minimizing the threat to the groundwater. The stabilizing compounds introduced into the waste chemically alter the waste constituents in order to make the contaminants insoluble.

Solidification, by contrast, is the process that produces a cohesion and structural stability *in the matrix*, which allows the waste to be handled for transport or burial. Additionally, solidification can be used along with stabilization to further encapsulate the waste. This fixing of the contaminants is most often accomplished by introduction of cementing materials to encapsulate the pit solids after having introduced stabilizing chemicals into the waste.

These processes are more common in hazardous waste applications than in the oil patch, but there may be times when this process may be of use. In Louisiana, wastes treated in this fashion must pass leachate testing requirements. A summary of those requirements is included in Table 8-5 and someone familiar with test parameters will see that these requirements may be difficult to meet.

Table 8-5
Louisiana Treated Waste Leachate Testing Requirements

REQUIRED PARAMETER	THRESHOLD VALUE
pH 6-12 s.u.	
Oil & Grease (Leachate)	<10mg/l
Metals (Leachate)	
Arsenic	<0.5 mg/l
Barium	<10 mg/l
Cadmium	<0.1 mg/l
Chromium	<0.5 mg/l
Lead	<0.5 mg/l
Mercury	<0.02 mg/l
Selenium	<0.1 mg/l
Silver	<0.5 mg/l
Zinc	<5 mg/l
Unconfined Compressive Strength (QU)	>20 lbs/in ^{2} (ASTM)
Permeability	< 1×10^6 cm/sec (ASTM)
Wet/Dry durability	>10 cycles to failure (ASTM)

As with dilution burial, the 29-B regulations stipulate that the top of the buried mixture must be 5 ft below the surface and covered with 5 ft of native soil. Likewise, the bottom of the cell must be at least 5 ft above the seasonal high water table. Burial requirements, again, have the effect of limiting the places where this option can be used.

It probably goes without saying that this option will be more complex and more expensive than landfarming or dilution burial, but if the choice is between this and off-site transport, this option may prove to be the more cost-effective.

SOIL AMENDMENTS

E&P wastes overwhelmingly consist of crude oil and produced salt water that have a particular effect on soil and groundwater. Likewise, factors such as pH can be affected. Metals can accumulate in soils and/or enter groundwater and cause a difficult remediation problem.

In this section, we will consider various problems and impacts of E&P wastes and the appropriate soil additive (or amendment) that can be used to correct the problem. Again, the exact soil amendment and quantity to be used requires sufficient data and proper calculation. Therefore, the discussion will be kept qualitative and general.

BRINE CONTAMINATION

A fresh, large quantity salt spill can represent the beginning of a difficult and long term problem. Salt is highly mobile in a soil profile and can migrate to the surface during dry seasons and concentrate in discrete layers during wet seasons. Production waste salt is overwhelmingly composed of Sodium Chloride (NaCl). As the salt is diluted by meteoric water, the contamination plume will move in a downgradient and lateral fashion. Dissolution of the salt over time will result in the chlorides being swept deeper into the soil profile and probably into the groundwater. The sodium can remain in the soil itself, trapped by clays, and can produce a long term deleterious effect on plant life called "sodic soil."

When a spill is fresh, a rinsing with fresh water is about the only way to deal with the problem in situ. Shallow interceptor trenches or wells can be installed, and the area of the contamination can be flushed and recovered. This has the effect of diluting the NaCl concentration and decreasing the residence time in the soil (the aim of which is to minimize soil sodicity). Where a soil is inherently low in hydraulic conductivity (permeability to water), this flushing process may be hindered. It is better not to spill it it in the first place, obviously.

Prior to the spill reaching equilibrium in the soil (when it is still fresh), there are additives that can be introduced that can have the effect of reducing the impact of the sodium on the soils by acting as an anti-dispersant on the clays.

SOIL SODICITY REMEDIATION. There are many places in the oil patch where large and chronic leaks of salt water have occurred in the past, however. These historic incidents have resulted in soils that are very high in sodium. As was noted in Chapter 4, sodicity in the soil reduces the structuring in the soil, which in turn reduces the movement of air and water through the soil profile. Therefore, something must be added to decrease the sodicity and reintroduce structuring to the soil.

Calcium is normally a good choice for sodic soils and can be introduced in the form of calcium sulfate ($CaSO_4$) where the soil is not highly calcareous. It will not have the effect of sterilizing the soil, and sulfates do not constitute a threat to the groundwater. The one main drawback with $CaSO_4$ is that it takes more time than some of the other potential additives. With $CaSO_4$ additive, the sodium, which is the cause of the soil disaggregation, is displaced by calcium. Simple gypsum can be used for this.[1]

Sulfur also is a good choice where the soil is calcareous. It is not as fast as $CaCl_2$, but has deep penetration ability and a higher solubility than $CaSO_4$. Once mechanically introduced to the soil it reacts with water to produce sulfuric acid, which in turn reacts with calcium carbonate ($CaCO_3$) in the soil to produce $CaSO_4$.[1] With sulfur, there is an additional step, chemically speaking, to get to the interaction of the calcium with the sodium in the soil.

Another amendment to consider is calcium nitrate ($CaNO_3$). It is faster acting than the other amendments and will favor calcium for replacement of the sodium cation, but will also have the possible effect of introducing higher levels of nitrates to the groundwater. Before going this route it is advisable to have completed some groundwater risk assessment. Potassium will, likewise, replace sodium, but it is monovalent and will not help ameliorate the soil structuring.

Organic materials can be very useful as structuring additives since the organic materials can have CECs of 100-300 meq/100 gm. Peat moss is very good for this purpose. It not only draws sodium to itself but has the effect of increasing soil moisture capacity. In this regard, the higher the field moisture capacity of the soil, the higher the potential for dilution of salts which are in solution in the soil.

Since the thing most commonly spilled in the oil patch is salt water, these additives can be a very important part of an operator's life. It is best to have an idea in your area of operations of what the soil conditions are like and what the salient groundwater characteristics are, because spills tend to take the form of crises, and when quick action is needed, it is not the time to begin a groundwater risk assessment.

HYDROCARBON CONTAMINATED SOIL REMEDIATION

There is, of course, the scoop it and haul it approach, but that is covered in the section on pits and is expensive. An available technology involves bioremediation. Bioremediation has been around for quite some time and has been sold both long and short.

In general, bioremediation will not prove to be effective on heavier hydrocarbon fractions. Very low gravity crudes and tars and weathered oils will show very little response and are better sent to the road builders (where legal and applicable).

Bioremediation, though not a cure-all, will work, given sufficient time and care. It relies on natural microorganisms that degrade the contaminant oil to acceptable limits within the soil. These microorganisms (hereafter known as "critters") can be introduced into the soil directly. In other cases, they are already present and merely need to be well-nourished.

Given the soil characteristics of a given location, the population of the appropriate critters may be weak and need to be bolstered by the addition of nitrogen, potassium, and phosphorus in the appropriate ratios. Attention must also be given to soil moisture and oxygen content during the remediation process. Many times, the failure of bioremediation effort is directly attributable to failure to keep the critters healthy.

The weaker the critter population, the slower the effect of the remediation will be. Likewise, it is important to track progress using the right yardstick. In crude oil remediation, for instance, some workers believe that it is better to use TPH GC than

TPH IR in tracking the progress of hydrocarbon degradation and that doing so will give a more accurate picture of the progress. Some regulatory bodies, in fact, require IR as opposed to GC.

COMPLICATIONS

Frequently, soil contamination incidents are a mixed bag of constituents, and this complicates the remediation process. In the case of metals contamination, treatment of one constituent can interfere with the treatment of another. Likewise, regulations may mandate the remediation of one contaminant and ignore the other. Where cash is short, a risked decision may need to be made in those cases to do a minimal remediation effort.

NORM can foul up one's plans if those plans involve transportation to a licensed NOW facility or involve dilution. It is still technically against the law in Louisiana to dilute NORM. That historic brine spill or old pit might cost you dearly. A treatment of NORM disposal options is included in Chapter 6.

SUMMARY

The following truths can be gleaned from the preceding discussion:

- On site treatment of wastes is generally less expensive than offsite transport of materials to a licensed facility.
- Soil and groundwater are parts of an integrated system and must frequently be concurrently remediated, particularly where the source of the groundwater contamination is a surface spill or impoundment.
- Groundwater remediation is usually of limited effectiveness and nearly always costs more than you anticipated.
- Choosing the proper type of pit closure depends on multiple factors, and multiple options should be considered before settling on a plan of action.
- Under the current RCRA exemption, options are more plentiful and less expensive than they will be if the exemption is lost.
- There are significant differences at this time in the way different oil producing states treat pit closure requirements.
- NORM can seriously foul up your life.

---

[1] Lloyd E. Deuel, Jr., Ph.D and George H. Holliday, Ph.D, Soil Remediation for Petroleum Extraction Industry, (unpublished training course materials, 1993).

Case Histories/Scenarios

This chapter is intended more for fun than anything else. Not only can the reader see what kinds of horrible things are happening out there to others, but he can take some of the information in other parts of the book and utilize it. The reader can see the data and play risk manager or environmental coordinator or entrepreneur or consultant or whatever he fancies.

It will be obvious that much of the documentation and background information has been deleted and that regulatory citations have been simplified or eliminated, which will give the impression, in some cases, that the author is stupid. While that perception may be very valid, hopefully the reader can glean something useful from looking at these scenarios despite having to work in somewhat of a vacuum.

In all the following scenarios there is a right answer. No one, however, knows what it is, so everyone is on safe ground here in the make-believe world. Good luck and watch your step!

SCENARIO 1

You are L'il Nell Oil's environmental coordinator, and your consultant brings you the following report on this particular site of a property you are about to buy. In fact, you are just 10 days away from closing. The property is a marginal producer. The boss wants it really badly, for reasons unfathomable to you. Apart from this little issue, nothing obvious (except some significant equipment NORM) was found by the Phase 1 audit. What are you going to do? What will you recommend? The seller will not indemnify you. He would like for you to indemnify him.

This site was included in this section to illustrate the importance of historical data research. The site looked pristine, but the well was a salt water gusher that had done so at one time (onto the ground).

RANGOON SITE #18
DALEK EVA BRAUN #1
SITE DESCRIPTION

(See Figure 9-1) The Eva Braun #1 well was shut in at the time of VEC's field inspection due to a problem with its heater treater. It appears to be in good condition on the surface. No obvious environmental problems were noted on the wellhead or the surrounding ground surface. It is located in a sugar cane field. No oil or salt water leaks were observed. There was little in the way of rust and no produced sand or paraffin was visible.

PROBLEM ANALYSIS

Despite a clean surface appearance, this is a well with a checkered past. There were apparently no cement returns to the surface when the surface casing was set, and the shoe was not tested. VEC can not, at this time, vouch for the integrity of the cement surrounding the surface casing. A "trouble" log follows:

- 2/22/54 – Channeling behind pipe was cited as the reason for excessive brine production.
- A casing leak was noted on 3/27/54.
- 2/10/55 – A storm blew down the derrick, bending the casing just beneath the wellhead and wrenching the flowline loose (Photo 9-2). An estimated 500 bbl of condensate and an unknown quantity of salt water were discharged onto the ground surface. The wellhead was straightened using a winch, which may have caused stress cracks to begin to develop in the casing.
- 5/15/57 – Cement *failure* was cited as the reason for *extreme* salt water production.

Severe pollution of the soil and, very possibly the aquifer, with brine and hydrocarbons has occurred at this site.

RECOMMENDATIONS

- Sample soil around wellhead.
- Dalek should retain any and all liability for environmental damage that may have occurred as a result of its operation of this well and agree to indemnify Lil Nell.

or

Dalek should pay a cash settlement to Lil Nell to cover the remediation of any existing environmental damage within some mutually agreeable, reasonable time frame.

Figure 9-1
Dalek Eva Braun Well Information Sheet

WELL INFORMATION

DATE:	11-18-92
SITE NUMBER:	18
OPERATOR:	Dalek
LEASE:	Eva Braun
WELL NUMBER:	1
API NUMBER:	—
ELEVATION:	2'
DATE DRILLING COMMENCED:	2-24-52
DATE DRILLING COMPLETED:	3-19-52

CASING PROGRAM

SURFACE CASING:	10 3/4" @ 2700'
PRODUCTION CASING:	5 1/2" @ 11998'
TUBING:	2 7/8" @ 10850'

TOTAL DEPTH:12,100'

PRESSURE READINGS

TUBING:	0 psig
FLOWLINE:	0 psig
CASING:	0 psig
GAS LIFT:	0 psig

WELL STATUS: Shut In due to work in progress on heater treater at Facilities Site at time of field inspection.

PLUGGING REPORT ON FILE: NA

DATE WELL PLUGGED: NA

OTHER COMMENTS: . Approximately 500 bbl condensate blown out on ground on 2-5-55 due to high winds. Derrick over wellhead fell over and bent wellhead and casing. Used winch line to pull wellhead back to vertical.

SCENARIO 2

Now you are a surface owner. You knew that there were oil operations on your property, but you never paid much attention to them. One day you notice that the operators are gone. Disappeared. But...they left something behind.

Actually, you did not notice on your own, strictly speaking. You sold the property sight unseen to a new surface owner who wants to use it for forestry and agriculture. The truth is that it was he who noticed. He also noticed that you had written in your contract of sale that you would be responsible for any environmental problems on the property.

Well, your enviro-guy just got back with this report after an extensive first phase of the study. What are you going to do now? What are your options?

It is interesting that the low chlorides belie the actual suitability of the soil for agriculture or tree farming. This is often the case. The fact that certain regulatory parameters are established may protect you from certain kinds of regulatory actions but not from litigation.

So, here you are: not having looked before you leaped. Do you do further study? Do you proceed with cleanup based on what you know? Do you have an option that will get you out of this mess?

PRICE FIELD SITE #7

SITE IDENTIFICATION AND DESCRIPTION

SOIL COVERAGE AND CONTAMINATION. Site #7 is a large cleared area between the Rooster Oil Harwell #3 well (Site #6) and the Rooster Oil Harwell #2 well (Site #8). Exposed flow lines lie on the east side of the clearing. Exposed flow lines observed at the site at the time of this report are 3 in. PVC pipe. It appears that a major break in one of these PVC flow lines has occurred at some time in the past, causing a pond of tar to accumulate in a low area at the edge of the site covering about 9,360 sq. ft. The oil contamination profile extends 3 ft into the subsurface in places (Figure 9-2).

Soil sample analysis indicates the soil at this site (from 0 to 3 ft deep below the tar) to be elevated in Electrical Conductivity (EC), Sodium Absorption Ratio (SAR) and Exchangeable Sodium Percentage (ESP) well beyond the regulatory limits established in Louisiana Statewide Order 29-B [LAC Title 43:Part XIX(B)(7)(d)(iii)]. SAR values of 19 to 19.5 and ESP of 19.6 to 21.7 were found, as well as an EC of 7.6. The chloride content of the soil is within regulatory limits but is elevated in the 0-3 ft depth range (Figure 9-3).

Soil samples taken from greater than 3 ft below the tar showed a relatively low pH value (4.2), which is abnormal even for this property. EC was highly elevated at 14.6 and the chlorides, while still within regulatory limits, increased to 1,022 ppm. SAR and ESP% are within limits below 3 ft, but are borderline. TOC values in the deeper soil samples were at 3.9%, and TPH was more than 18,000.

Other areas of Site #7 show localized patchy tar mats. The soil is extremely sandy and low in clay content here, and there is very little new tree growth in the cleared area. No spill report for this site was located, making this a probable spill reporting violation.

NORM. No NORM levels in excess of proposed or existing regulatory thresholds were found at this site.

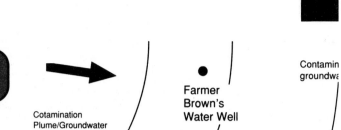

Snidely Whiplash
Production Pit

Cotamination
Plume/Groundwater
flow direction

Farmer
Brown's
Water Well

Contamin
groundwa

Contaminattion
surface water

Uptha Creek

Figure 9-2
Price Field Site #7

PROBLEM ANALYSIS

The tar pond located downgradient from the PVC flowline leak-point is retentive of sufficient volatile hydrocarbon fraction to have not only penetrated the soil to a depth of 3 ft, but to present a hazard to wildlife on the surface. This leak was probably not a short term event and is probably attributable to the use of the relatively weaker PVC pipe instead of metal as flowline material.

More significant than the surface tar itself is the chloride content of the soil, which increases down into the soil profile, and the other above-mentioned parameters, which indicate that brine and lighter fraction crude oil components probably have filtered well below the surface of the soil. A brine leak would result in salt being leached progressively deeper into the soil until it encounters an impermeable layer, and this appears to be the case in this location. The sandy soil in this area would present ideal conditions for this scenario and allow shallow rooted vegetation to grow while preventing the new growth of deep rooted vegetation. Existing deep rooted plants would be threatened by a saline front moving downgradient through the permeable soil.

Likewise, lighter fraction crude components have filtered down and spread into the deeper soil profile from the surface spill. There is also concern at this site about aquifer contamination as well as inhibited and threatened plant life.

Furthermore, the *scope* of the problem parameters have implications for remediation actions at Site #7. Given the uncertainty of the direction of the Texokarkla state oil spill clean-up regulation effort, any prudent remediation effort should be designed with these parameters in mind. Post-remediation values for EC, SAR, ESP%, TOC, and TPH should be reduced to well below the applicable regulatory threshold values (preferably background).

Finally, it should be considered that in some cases regulatory thresholds do not speak to the problem. The chloride levels are below relevant regulatory limits here, but there is some indication on the Little Jewell property that deeper rooted vegetation can be affected where samples register chloride values well below threshold, such as at Rita Field Site #5 in the northern area of the Little Jewell property. The samples in this report have been obtained and composited to get an indication of the potential for problems but are not intended to be detailed incremental depth samples. There are likely to be zones within the soil profile that would be more concentrated but would be diluted by the technique of composite sampling. Therefore, the values registered in this report should be considered as minimum values.

RECOMMENDATIONS

VEC recommends the following remedial actions be implemented by the appropriate responsible party or parties on this site:

1) Removal of the tar mat and remediation of oil contaminated soil.

2) Recycling and blending of the tar for roadspreading.

3) Deep soil borings and incremental depth sampling to delineate the level and extent of the brine contamination front.

4) Remediation of the brine parameters.

Figure 9-3

Company:
Submitted by:
Project Name:
Received:
Reference #:
Report Date:

Parameter	S7-1S	S7-2S	S7-3S	Tech	Date	Regulatory Threshold
Moisture, %	3.3	3.0	3.6	BW	08/25	– –
SP Moisture, %	20.9	20.6	25.6	LF	09/05	– –
pH	7.8	7.6	4.2	SBC	09/02	6.0 9.0+
SP EC, mmhos/cm	7.6	7.7	14.6	SBC	09/02	4.0+
Chloride, ppm	494	484	119	KM	09/07	3,000++
Soluble Cations, meq 1						
Sodium	12.7	12.2	27.6	ALB	09/08	– –
Calcium	0.5	0.4	6.7	ALB	09/08	– –
Magnesium	0.4	0.4	4.1	ALB	09/08	– –
SAR	19.0	19.5	11.9		Calculation	12.0+
CEC, meq/100g	1.0	0.9	1.1	ALB	09/08	– –
Exchangable Cations, meq/100g						
Sodium	0.2	0.2	0.2	AJA	09/08	– –
Calcium	0.6	0.5	<0.1	AJA	09/08	– –
Magnesium	<0.1	<0.1	<0.1	AJA	09/08	– –
ESP, %	21.7	19.6	14.3		Calculation	15.0+
Total Metals, ppm						
Arsenic	3.2	3.4	3.6	AJA	09/09	10+
Barium	31.7	32.8	46.7	AJA	09/08	40,000+
True Total Ba	367.9	450.7	297.4	AJA	09/08	40,000+
Cadmium	1.1	1.1	1.7	AJA	09/08	10+
Chromium	<5.0	<5.0	<5.0	AJA	09/08	500+
Lead	28.4	21.0	12.0	AJA	09/08	500+
Mercury	0.1	0.1	<.1	AJA	09/09	10+
Selenium	0.3	0.3	0.3	AJA	09/09	10+
Silver	<5.0	<5.0	<5.0	AJA	09/08	200+
Zinc	5.2	5.8	8.2	AJA	09/08	500+
TOC, %	<0.1	<0.1	3.9	KM	09/08	– –
TPH by IR, mg/kg	42.20	– –	18,042	KO	08/31	10,000+
PCB's mg/kg	<1.0	– –	<1.0	CAW	09/01	– –

* Analysis Methods are from Laboratory Procedures for Analysis of Oilfield
  Waste Louisiana DNR, August, 1988
+ Louisiana 29-B Regulatory Threshold
++ Texas Rule 8 Regulatory Threshold

Price Field Site #7 Soil Sample Analysis

SCENARIO 3

Just down the road from the flowline leak, this situation exists. Here, a real pH anomaly was found (in addition to other potential cleanup liability). How can one account for it? How would you classify it?. It is in the oil field, but is it RCRA D or RCRA C? Was TCLP a good suggestion recommendation?

A notable aspect of this site is that there is no one to explain the past operation. Whoever did this is gone. In fact, he's out of business. The operation must be reconstructed as well as possible from relics. There are some puzzles here.

PRICE FIELD SITE #12

SITE IDENTIFICATION AND DESCRIPTION

OIL WELL. Site #12 is notable for its complexity and somewhat enigmatic production facilities and installations (Figure 9-4). The well was completed in 1956 and produced oil from the Zydeco formation until it went off production and was abandoned. A plugging report was on file for the well and gives a plugging date of April 7, 1976. Surface casing was set at 900 ft which may or may not adequately cover the fresh water in the underlying aquifer. The concrete support pads for the derrick and the rod pump have been left on the site by the operator.

STORAGE TANK/WATER WELL. There is a tall steel storage tank on the east side of the location that is identical to the one used for produced brine storage at Site #3 and might have been used for salt water storage. This tank sits next to an unplugged water well, the metal casing of which has been crimped below the surface (Figure 9-5). It is uncertain, at this time, what this tank and well were used for, but soil sampling tended to strengthen VEC's theory that the tank was used for salt water storage and oil/water separation. Tar has leaked from the base of the tank, but this could be residual oil remaining after the brine has leaked out or has been drained from the tank. No record of the water well in question was found in the regulatory files. Repeated attempts were made to retrieve a water sample from this well, but the crimp in the casing made it impossible to recover.

OIL STORAGE TANKS. Two additional tanks clearly used as oil storage tanks are located on the west half of the site. These are of the usual steel variety, with asbestos and Styrofoam insulation lying in ruin around them.

SOIL COVERAGE.

- **GENERAL.** An estimated 80% of the site is covered with tar and tar/sand aggregate, which translates into an aerial coverage of about 40,300 sq. ft. The contamination profile is as deep as 2 ft in places, giving the site a paved appearance. No spill reports have been found for this site. Soil samples were taken from below the tar and tar/sand aggregate mat and the results can be found in the sample analysis results in Figure 9-6. Indications from the sample analysis are that a soil problem exists in areas proximal to the oil storage tanks and the storage tank/water well combination.

Figure 9-4
Price Field Site #12 well information

WELL INFORMATION

SITE NUMBER: 12

OPERATOR: Rooster Oil, Inc.

LEASE: Harwell

WELL NUMBER: 3

API NUMBER: 699 8346

ELEVATION: 427' GL

DATE DRILLING COMMENCED: 3-23-54

DATE DRILLING COMPLETED: 4-4-54

<u>CASING PROGRAM</u>

    SURFACE CASING: 10 3/4" @ 828'

    PRODUCTION CASING: 5 1/2" @ 5917'

    TUBING: —

TOTAL DEPTH: 5917'

WELL STATUS: P & A

PLUGGING REPORT ON FILE: Yes

DATE WELL PLUGGED: 6-7-74

- **OIL STORAGE TANKS.** A pH of 2.1 was registered in the soil sample taken near the storage tanks.
- **STORAGE TANK/WATER WELL.** On the east side of the site, near the storage tank/water well combination, a definite fingerprint of brine contamination was discovered. EC was significantly elevated. Chlorides are well below 3,000 ppm, but nevertheless are elevated. The SAR and the ESP% were 27.9 and 21.6, respectively, and both values are elevated beyond the Louisiana 29-B threshold.

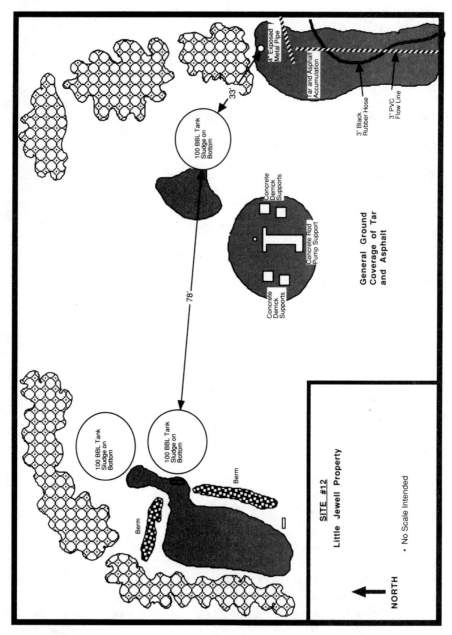

Figure 9-5
Price field site #12

Company:
Submitted by:
Project Name:
Received:
Reference #:
Report Date:

Parameter	S12-2S	S12-2S	S12-3S	S12-5ST	Tech	Regulatory Date	Threshold
Moisture, %	4.3	– –	4.2	3.0	BW	08/25	– –
SP Moisture, %	21.5	– –	20.7	20.6	LF	09/05	– –
pH	6.8	– –	6.8	2.3	SBC	09/02	6.09.0+
SP EC, mmhos/cm	1.1	– –	6.1	2.1	SBC	09/02	4.0+
Chloride, ppm	85	– –	392	119	KM	09/07	3,000++
Soluble Cations, meq 1							
Sodium	0.9	– –	12.3	2.5	ALB	09/08	– –
Calcium	2.4	– –	0.3	0.4	ALB	09/08	– –
Magnesium	0.2	– –	<0.1	<0.1	ALB	09/08	– –
SAR	0.8	– –	27.9	5.3		Calculation	12.0+
CEC, meq/100g	1.2	– –	0.9	0.7	ALB	09/08	– –
Exchangable Cations, meq/100g							
Sodium	<0.1	– –	0.2	<0.1	AJA	09/08	– –
Calcium	1.4	– –	0.4	0.3	AJA	09/08	– –
Magnesium	<0.1	– –	<0.1	<0.1	AJA	09/08	– –
ESP, %	2.0	– –	21.6	5.2		Calculation	15.0+
Total Metals, ppm							
Arsenic	0.0	– –	4.3	4.0	AJA	09/09	10+
Barium	41.4	– –	46.6	18.7	AJA	09/08	40,000+
True Total Ba	506.0	– –	554.0	336.0	AJA	09/08	40,000+
Cadmium	<0.1	– –	1.4	1.5	AJA	09/08	10+
Chromium	<5.0	– –	<5.0	<5.0	AJA	09/08	500+
Lead	<5.0	– –	51.7	56.7	AJA	09/08	500+
Mercury	0.0	– –	0.1	0.1	AJA	09/09	10+
Selenium	0.0	– –	0.2	0.3	AJA	09/09	10+
Silver	<5.0	– –	<5.0	<5.0	AJA	09/08	200+
Zinc	7.0	– –	6.5	4.7	AJA	09/08	500+
TOC, %	<0.1	– –	<0.1	0.2	KM	09/08	– –
TPH by IR, mg/kg	25.34	24.52	25.70	706.9	KO	08/31	10,000+
PCB's mg/kg	<1.0	– –	<1.0	<1.0	CAW	09/01	– –

* Analysis Methods are from Laboratory Procedures for Analysis of Oilfield
  Waste Louisiana DNR, August, 1988
+ Louisiana 29-B Regulatory Threshold
++ Texas Rule 8 Regulatory Threshold

Figure 9-6
Price field site #12 Soil Analysis

- **FLOWLINE EASEMENT.** A 3 in. PVC flow line and a 3 in. black rubber hose were run from the southeast edge of this site down to Site #13. Several flow line leaks have occurred along this easement. The black rubber hose was probably used for transporting produced salt water.

PROBLEM ANALYSIS

OIL WELL. Although the well is apparently plugged, the status of the plugging is in question, and the casing possibly does not cover all of the aquifer. This could represent a contamination threat to the aquifer, but it is not necessarily the major concern at this location.

STORAGE TANK/WATER WELL

A primary concern at Site #12 is the bent and unplugged water well sitting next to what may have been a salt water storage tank. It is possible that brines were being directly disposed into this water well or that this was a salt water disposal well. If this well is indeed a fresh water well and has been receiving salt water (and particularly over a long period of time), then this represents a violation of both state and federal regulations such as those under the SDWA and Texokarkla State Groundwater Quality Standards.

SOIL

- **GENERAL.** The tar and tar/sand aggregate on the ground are detrimental to plant growth and represent one of the worse cases of surface contamination on the property.

- **OIL STORAGE TANKS.** The extremely low pH found near the oil storage tank battery is difficult to explain by natural processes or oil spills, even in this area. It creates concern because one very possible explanation for it is the dumping or spillage of acids such as HCl or some other substance, which would not be covered by the oil industry's RCRA exemption. If this is the case, then the affected areas could be classified as hazardous rather than NOW. Hazardous waste stream areas would then have to be distinguished from NOW waste and treated separately and differently.

- **STORAGE TANK/WATER WELL.** The distinctive brine contamination signature in the soil samples of this area indicate that brines have leaked or spilled onto the soil. It is the same problem discussed previously on Sites #2, #3, and #7. Salt from produced brines could be leached deeper into the soil profile, where it could possibly remain as poison to deeper rooted vegetation. The extent and level of contamination would need to be delineated and the soil remediated before vegetation could regain a foothold.

FACILITIES AND INSTALLATIONS. The tanks, concrete support pads, and installations at this site are an obstruction to tree farming and other land use activities.

RECOMMENDATIONS

VEC advises that the appropriate responsible party or parties take the following actions at this site:

1) Take samples near the oil storage tank battery and perform Toxicity Leachate Characteristics Procedure (TCLP).

2) Take soil borings and detailed samples to delineate brine contamination in the soil.

3) Check the plugging status of the well and test the casing integrity and fluid levels in the well.

4) Sample the water well and analyze for brine and hydrocarbon contamination.

5) Plug the water well and determine the makeup of the well as regards casing, bridge plugs, etc.

6) Install monitoring wells to obtain water samples from the aquifer.

7) Remove the tar and tar/sand aggregate.

8) Recycle and blend tar for road spreading on the property.

9) Remove unusable portions of contaminated soil (if any) to a licensed NOW facility or remediate in situ using soil amendments.

10) Remove all steel tanks after evacuating any residual bottom material.

11) Remove concrete pads, exposed flowlines, other debris, and production installations.

SCENARIO 4

This baby is making some oil. It would be a real money maker. Your consultant failed to notice the glowing clean bill of health afforded the property by the seller's audit and went out and found a few problems. Up 'til now everyone was happy. The seller does want a few things from you, however. For instance, there is an indemnification agreement that he is demanding you sign. After signing it, you will be totally responsible for everything and will have to spend your money to defend the seller for everything up to and including the Franco-Prussian War.

You really like this property. The seller tells you that your consultant is a dingbat. What will you do? There is a fairly mixed bag of issues at this location on the property.

Do you walk away from the deal?

WHOPPER SITE #1

SITE DESCRIPTION

DEFORESTATION. Site 1 is an area of deforestation behind Tank Batteries 1 and 2 and across the canal from the Whopper Field Office complex. It is about 186 acres in area. Flow line runs, two salt water disposal wells, and two tank batteries border the area on the south.

Spoil banks, produced by dredging of the canals, have isolated the internal area of the Site 1 and have restricted the circulation of water. Beluga Field Foreman Martin Tolstoy stated that, prior to underground injection of produced water, it was common to discharge directly into the swamp behind the tank batteries.

Some of the dead tree stumps are still standing, but the oldest contaminated[1] areas (nearest the tank batteries) no longer have standing stumps (Photos 9-1 through 9-4).

PITS. Two discharge pit complexes were active in this area at one time (Figure 9-7). Each of the two presently active facilities had its own designated pit complex. Both have been closed by Beluga and their pre and post-closure sample results are included in Appendix A

FACILITIES.

TANK BATTERY #1: Bordering Site 1 to the southwest is the #1 Tank Battery. It is consists of two separate platforms, one for storage tanks and one for heater-treaters.

The deck of the heater treater platform is concrete in part and steel grating in part (Photos 9-5, 9-6). The support platform for the storage tanks has a wooden deck, and the spill containment is provided by individual drain pans for each tank. Oil staining was observed on the wooden deck (Photo 9-7).

None of the vessels appeared to be actively leaking during the field inspection. Salt Water Disposal Well #1 is located about 750 ft west of Tank Battery #1 and is an active injector. It sits on a platform over water, like the tank battery (Photo 9-8).

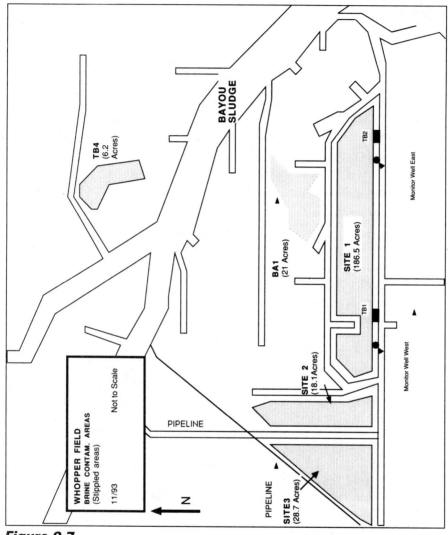

Figure 9-7
Whopper Site #1 aerial view

TANK BATTERY #2: A second active tank battery is located about 4,000 ft east of Tank Battery #1, bordering Site 1 to the southeast. Like the #1 Tank Battery, the #2 consists of two structures (Photos 9-10, 9-11). There is a separate heater treater platform with both wooden and steel grating for decking and a storage tank platform with wooden decking (Photos 9-12, 9-13, 9-14).

Here also, individual drain pans on the storage tanks seem to be the primary spill containment (Photo 9-15). Oil staining was observed on deck of this platform, although none of the vessels appeared to be leaking during the field visit. The R. Barclay C-7 (SWD #7) is located about 1,500 ft west of the tank battery and is active as a salt water disposal well.

INDIVIDUAL STORAGE TANK: A large single storage tank was observed on the south side of the SA1 area near the center. No active leaks were observed at this location.

PROBLEM ANALYSIS

Four environmental problems are noted in this area/system. They are:

- Soil contamination/deforestation.
- Groundwater contamination.
- Oil and grease in closed pit.
- NORM contamination.

It is important to see and note the relationship among items 1, 2, and 3. These items are part of a system and probably not completely separate issues. Item 4 (NORM) is a separate issue. Each of these four items will be discussed in greater detail.

SOIL CONTAMINATION/DEFORESTATION.

PROBLEM STATEMENT. Sampling of this 186 acre area indicates that the probable cause for the deforestation is contamination by produced brines. EC, SAR, and ESP all indicate past contamina-tion (See sample analysis data sheets in Appendix B). This would fit well with the testi-mony of Beluga Field Foreman Martin Tolstoy who stated that past practice was to discharge directly into the swamp. Additionally, sampling of this area by VEC found oil and grease contamination that could be affecting plant growth in the Site 1 internal area.

CAVEAT. It is important to understand that the soil contamination is a relatively old event and that the values present in the samples are, very possibly, well below the peak levels. It should be further noted that all of the samples come from the upper portion of the soil profile and represent the portion of the soil profile most likely to be flushed by fluctuating water levels. Therefore, it is possible that the severity of the existing brine contamination could increase with depth. Furthermore, the extent of oil and grease contamination can not be delineated until low water conditions exist and further sampling can be undertaken.

REMEDIATION. It is likely that a sodic soil condition could exist in the tree rooting zone of all or parts of the site and that remediation would be required for reforestation. Further sampling at multiple depths would be needed to prescribe the proper soil amendment. Extensive oil and grease contamination would make the soil remediation more complex than for brine contamination alone.

In addition, it is possible that there are other contaminants such as boron or molybdenum that would not be detected by the existing sampling, but which might be the cause of the tree death. These possibilities would also need to be tested in order to arrive at a final remediation plan.

An area this large would require a farming/soil amendment option. Likewise, the size of the area makes it a significant source for groundwater contamination.

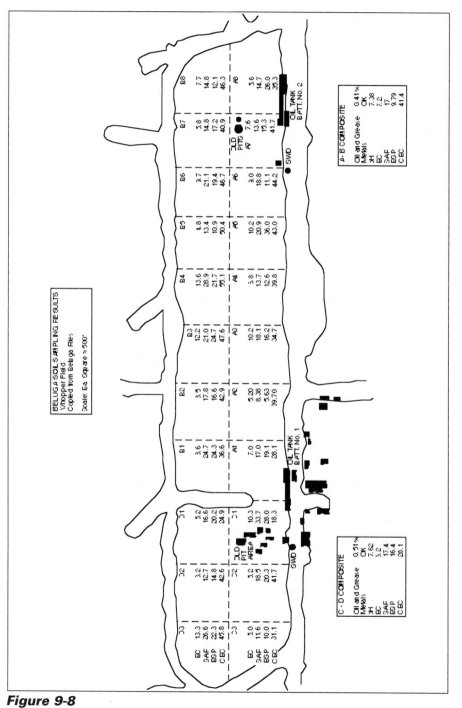

Figure 9-8
Whopper Site #1 Soil Sampling Results

OIL AND GREASE IN CLOSED PIT. Two discharge pit complexes were, at one time, operative within the SA1 (Figure 9-7). Both pits have been closed by Beluga. However, sampling of the closed discharge pit for Tank Battery #1 indicates that the oil and grease content is still above the permissible post-closure limits prescribed by Texmissiarkla regulations. This represents a continuing environmental/regulatory problem that might require further remediation. Remediation figures for this work are attached.

GROUNDWATER CONTAMINATION. Due to the large potential source area (186 acres) resulting from the soil contamination of Site 1, VEC drilled two shallow (5 ft) monitor wells on the south side and downgradient of the site (Figure 9-7). Sample analysis of the recovered water showed contamination of the shallow groundwater of the unconfined zone. The contamination consisted of benzene and metals contamination. (See sample analysis data sheets in Appendix B). The problem parameters are shown in Table 9-1 in relation to the monitoring well from which each sample was taken.

Table 9-1
Site #1 Contamination

MONITORING WELL	PROBLEM PARAMETER
Tank Battery #1 (West)	*Benzene, Xylenes, Barium, Chloride, Chromium*
Tank Battery #2 (East)	*Arsenic, Barium, Chromium, Mercury*

It should be noted that both monitoring wells discovered contamination in excess of proposed federal levels set forth in 40 CFR Part 264 "Subpart S." Subpart S levels, although not final, were cited by two Texmissisarkla representatives as applicable action levels that would be used as standards for groundwater contamination as regulated by the Texmissisarkla under TXMIS Code 42:XXI,45.3(a). The contaminant levels also exceed the Maximum Contaminant Levels (MCL) established under the SDWA in 40 CFR 141.11 & 61-62.

It is unknown whether the contamination has reached and involved major aquifers such as the Hotchachacha or the Chihuahua. The high CEC in the soil samples (ranging 25-50 meq/100 gm) give reason to hope that the soil buffering would be sufficient to mitigate such a possibility. Further investigation would be needed to delineate the level and extent of the groundwater contamination and to estimate a remediation cost, should remediation become necessary. Therefore, no estimate for remediation cost is included in this study.

NORM. Both of the tank batteries associated with this site have equipment NORM according to a 7/93 survey by GDGD (Figures 9-9, 9-10). Estimates for the disposal cost of equipment NORM are attached.

Additionally, there appears to have been a serious leakage from the NW storage tank on Tank Battery #1, leaving possible contamination on the deck of the platform and on the soil below. GDGD found readings as high as 150 µR/hr. on the soil and 65µR/hr on the deck itself. VEC took a confirmation composite soil sample and found Ra 226 to be at 11.95 pCi/gm

This NORM possibly will have to be remediated at the release of the property.

RECOMMENDATIONS

1) Beluga should retain liability for at least the groundwater contamination at this location. In lieu of that, a cash settlement/price reduction should be negotiated to mitigate the impact on High Roller in the event that remediation is required.

2) The contaminated soil should be bioremediated and landfarmed. Reforestation should be undertaken.

3) Further study of the groundwater contamination.

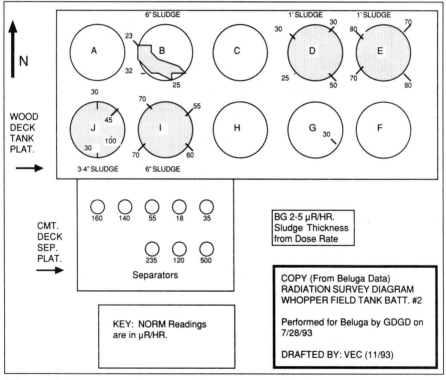

Figure 9-9
Site #1 Tank battery NORM survey

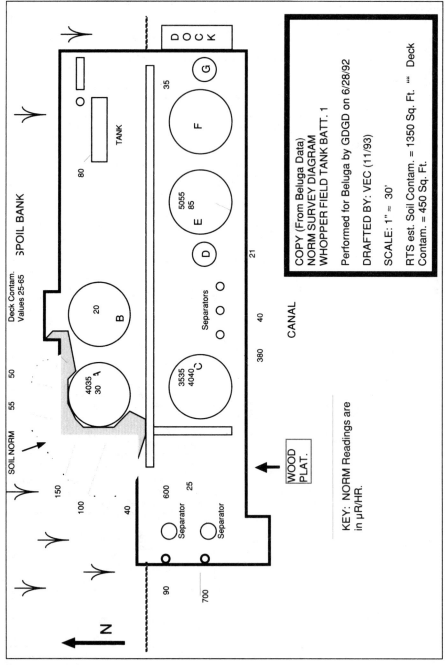

Figure 9-10
Site #1 tank battery NORM survey

SCENARIO 5

You are back to being the surface owner. Being a noble sort, you have located a property on which you plan to build a subdivision: little bungalows for America's hard working families. There is good possibility that you will have to drill a community water well for your subdivision somewhere on the property.

You were pretty confident so you told your consultant to just do a "quick and dirty." Now you are looking at his preliminary report. What do you do? You have only 20 days to closing. There are these oil and gas operations sitting at the highest topographic point right on the edge of your property.

Sometimes one finds oneself in a situation of having minimal data with which to work. Limited by time and circumstances, decisions must be made anyway. What can be gleaned from the report to help you know what to do?

SUMMARY

SECTION D PROPERTY, ENVIRONMENTAL ISSUES AND CONCERNS

Three categories of environmental and/or regulatory liability and concerns were noted during Vigilant Environmental Consulting's preliminary work on the property. They are:

- Soil contamination from RCRA D materials.
- Potential contamination of the fresh water aquifer and surface water by RCRA D materials.
- Potential contamination of the fresh water aquifer by hazardous materials, as regulated under RCRA C and CERCLA.

Each of these categories will be covered in detail. Some of the specific sites will be treated individually later in the report.

SOIL CONTAMINATION FROM RCRA D MATERIALS.

Two sites were examined visually. Both showed evidence of contamination by brine, hydrocarbons, and (possibly) other production related fluids. Site #1 is the wellhead, which sits approximately 30 ft south of the drainage canal at the end of the lease road, which diverges north from Rocky Road. Site #2 is the Winger #1 separation and storage facility located at the extreme south end of the property next to Rocky Road.

Both sites probably predate 1960 and have had a long history of use in regard to production and storage of oil and gas related materials.

POTENTIAL POLLUTION OF THE SURFACE WATER AND GROUNDWATER BY RCRA D MATERIALS

GROUNDWATER. Both of the listed sites also are potential point sources for groundwater contamination of the fresh water aquifer of the property, based upon age, use, and conditions observed at the site.

In the report area, the Chihuahua, Hotchachacha, and Darby zones are all fresh. The top of the fresh water phreatic zone can be well above 100 ft and perched aquifers are common. Fresh water can extend to depths of 1,400-1,500 ft.

The soil covering appears to be of a type that would have low cation exchange capacity, thus reducing any buffering effect. Spills on the ground surface and in the shallow subsurface would tend to pass through to the groundwater with little impediment (in lieu of some laterally extensive aquitard).

There are several water wells in the vicinity, that may be affected by contaminant plumes emanating from the facilities noted in this report. There was not time to compile a complete listing of area wells, so there are probably others in the area.

The Winger #1 Tank Battery (Site #2) is a particular threat to the groundwater under the property because of its location. It sits several feet upgradient from the main body of the property and at least some component of the groundwater gradient would be north and northwest into the heart of the property.

SURFACE WATER. In addition to a potentially compromised aquifer, the well at Site #1 has no firewall and is within 50 ft of a drainage canal that opens to state waters. A flowline leak at this location could enter the waters of the canal and from there move into state waters.

Two drums labeled "Demulsifier" were found in the canal below the well site and were shot full of holes.

GROUNDWATER CONTAMINATION BY HAZARDOUS MATERIALS

Frank Cameron and Art Smedley of BM Corp. reported that a hazardous dump site existed adjacent the property and across the Missouri Pacific Railroad to the east. Allegedly, this site has been cleaned up.

However, checking of the relevant regulatory files has not yet shown any indication that any proper cleanup measures were undertaken or that proper notification of such a site was given. More extensive file searching may reveal proper handling, but without further information, it seems probable that (if the site actually existed) no proper cleanup measures were ever taken.

No such site has yet been located on the ground, but there is a very likely candidate that was observed by Vigilant representatives. Contamination from such a source could threaten the groundwater of the Section C property. This possibility, due to the number of unknowns, makes the purchase of this property a very sensitive issue.

MISCELLANEOUS CONCERNS

Other concerns have surfaced in the investigation to date. A brief listing would include, but not be limited to, the following:

- Naturally Occurring Radioactive Material (NORM)
- Two hydrocarbon transmission pipelines (one dating from before 1960).
- At least one other active well site (which may be an injector well) and the possibility of other abandoned sites that might be contaminated.
- Gas, observed leaking to the surface from an unknown source at Site #1.

SECTION D SITE #1

SITE DESCRIPTION

An unidentified active wellhead sits at this location, about 30 ft from the edge of a dredged drainage canal (Photo 9-14). No firewall was in existence at the time of the visual inspection. Chemical drums, one of which was hooked up as a demulsifier unit, were present on the location. The fencing around the site was partially down, leaving open access to the chemicals and the wellhead.

A bog lacking any vegetation (and surrounded by stressed and dead vegetation) was observed on the east and south sides of the wellsite. The water contained by the bog was cloudy and may be produced brine that has leaked. Additionally, there were oil stains in the bog and on pipe surfaces that may be indicative of leaks (Photos 9-15 through 9-19).

Immediately south of the wellsite, in the bottom of the drainage canal, perforated drums labeled "Demulsifier" were observed (Photo 9-18, 9-19). Almost certainl, this is the result of vandalism. The downed fence (which might itself be the result of vandalism) would easily allow access to the chemicals and the wellhead.

PROBLEM ANALYSIS

Soil, groundwater, and surface water are potentially jeopardized by the operation at this location. The spill indications at the surface suggest that the soil is *already* contaminated.

Spills at this location would tend to move downgradient and laterally through the soil profile and enter the groundwater or possibly directly enter the nearby dredged canal. The absence of a firewall makes it easier for spills to enter the canal from the surface.

Brine, in particular, is a problem in that the salt may take up long term residence in the soil or sodic soil development may occur. Either of the two conditions will, unless remediated, prevent the healthy growth of plant/tree life on a long term basis.

SECTION D SITE #2
WINGER #1 TANK BATTERY
SITE DESCRIPTION

GENERAL. This is a production facility site used for separation and storage of oil and brine being severed from the Winger #1 Lease. Three oil storage tanks and three heater treaters are present as well as a production pit (Figure 9-11 and Photo 9-20). The production pit seems to be in use at the present time as an emergency saltwater storage pit and/or a basic sediment pit.

Parts or all of this facility, including the pit, may have been in use since before 1960. The tanks and heater treaters are surrounded by a firewall, which in turn has an older post and cable enclosure surrounding it. The entire facility is surrounded by a newer chain-link/barbed wire fence. On both occasions, where Vigilant representatives observed the site, the gates were open.

WATER AND FREE OIL. Inside the firewall, there was a great deal of water and free oil. About 50% of the sub-enclosure around the heater treaters was covered with water and free oil. Oil staining of the soil was widespread in some cases coming nearly to the top of the firewall (Photos 9-21 through 9-25).

One of the stock tanks has recently overflowed (Photo 9-23). This may be a result of a problem with the salt water disposal system.

PRODUCTION PIT. The production pit, which sits on the east side of the facility outside the chain link fence, is water filled and has dimensions of about 60 ft by 60 ft. A flowline from inside the firewall area extends into the pit (Photos 9-26, 9-27).

SOIL CONTAMINATION SURROUNDING FACILITY. On the west and northwest side of the facility is a barren, boggy area that shows strong evidence of contamination (Photos 9-28 through 9-31). The soil is largely barren of vegetation. It has cloudy water standing in pools. The surrounding ground vegetation is dead and dying. Pine trees in the boggy area itself are dead, and others, on the periphery, are turning brown. This would tend to indicate elevated electrical conductivity perhaps (>4 mmhos/cm). In addition, there is oil staining of the soil in places, particularly near the valves just west of the chain link fence.

There is general oil staining of the soil just outside the fenced area north of the site around the flowlines (Photos 9-32, 9-33). In addition, gas was escaping to the surface from underground near the southeast corner of the site by the meter loop.

MISCELLANEOUS. A 4 in. flowline, running from the stock tanks to the fence on the south side of the tank battery, apparently serves as the shipping terminal. The flowline was dripping oil into a partially buried drum. A nearby standpipe was nearly full of oil, and the ground was stained with oil (Photo 9-34).

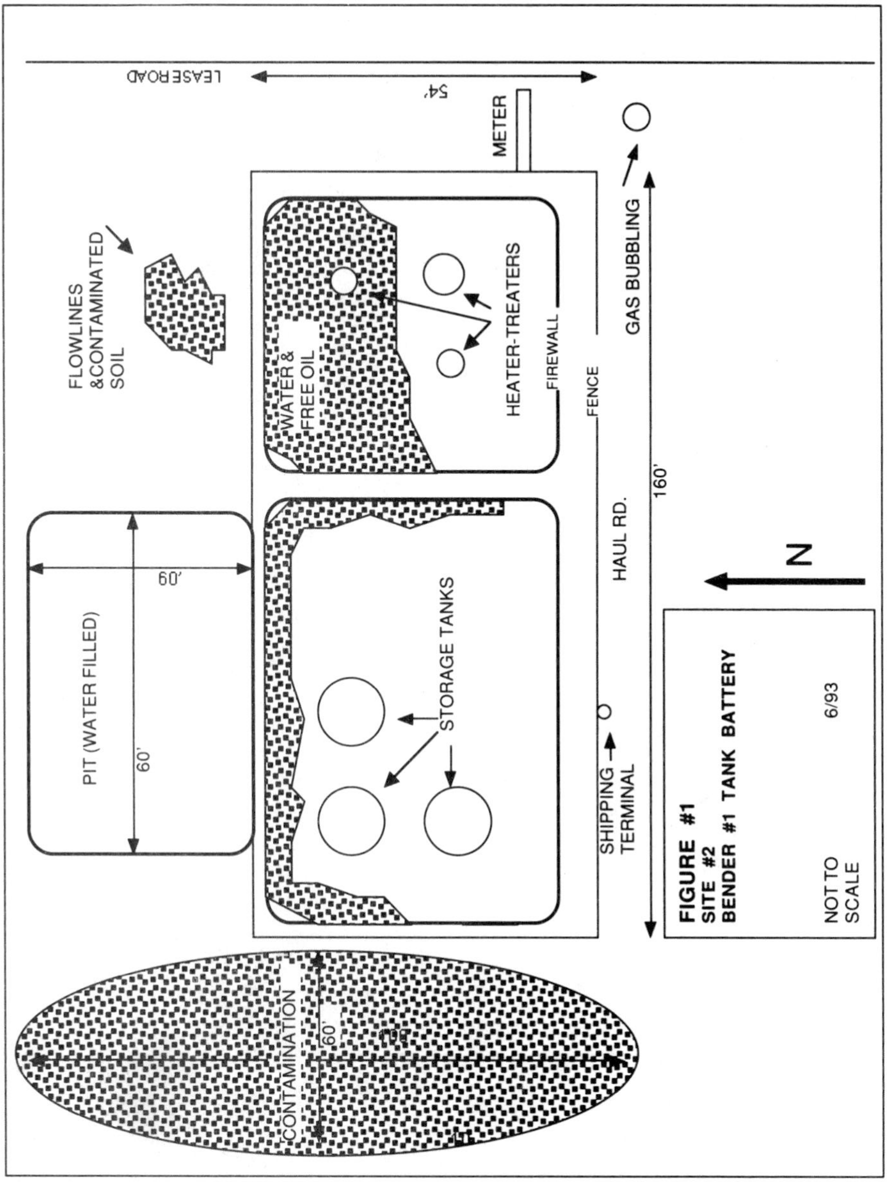

Figure 9-11
Site #2 Winger #1 Tank Battery

PROBLEM ANALYSIS

The Winger #1 Tank Battery (Site #1) constitutes a serious environmental concern for the Section D Property. Three factors converge to make it so. They are:

- Its age (possibly pre-1960) and use.
- Its location (upgradient from the remainder of the property).
- The visual evidence (existing soil contamination).

A large volume of fluids has been handled by this facility over several decades. There is evidence of at least one contamination incident on the ground surface at the time of this report, and it is not unreasonable to believe that there may have been others.

Topographically, this site is located several feet above the remainder of the property. It is likely that the groundwater gradient would be toward the north and northwest. This would put a groundwater contamination plume, derived from this site, directly under the main body of the Section D Property.

It has not yet been ascertained whether or not the aquifer actually has been compromised by this site, but it must be regarded as a significant possibility.

Finally, there is probably a great deal of old plumbing buried around this site that may be leaking, as evidenced by the valves on the west end of the site and the bubbling gas in the southeast corner of the site.

APPENDIX A

WHOPPER SITE #1 PRE AND POST-CLOSURE SAMPLE RESULTS

PARAMETER	ANALYTICAL RESULTS				ANALYST
	PW	PBS	BG	SAL	
pH (Std. Units)	6.58	7.14	5.74	– –	VLS
METALS: (ppm)					
Arsenic	<0.010	7.97	10.8	– –	RDH
Barium	770	6659	1198	– –	RDH
Cadmium	0.40	<3.30	<1.42	– –	RDH
Chromium	<0.05	42.9	47.1	– –	RDH
Lead	1.03	70.4	28.6	– –	RDH
Mercury	<0.001	1.52	<0.34	– –	RDH
Selenium	0.010	<3.32	<1.43	– –	RDH
Silver	<0.04	<13.3	<5.71	– –	RDH
Zinc	0.15	262	132	– –	RDH
Oil & Grease (ppm)	35.5	221,000	2940	– –	VLS/KLJ
Conductivity (mmhos/cm)	172	4.86	3.05	– –	VLS/KLJ
Salinity (as Chloride) (ppm)	66,900	– –	– –	38.3	KLJ
SAR	– –	132	24.0	– –	RDH
ESP (%)	– –	66.0	25.4	– –	HNL
CEC (meg/100g)	– –	19.7	28.1	– –	VLS
Moisture (%)	– –	70.9	38.4	– –	VLS

CERTIFICATION:

APPENDIX A

WHOPPER SITE #1 PRE AND POST-CLOSURE SAMPLE RESULTS

TO: DATE: 6/22/90

Analysis of OTB #1 PIT #1 – POST CLOSURE SOIL COMPOSITE – 0'-3' DEPTH collected on 6/08/90 at 0730 by and received at lab on 6/08/90 at 1320. Sample was assigned and analyzed in accordance with procedures outlined in Statewide Order 29-B.

Percent (%) Moisture	34.49
Oil & Gas (% Dry Wt.)	0.73

<u>TOTAL METAL CONTENT (ppm)</u>

Arsenic	7.142	Chromium	15.56	Seleniumm	0.048
Barium	495.8	Lead	<0.050	Silver	<0.010
Cadmium	<0.010	Mercury	0.034	Zinc	88.18

pH (Std. Units)	8.16
Electrical Conductivity (mmhos/cm)	7.80
Sodium Adsorption Ratio (SAR)	19.53
Paste Saturation Percentage (%)	84.21

<u>SOLUBLE CATIONS (meq/1)</u>

Calcium	14.2365
Magnesium	5.6895
Sodium	61.6743

Exchangeable Sodium (meq/100g)	6.81
Exchangeable Sodium Percentage (%)	32.49
Cation Exchange Capacity (meq/100g)	20.97

APPENDIX A
WHOPPER SITE #1 PRE AND POST-CLOSURE SAMPLE RESULTS

	-OTB # 1-2		
PARAMETER	ANALYTICAL RESULTS		ANALYST
	PW	PBS	
pH (Std. Units)	6.95	6.51	VLS
METALS: (ppm)			
Arsenic	<0.010	1.70	RDH
Barium	482	4639	RDH
Cadmium	0.40	<1.41	RDH
Chromium	<0.05	25.0	RDH
Lead	1.05	29.1	RDH
Mercury	<0.001	<0.38	RDH
Selenium	<0.010	<1.41	RDH
Silver	<0.04	<5.66	RDH
Zinc	0.15	91.5	RDH
Oil & Grease (ppm)	11.3	240,000	VLS/KLJ
Conductivity (mmhos/cm)	140	169	VLS/KLJ
Salinity (as Chloride) (ppm)	62,500	– –	KLJ
SAR	– –	8.53	RDH
ESP (%)	– –	10.2	HNL
CEC (meg/100g)	– –	9.85	VLS
Moisture (%)	– –	30.7	VLS

CERTIFICATION:

APPENDIX A
WHOPPER SITE #1 PRE AND POST-CLOSURE SAMPLE RESULTS

TO: DATE: 6/22/90

Analysis of OTB #1 PIT #2 – POST CLOSURE SOIL collected on 6/22/90 at
0830 by and received at lab on 6/22/90 at 1300. Sample was assigned and
analyzed in accordance with procedures outlined in Statewide Order 29-B.

Percent (%) Moisture   37.02
Oil & Gas (% Dry Wt.)   0.43

<u>TOTAL METAL CONTENT (ppm)</u>

Arsenic	7.1678	Chromium	18.00	Seleniumm	0.147
Barium	1,250.0	Lead	<0.050	Silver	<0.010
Cadmium	<0.010	Mercury	0.185	Zinc	386.6

pH (Std. Units)   8.47
Electrical Conductivity (mmhos/cm)   5.40
Sodium Adsorption Ratio (SAR)   9.10
Paste Saturation Percentage (%)   64.12

<u>SOLUBLE CATIONS (meq/1)</u>

Calcium   25.3292
Magnesium   2.5386
Sodium   33.9735

Exchangeable Sodium (meq/100g)   2.70
Exchangeable Sodium Percentage (%)   10.02
Cation Exchange Capacity (meq/100g)   26.97

APPENDIX A
WHOPPER SITE #1 PRE AND POST-CLOSURE SAMPLE RESULTS

TO: DATE: 6/22/90

Analysis of #2 PIT #1 – POST CLOSURE SOIL collected on 6/26/90 at 0800 by
and received at lab on 6/26/90 at 1000. Sample was assigned and analyzed in
accordance with procedures outlined in Statewide Order 29-B.

Percent (%) Moisture   29.12
Oil & Gas (% Dry Wt.)   0.09

<u>TOTAL METAL CONTENT (ppm)</u>

Arsenic	5.780	Chromium	14.00	Seleniumm	0.022
Barium	422.0	Lead	<0.050	Silver	<0.010
Cadmium	<0.010	Mercury	0.115	Zinc	48.66

pH (Std. Units)   7.93
Electrical Conductivity (mmhos/cm)   2.40
Sodium Adsorption Ratio (SAR)   4.44
Paste Saturation Percentage (%)   42.84

<u>SOLUBLE CATIONS (meq/l)</u>

Calcium   10.9131
Magnesium   5.1546
Sodium   12.5889

Exchangeable Sodium (meq/100g)   0.59
Exchangeable Sodium Percentage (%)   4.02
Cation Exchange Capacity (meq/100g)   14.70

APPENDIX A
WHOPPER SITE #1 PRE AND POST-CLOSURE SAMPLE RESULTS

	-OTB # 2-1		
PARAMETER	ANALYTICAL RESULTS		ANALYST
	PW	PBS	
pH (Std. Units)	7.05	6.70	VLS
METALS: (ppm)			
Arsenic	0.010	<1.39	RDH
Barium	364	6840	RDH
Cadmium	0.25	<1.39	RDH
Chromium	<0.05	34.3	RDH
Lead	0.74	84.4	RDH
Mercury	<0.001	<0.25	RDH
Selenium	<0.010	<1.39	RDH
Silver	<0.04	<5.55	RDH
Zinc	0.11	142	RDH
Oil & Grease (ppm)	20.7	185,000	VLS/KLJ
Conductivity (mmhos/cm)	102	160	VLS/KLJ
Salinity (as Chloride) (ppm)	43,500	– –	KLJ
SAR	– –	16.6	RDH
ESP (%)	– –	19.1	HNL
CEC (meg/100g)	– –	20.25	VLS
Moisture (%)	– –	43.4	VLS

CERTIFICATION:

APPENDIX A
WHOPPER SITE #1 PRE AND POST-CLOSURE SAMPLE RESULTS

PARAMETER	-OTB # 2-2 ANALYTICAL RESULTS		ANALYST
	PW	PBS	
pH (Std. Units)	7.75	7.11	VLS
METALS: (ppm)			
Arsenic	<0.010	3.34	RDH
Barium	425	3012	RDH
Cadmium	0.22	<1.85	RDH
Chromium	<0.05	13.4	RDH
Lead	0.69	29.7	RDH
Mercury	<0.001	<0.48	RDH
Selenium	<0.010	<1.85	RDH
Silver	<0.04	<7.426	RDH
Zinc	0.05	113	RDH
Oil & Grease (ppm)	3.0	149,600	VLS/KLJ
Conductivity (mmhos/cm)	92.0	192	VLS/KLJ
Salinity (as Chloride) (ppm)	37,900	--	KLJ
SAR	--	31.1	RDH
ESP (%)	--	30.9	HNL
CEC (meg/100g)	--	20.6	VLS
Moisture (%)	--	48.3	VLS

CERTIFICATION:

APPENDIX A
WHOPPER SITE #1 PRE AND POST-CLOSURE SAMPLE RESULTS

TO: DATE: 6/22/90

Analysis of OTB #2 PIT #2 – POST CLOSURE SOIL collected on 6/22/90 at
0815 by and received at lab on 6/22/90 at 1300. Sample was assigned and
analyzed in accordance with procedures outlined in Statewide Order 29-B.

Percent (%) Moisture   34.63
Oil & Gas (% Dry Wt.)   0.24

TOTAL METAL CONTENT (ppm)

Arsenic	8.686	Chromium	28.423	Seleniumm	0.312
Barium	544.6	Lead	<0.050	Silver	<0.010
Cadmium	<0.010	Mercury	0.081	Zinc	84.08

pH (Std. Units)   8.16
Electrical Conductivity (mmhos/cm)   1.98
Sodium Adsorption Ratio (SAR)   3.55
Paste Saturation Percentage (%)   76.27

SOLUBLE CATIONS (meq/1)

Calcium   14.2365
Magnesium   5.6895
Sodium   61.6743

Exchangeable Sodium (meq/100g)   0.81
Exchangeable Sodium Percentage (%)   3.61
Cation Exchange Capacity (meq/100g)   22.45

APPENDIX A
WHOPPER SITE #1 PRE AND POST-CLOSURE SAMPLE RESULTS

Page 3   Report   Work Order #93-10-356
Received: 10/20 93   10/29/93 09:24:33

VIGILANT ENVIRONMENTAL

Analysis of OTB BATTERY 1 NORM AREA collected on 10/15/93 at 1100 and received at lab on 10/18/93 at 1500. Sample was assigned No. 9310356-19A and analyzed for Radioactivity as follows:

TEST DESCRIPTION	RESULT (pCi/g)
Radium 226	11.95
Radium 228	2.597

COMMENTS: EPA Method 9315A, 9310, 9320.

APPENDIX A

WHOPPER SITE #1 PRE AND POST-CLOSURE SAMPLE RESULTS

LAB I.D. _____ DATE REPORTED: <u>11/02/93</u>

SAMPLE DESCRIPTION _____

DATE COLLECTED: <u>10/19/93   12:00</u>

ANALYTE	ANALYSIS INITIALS	DATE COMPLETED	REFERENCE METHOD	DETECTION LIMIT	CONCENTRATION mg/1 (ppm)
ARSENIC	TS	10/25/93	EPA 206.3	0.0004 ppm	0.0372
BARIUM	TS	10/22/93	EPA 200.7	0.004 ppm	13.1
CADMIUM	TS	10/22/93	EPA 200.7	0.003 ppm	BDL
CHLORIDE	MF	10/28/93 14:00	EPA 325.3	2.0 ppm	7,020
CHROMIUM	TS	10/22/93	EPA 200;.7	0.007 ppm	0.219
MERCURY	TS	10/20/93	EPA 245.1	0.00002 ppm	0.00048
LEAD	TS	10/22/93	EPA 200.7	0.050 ppm	BDL
pH MEASUREMENT	NP	10/20/93 10:55	EPA 150/1	0.1 s.u.	6.77 s.u.

APPENDIX A
WHOPPER SITE #1 PRE AND POST-CLOSURE SAMPLE RESULTS

LAB I.D. _____ DATE REPORTED: 11/02/93

SAMPLE DESCRIPTION _____

DATE COLLECTED: 10/19/93 12:00

ANALYTE	ANALYSIS INITIALS	DATE COMPLETED	REFERENCE METHOD	DETECTION LIMIT	CONCENTRATION mg/l (ppm)
TOTAL XYLENEs	SF	10/26/93	SW846-8020	0.002 ppm	0.075
BENZENE	SF	10/26/93	SW846-8020	0.002 ppm	0.106
ETHYL BENZENE	SF	10/26/93	SW846-8020	0.002 ppm	0.106
TOLUENE	SF	10/26/93	SW846-8020	0.002 ppm	BDL
TPH - DIESEL	SF	10/28/93	SW846-8015	10.0 ppm	BDL

APPENDIX A
WHOPPER SITE #1 PRE AND POST-CLOSURE SAMPLE RESULTS

LAB I.D. _____ DATE REPORTED: 11/02/93

SAMPLE DESCRIPTION _____

DATE COLLECTED: 10/19/93   16:00

ANALYTE	ANALYSIS INITIALS	DATE COMPLETED	REFERENCE METHOD	DETECTION LIMIT	CONCENTRATION mg/l (ppm)
ARSENIC	TS	10/25/93	EPA 206.3	0.0004 ppm	0.1046
BARIUM	TS	10/22/93	EPA 200.7	0.004 ppm	6.05
CADMIUM	TS	10/22/93	EPA 200.7	0.003 ppm	BDL
CHLORIDE	MF	10/28/93 14:00	EPA 325.3	2.0 ppm	234
CHROMIUM	TS	10/22/93	EPA 200;.7	0.007 ppm	0.360
MERCURY	TS	10/20/93	EPA 245.1	0.00002 ppm	0.00572
LEAD	TS	10/22/93	EPA 200.7	0.050 ppm	BDL
pH MEASUREMENT	NP	10/20/93 10:55	EPA 150/1	0.1 s.u.	6.93 s.u.

APPENDIX A
WHOPPER SITE #1 PRE AND POST-CLOSURE SAMPLE RESULTS

LAB I.D. _____ DATE REPORTED: 11/02/93

SAMPLE DESCRIPTION _____

DATE COLLECTED: 10/19/93   16:00

ANALYTE	ANALYSIS INITIALS	DATE COMPLETED	REFERENCE METHOD	DETECTION LIMIT	CONCENTRATION mg/l (ppm)
TOTAL XYLENEs	SF	10/27/93	SW846-8020	0.002 ppm	BDL
BENZENE	SF	10/27/93	SW846-8020	0.002 ppm	BDL
ETHYL BENZENE	SF	10/27/93	SW846-8020	0.002 ppm	BDL
TOLUENE	SF	10/27/93	SW846-8020	0.002 ppm	BDL
TPH - DIESEL	SF	10/28/93	SW846-8015	10.0 ppm	BDL

APPENDIX B
SAMPLE ANALYSIS

Name   A-1   **DATE:** 7/28/93

NORM

     BG:

     READING:

%MOISTURE:

OIL&GREASE (%Dry Weight): 0.35

TOTAL METAL CONTENT (ppm):

Arsenic:	Chromium:	Selenium:
Barium:	Lead:	Silver:
Cadmium:	Mercury:	Zinc:

pH(standard units):

EC(mmhos/cm): 7

SAR: 17

Paste Saturation %:

SOLUBLE CATIONS:

Ca: 19.8

Mg: 7.09

Na: 62.3

EXCHANGEABLE Na (Meq./100g): 19.8

ESP (%):

CEC (Meq./100g): 28.1

TRUE TOTAL Ba (ppm):

   Ra 226:

   Ra 228:

APPENDIX B
SAMPLE ANALYSIS

Name   A-2   **DATE:**7/28/93

NORM

      BG:

      READING:

%MOISTURE:

OIL&GREASE (%Dry Weight):

TOTAL METAL CONTENT (ppm):

Arsenic:	Chromium:	Selenium:
Barium:	Lead:	Silver:
Cadmium:	Mercury:	Zinc:

pH(standard units):

EC(mmhos/cm): 5.2

SAR: 8.38

Paste Saturation %:

SOLUBLE CATIONS:

Ca: 12

Mg: 7.75

Na: 26.3

EXCHANGEABLE Na (Meq./100g): 5.63

      TRUE TOTAL Ba (ppm):

ESP (%):

CEC (Meq./100g): 39.7

  Ra 226:

  Ra 228:

APPENDIX B
SAMPLE ANALYSIS

Name   A-3   **DATE:**7/28/93

NORM

    BG:

    READING:

%MOISTURE:

OIL&GREASE (%Dry Weight): 1.02

    TOTAL METAL CONTENT (ppm):

Arsenic:	Chromium:	Selenium:
Barium:	Lead:	Silver:
Cadmium:	Mercury:	Zinc:

pH(standard units):

EC(mmhos/cm): 10.2

SAR: 18.1

Paste Saturation %:

SOLUBLE CATIONS:

Ca: 25.8

Mg: 12.9

Na: 79.6

EXCHANGEABLE Na (Meq./100g): 16.2

ESP (%):

TRUE TOTAL Ba (ppm):

CEC (Meq./100g): 34.7

  Ra 226:

  Ra 228:

APPENDIX B
SAMPLE ANALYSIS

Name   A-6   **DATE**:7/28/93

NORM

    BG:

    READING:

%MOISTURE:

OIL&GREASE (%Dry Weight): 2.03

    TOTAL METAL CONTENT (ppm):

Arsenic:	Chromium:	Selenium:
Barium:	Lead:	Silver:
Cadmium:	Mercury:	Zinc:

pH(standard units):

EC(mmhos/cm): 9

SAR: 18.8

Paste Saturation %:

SOLUBLE CATIONS:

Ca: 20

Mg: 10.5

Na: 73.4

EXCHANGEABLE Na (Meq./100g): 11.1

ESP (%):

CEC (Meq./100g): 44.2

TRUE TOTAL Ba (ppm):

Ra 226: 2.896

Ra 228: 0.7336

APPENDIX B
SAMPLE ANALYSIS

Name   A-5   **DATE:**7/28/93

NORM

   BG:

   READING:

%MOISTURE:

OIL&GREASE (%Dry Weight):0.81

TOTAL METAL CONTENT (ppm):

Arsenic:	Chromium:	Selenium:
Barium:	Lead:	Silver:
Cadmium:	Mercury:	Zinc:

pH(standard units):

EC(mmhos/cm): 10.2

SAR: 20.9

Paste Saturation %:

SOLUBLE CATIONS:

Ca: 17.2

Mg: 10.7

Na: 78

EXCHANGEABLE Na (Meq./100g):36

ESP (%):

CEC (Meq./100g):43

TRUE TOTAL Ba (ppm):

Ra 226: 2.896

Ra 228: 0.7336

APPENDIX B
SAMPLE ANALYSIS

Name   A-6   DATE:7/28/93

NORM

    BG:

    READING:

%MOISTURE:

OIL&GREASE (%Dry Weight): 2.03

TOTAL METAL CONTENT (ppm):

Arsenic:	Chromium:	Selenium:
Barium:	Lead:	Silver:
Cadmium:	Mercury:	Zinc:

pH(standard units):

EC(mmhos/cm): 9

SAR: 18.8

Paste Saturation %:

SOLUBLE CATIONS:

Ca: 20

Mg: 10.5

Na: 73.4

EXCHANGEABLE Na (Meq./100g): 11.1

TRUE TOTAL Ba (ppm):

ESP (%):

CEC (Meq./100g): 44.2

Ra 226: 2.896

Ra 228: 0.7336

APPENDIX B
SAMPLE ANALYSIS

Name   A-7   **DATE:**7/28/93

NORM
   BG:
   READING:

%MOISTURE:

OIL&GREASE (%Dry Weight): 0.04

TOTAL METAL CONTENT (ppm):

Arsenic:	Chromium:	Selenium:
Barium:	Lead:	Silver:
Cadmium:	Mercury:	Zinc:

pH(standard units):

EC(mmhos/cm): 7.6

SAR: 13.6

Paste Saturation %:

SOLUBLE CATIONS:

Ca: 18.4

Mg: 12.4

Na: 53.4

EXCHANGEABLE Na (Meq./100g): 15.3

ESP (%):

CEC (Meq./100g): 41.7

TRUE TOTAL Ba (ppm):

Ra 226: 2.858

Ra 228: 0.7439

APPENDIX B
SAMPLE ANALYSIS

Name A-8   **DATE:** 7/28/93

NORM

> **BG:**
>
> **READING:**

%MOISTURE:

OIL&GREASE (%Dry Weight):

TOTAL METAL CONTENT (ppm):

Arsenic:	Chromium:	Selenium:
Barium:	Lead:	Silver:
Cadmium:	Mercury:	Zinc:

pH(standard units):

EC(mmhos/cm): 5.6

SAR: 14.7

Paste Saturation %:

SOLUBLE CATIONS:

Ca: 10.8

Mg: 4.61

Na: 40.9

EXCHANGEABLE Na (Meq./100g): 26

ESP (%):

TRUE TOTAL Ba (ppm):

CEC (Meq./100g): 35.3

Ra 226:

Ra 228:

APPENDIX B
SAMPLE ANALYSIS

Name   B-I

DATE:7/28/93

NORM

   BG:

   READING:

%MOISTURE:

OIL&GREASE (%Dry Weight):0.34

TOTAL METAL CONTENT (ppm):

Arsenic:	**Chromium:**	**Selenium:**
Barium:	**Lead:**	**Silver:**
Cadmium:	**Mercury:**	**Zinc:**

pH(standard units):

EC(mmhos/cm): 8.6

SAR: 24.7

Paste Saturation %:

SOLUBLE CATIONS:

Ca: 12.2

Mg: 5.25

Na: 73

EXCHANGEABLE Na (Meq./100g):24.3

ESP (%):

CEC (Meq./100g):36.6

TRUE TOTAL Ba (ppm):

   Ra 226:

   Ra 228:

APPENDIX B
SAMPLE ANALYSIS

Name   B-2   **DATE:** 7/28/93

NORM

    BG:

    READING:

%MOISTURE:

OIL&GREASE (%Dry Weight): 0.34

    TOTAL METAL CONTENT (ppm):

Arsenic:	Chromium:	Selenium:
Barium:	Lead:	Silver:
Cadmium:	Mercury:	Zinc:

pH(standard units):

EC(mmhos/cm): 8.5

SAR: 17.8

Paste Saturation %:

SOLUBLE CATIONS:

Ca: 17.1

Mg: 9.72

Na: 65.2

EXCHANGEABLE Na (Meq./100g): 16.6

ESP (%):

CEC (Meq./100g): 42.9

TRUE TOTAL Ba (ppm):

  Ra 226:

  Ra 228:

APPENDIX B
SAMPLE ANALYSIS

Name . B-3   DATE:7/28/93

NORM

    BG:

    READING:

%MOISTURE:

OIL&GREASE (%Dry Weight): 0.07

    TOTAL METAL CONTENT (ppm):

Arsenic:	**Chromium:**	**Selenium:**
Barium:	**Lead:**	**Silver:**
Cadmium:	**Mercury:**	**Zinc:**

pH(standard units):

EC(mmhos/cm): 12.2

SAR: 21

Paste Saturation %:

SOLUBLE CATIONS:

Ca: 27

Mg: 16.3

Na: 97.8

EXCHANGEABLE Na (Meq./100g): 24.7

ESP (%):

CEC (Meq./100g): 47.6

TRUE TOTAL Ba (ppm):

Ra 226: 3.395

Ra 228: 0.5558

APPENDIX B
SAMPLE ANALYSIS

Name   B-4   **DATE:** 7/28/93

NORM

       BG:

       READING:

%MOISTURE:

OIL&GREASE (%Dry Weight): 0.13

TOTAL METAL CONTENT (ppm):

Arsenic:	Chromium:	Selenium:
Barium:	Lead:	Silver:
Cadmium:	Mercury:	Zinc:

pH(standard units):

EC(mmhos/cm): 13.6

SAR: 28.9

Paste Saturation %:

SOLUBLE CATIONS:

Ca: 23.2

Mg: 15.1

Na: 126

EXCHANGEABLE Na (Meq./100g): 21.7

ESP (%):

CEC (Meq./100g): 55.1

TRUE TOTAL Ba (ppm):

Ra 226: 3.395

Ra 228: 0.5558

APPENDIX B
SAMPLE ANALYSIS

Name   B-5   **DATE:** 7/28/93

NORM

 BG:

 READING:

%MOISTURE:

OIL&GREASE (%Dry Weight): 1.14

 TOTAL METAL CONTENT (ppm):

Arsenic:	Chromium:	Selenium:
Barium:	Lead:	Silver:
Cadmium:	Mercury:	Zinc:

pH(standard units):

EC(mmhos/cm): 4.8

SAR: 13.4

Paste Saturation %:

SOLUBLE CATIONS:

Ca: 8.94

Mg: 4.95

Na: 35.3

EXCHANGEABLE Na (Meq./100g): 10.9

ESP (%):

TRUE TOTAL Ba (ppm):

CEC (Meq./100g): 50.4

 Ra 226: 2.882

 Ra 228: 0.9776

APPENDIX B
SAMPLE ANALYSIS

Name   B-6   **DATE:** 7/28/93

NORM

    BG:

    READING:

%MOISTURE:

OIL&GREASE (%Dry Weight):

TOTAL METAL CONTENT (ppm):

Arsenic:	Chromium:	Selenium:
Barium:	Lead:	Silver:
Cadmium:	Mercury:	Zinc:

pH(standard units):

EC(mmhos/cm): 9.7

SAR: 21.1

Paste Saturation %:

SOLUBLE CATIONS:

Ca: 16.8

Mg: 9.43

Na: 76.6

EXCHANGEABLE Na (Meq./100g): 19.4

ESP (%):

TRUE TOTAL Ba (ppm):

CEC (Meq./100g): 46.7

  Ra 226:

  Ra 228:

APPENDIX B
SAMPLE ANALYSIS

Name   B-7   **DATE:**7/28/93

NORM

    BG:

    READING:

%MOISTURE:

OIL&GREASE (%Dry Weight):

   TOTAL METAL CONTENT (ppm):

Arsenic:	Chromium:	Selenium:
Barium:	Lead:	Silver:
Cadmium:	Mercury:	Zinc:

pH(standard units):

EC(mmhos/cm): 5.8

SAR: 14.8

Paste Saturation %:

SOLUBLE CATIONS:

Ca: 10.2

Mg: 5.5

Na: 41.4

EXCHANGEABLE Na (Meq./100g): 17.2

ESP (%):

CEC (Meq./100g): 40.9

TRUE TOTAL Ba (ppm):

Ra 226:

Ra 228:

APPENDIX B
SAMPLE ANALYSIS

Name   B-8   **DATE:**7/28/93

NORM
   BG:
   READING:

%MOISTURE:

OIL&GREASE (%Dry Weight):

TOTAL METAL CONTENT (ppm):

Arsenic:	Chromium:	Selenium:
Barium:	Lead:	Silver:
Cadmium:	Mercury:	Zinc:

pH(standard units):

EC(mmhos/cm): 7.7

SAR: 14.8

Paste Saturation %:

SOLUBLE CATIONS:

Ca: 17.4

Mg: 11.4

Na: 56

EXCHANGEABLE Na (Meq./100g):12.1

ESP (%):

TRUE TOTAL Ba (ppm):

CEC (Meq./100g):46.3

   Ra 226:
   Ra 228:

APPENDIX B
SAMPLE ANALYSIS

Name  C-1   **DATE:** 7/28/93

NORM

    BG:

    READING:

%MOISTURE:

OIL&GREASE (%Dry Weight): 0.73

    TOTAL METAL CONTENT (ppm):

Arsenic:	Chromium:	Selenium:
Barium:	Lead:	Silver:
Cadmium:	Mercury:	Zinc:

pH(standard units):

EC(mmhos/cm): 10.3

SAR: 33.7

Paste Saturation %:

SOLUBLE CATIONS:

Ca: 14.7

Mg: 4.3

Na: 104

EXCHANGEABLE Na (Meq./100g): 28

ESP (%):

CEC (Meq./100g): 18.3

TRUE TOTAL Ba (ppm):

Ra 226: 4.171

Ra 228: 0.7521

APPENDIX B
SAMPLE ANALYSIS

Name   C-2   **DATE:** 7/28/93

NORM

  BG:

  READING:

%MOISTURE:

OIL&GREASE (%Dry Weight): 0.33

TOTAL METAL CONTENT (ppm):

Arsenic:	Chromium:	Selenium:
Barium:	Lead:	Silver:
Cadmium:	Mercury:	Zinc:

pH(standard units):

EC(mmhos/cm): 5.2

SAR: 18.5

Paste Saturation %:

SOLUBLE CATIONS:

Ca: 6.91

Mg: 4.33

Na: 43.9

EXCHANGEABLE Na (Meq./100g): 20.3

TRUE TOTAL Ba (ppm):

ESP (%):

CEC (Meq./100g): 41.7

  Ra 226:

  Ra 228:

APPENDIX B
SAMPLE ANALYSIS

Name   C-3   **DATE:**7/28/93

NORM

    BG:

    READING:

%MOISTURE:

OIL&GREASE (%Dry Weight):0.33

TOTAL METAL CONTENT (ppm):

Arsenic:	Chromium:	Selenium:
Barium:	Lead:	Silver:
Cadmium:	Mercury:	Zinc:

pH(standard units):

EC(mmhos/cm): 5

SAR: 11.6

Paste Saturation %:

SOLUBLE CATIONS:

Ca: 12.3

Mg: 6.99

Na: 36.1

EXCHANGEABLE Na (Meq./100g):10

ESP (%):

CEC (Meq./100g):31.3

TRUE TOTAL Ba (ppm):

Ra 226:

Ra 228:

APPENDIX B
SAMPLE ANALYSIS

SAMPLE ANALYSIS

Name   D-1   **DATE:** 7/28/93

NORM

    BG:

    READING:

%MOISTURE:

OIL&GREASE (%Dry Weight): 0.3

TOTAL METAL CONTENT (ppm):

Arsenic:	Chromium:	Selenium:
Barium:	Lead:	Silver:
Cadmium:	Mercury:	Zinc:

pH(standard units):

EC(mmhos/cm): 5.2

SAR: 16.6

Paste Saturation %:

SOLUBLE CATIONS:

Ca: 9.39

Mg: 3.76

Na: 42.6

EXCHANGEABLE Na (Meq./100g): 20.2

ESP (%):

TRUE TOTAL Ba (ppm):

CEC (Meq./100g): 24.9

    Ra 226:

    Ra 228:

APPENDIX B
SAMPLE ANALYSIS

Name D-2   **DATE:** 7/28/93

NORM

    BG:

    READING:

%MOISTURE:

OIL&GREASE (%Dry Weight): 0.3

TOTAL METAL CONTENT (ppm):

Arsenic:	Chromium:	Selenium:
Barium:	Lead:	Silver:
Cadmium:	Mercury:	Zinc:

pH(standard units):

EC(mmhos/cm): 3.2

SAR: 12.7

Paste Saturation %:

SOLUBLE CATIONS:

Ca: 5.29

Mg: 3.62

Na: 26.8

EXCHANGEABLE Na (Meq./100g): 14.8

ESP (%):

CEC (Meq./100g): 42.6

TRUE TOTAL Ba (ppm):

  Ra 226:

  Ra 228:

APPENDIX B
SAMPLE ANALYSIS

Name D-3   **DATE:**7/28/93

NORM

    BG:

    READING:

%MOISTURE:

OIL&GREASE (%Dry Weight):0.13

    TOTAL METAL CONTENT (ppm):

Arsenic:	Chromium:	Selenium:
Barium:	Lead:	Silver:
Cadmium:	Mercury:	Zinc:

pH(standard units):

EC(mmhos/cm): 13.3

SAR: 26.6

Paste Saturation %:

SOLUBLE CATIONS:

Ca: 23.1

Mg: 13.8

Na: 114

EXCHANGEABLE Na (Meq./100g):22.3

ESP (%):

CEC (Meq./100g):45.8

TRUE TOTAL Ba (ppm):

Ra 226: 2.727

Ra 228: 0.7511

APPENDIX B
SAMPLE ANALYSIS

Name   A1-8 & B1-8 Composite   **DATE**:7/28/93

NORM

    BG:

    READING:

%MOISTURE: 54.69

OIL&GREASE (%Dry Weight): 0.41

    TOTAL METAL CONTENT (ppm):

Arsenic: 6.58	**Chromium:** 27.1	**Selenium:** 0.186
Barium: 500	**Lead:** <5.00	**Silver:** <0.700
Cadmium: <0.300	**Mercury:** 0.198	**Zinc:** 87.7

pH(standard units): 7.38

EC(mmhos/cm): 7.2

SAR: 17

Paste Saturation %: 112

SOLUBLE CATIONS:

Ca: 14.3

Mg: 8.31

Na: 57.3

EXCHANGEABLE Na (Meq./100g):

    ESP (%): 9.79

CEC (Meq./100g): 41.4

TRUE TOTAL Ba (ppm): 786

  Ra 226:

  Ra 228:

APPENDIX B
SAMPLE ANALYSIS

Name   C1-3 & D1-3 Composite   **DATE:** 7/28/93

NORM

    BG:

    READING:

%MOISTURE: 40.66

OIL&GREASE (%Dry Weight): 0.51

TOTAL METAL CONTENT (ppm):

Arsenic: 6.61	Chromium: 24.	Selenium: 0.190
Barium: 609	Lead: <5.00	Silver: <0.700
Cadmium: <0.300	Mercury: 0.236	Zinc: 78.7

pH(standard units): 7.62

EC(mmhos/cm): 6.2

SAR: 17.4

Paste Saturation %: 79

SOLUBLE CATIONS:

Ca: 10.1

Mg: 5.13

Na: 47.9

EXCHANGEABLE Na (Meq./100g):

ESP (%): 16.4

CEC (Meq./100g): 28.1

TRUE TOTAL Ba (ppm): 911

Ra 226:
Ra 228:

GLOSSARY OF TERMS

ADSORPTION: The proces whereby ions are attracted and trapped by open bonds on the surface of the adsorbent material. Moreover, it may be the exchange of one cation or anion for another at the surface.

ALPHA PARTICLES: A positively charged particle consisting of two protons and two neutrons (equal to a helium nucleus) that is emitted from a radioactive isotope.

ANION: A negatively charged ion.

ANNULUS: The space between the casing and the formation or, sometimes, the space inside the casing and outside the tubing.

API NUMBER: American Petroleum Institute unique number identifying the individual well.

AQUICLUDE: A geologic unit that is incapable of transmitting water under normal hydraulic gradients.

AQUITARD: Ageologic unit in the stratigraphic sequence in the area that is less permeable than an aquifer, although some amount of water may be able to move through it.

ASYMPTOTIC: A state where a decline curve approaches its horizontal (or X axis with time but flatterns and does not intercept.

BETA PARTICLES: An electron sized particle emitted from the nucleus of a radioactive isotope having either positive or negative charge.

BIOAVILABILITY: A substance that is in such a state that it can be taken up into the systems of organic life.

BIOLOGICAL HALF-LIFE: The time required for the body to eliminate (through natural processes) one half of the atoms of radioactive material ingested.

BULK DENSITY: A measure of the mass of a substance per unit bulk volume.

CALCAREOUS: Containing significant calcium carbonate ($CaCO_3$).

CESIUM^{137} (Cs^{137}): A radiosactive isotope used as a check source for radiation detectors.

CaCl$_2$: Calcium chloride.

CaCO$_3$: Calcium carbonate.

CaNO$_4$: Calcium nitrate.

CaSO$_4$: Calcium sulfate. Also the chemical formula for the mineral anhydrite.

CATION EXCHANGE CAPACITY: A measurement of the total amount of exchangeable cations (such as sodium, magnesium, and calcium) that a soil is able to absorb.

CHANNELING: An empty space between the casing and the formation that results from defective or incomplete cementing.

DIVALENT: Having an electrical charge of +2.

EFFECTIVE HALF-LIFE: The result of a combination of the normal radioactive decay process and the biological reduction in the amount of radioactive atoms in the system.

FAUNAL DIVERSITY: The abundance (or lack thereof) of species in a given area or ecosystem.

FLOWLINE: Part of the oil & gas intrafield gathering system that transports produced fluids to primary seperation and/or to the field sale point.

FRIABLE: Unconsolidated rock material or sediment.

GRADIENT: The rate of drop in elevation.

H$_2$S: Hydrogen sulfide, a poisonous gas associated with oil and gas production in some areas.

HORIZON A: The uppermost soil horizon, usually enriched in organic materials.

HORIZON B: Middle layer of soil, lower in organic materials than Horizon A, but higher in clay content.

HORIZON C: Bottom soil layer consisting of weathered and displaced bedrock.

HYDRAULIC CONDUCTIVITY: The constant of proportionality in Darcy's Law. Used to describe the ease with which fluid moves through a porous medium and roughly equivalent to permeability.

INDURATED: Having undergone rock diagenesis and having the quality of being cemented and cohesive.

ISOMORPHOUS SUBSTITUTION: An process by which ions with similar characteristics such as coordination number (but not necessarily charge) will substitute for one another in the crystalline lattice of a mineral and yet retain the same crystallographic form.

ISOTOPES: An atom that differs in mass from other like atoms due to the number of neutrons in its nucleus.

JUG TEST: A kind of Pressure Integrity Test (PIT) run on casing shoe that does not break down the formation.

KAOLINITE: A clay mineral enriched in aluminium that is formed from the weathering or hydrothermal alteration of aluminum silicates.

LEAKOFF TEST: A kind of Pressure Integrity Test (PIT) that breaks down the formation.

LOAM: A soil type midway on the continuum between pure sand and pure clay.

MACROPOROSITY: A type of porosity characterized by pore throats that can be observed with the naked eye or with simple magnification.

MICROPOROSITY: Porosity characterized by very small pore throats that require the aid of microscopic techniques to observe.

MONTMORILLONITE: A mixed layer clay characterized by susceptibility to isomorphous substitution in the tetrahedral layer and swelling due to introduction of water.

MUCK SOIL: A soil containing very high percentages of organic matter.

PERCHED AQUIFER: An aquifer of limited areal extent seperated from underlying aquifers by an aquiclude or aquitard, having unsaturated conditions below it.

PHOTONS: A quantum of light energy the energy of which is directly proportional to its frequency.

PHYLLOSILICATES: Silicate minerals characterized by a sheet structure caused by the linkage of the SiO_4 in the tetrahedral layer.

POINT SOURCE: The point of origin for contaminant plumes.

RADIOSOTOPE: An unstable (or radioactive) isotope.

RADIONUCLIDE: A type of atom having a characteristic nucleus and a measurable lifespan that is unstable (or radioactive).

RECOMPLETION: A type of workover where one productive zone is abandoned and a new geologic interval is perforated with the intent of production.

REGOLITH: A layer or blanket of loose rock material that covers the bedrock and forms the lowest horizon of soil.

SATURATED ZONE: The section of soil and/or rock below the water table where the pore spaces are completely saturated with water. Analogous to the phreatic zone.

SOLAR INSOLATION: The solar radiation that not only enters the earth's atmosphere, but also reaches the surface.

SOLVATION: The process of dissolution of a chemical or constituent by a solvent to form a compound.

SQUEEZE PERFORATIONS: The process of cementation and abandonment of perforations in the casing.

SUBAERIALLY EXPOSED: Exposed to the chemical and mechanical processes active at the interface of the earth's surface with its atmosphere.

TANK BATTERY: A facility consisting of storage tanks.

TETRAHEDRAL LAYER: The sheet layer in phyllosilicates formed by the linkage of SiO_4 tetrahedrons.

UNSATURATED ZONE: The zone above the water table in which the pore spaces are partially filled with air and partially filled with water. Analogous to the vadose zone.

VALENCE: The ability of an atom to chemically combine with other atoms by means of an electrical charge.

WATER TABLE: Essentially the top of the saturated zone. The surface where the fluid pressure in the pore spaces is exactly atmospheric. Due to capillary effects in a porus medium it is not always exactly coincident with the top of the saturated zone.

WEATHERING: The breakdown and degradation of rocks and materials that are exposed at the earth's surface, whether by chemical or mechanical means.

INDEX

A

Abandoned/idle well, xvi, 7, 60, 89, 101
Aboveground storage tank, 13
Acetic acid, 48
Acid rain, 14
Acidity/alkalinity. SEE pH.
Acquisition mode, 5
Acronyms, xi-xiii
Action levels, 50, 68
Aerial photography, 35
After federal income tax, 67
Aggregation, 41-42
Air quality issue, xxi
Air supply monitoring, 94
Air toxics, 14
Alpha particle, 75-76, 86, 94
American Society for Testing and Materials, 36-37
Annual limit on intake, 86
Annular disposal, 83
Appraisal (environmental), 5
Appropriate inquiry, 37
Aquifer discharge point, 55
Aquifer recharge area, 55
Aquifer, 25, 28, 55, 102-103, 135
Aquitard, 103
Arsenic, 46, 48, 68-69, 96, 132
As low as reasonably achievable principle, 84
Asbestos, 22
As-is where-is contract, 6, 98
Atomic Energy Commission, 84

Attorney, 9, 25
Auditing, 5-6, 26-35:
    example (tank battery), 28-33;
    procedure, 33-35
Audubon Society, xvi
Authority to act, 9

B

Barite, 46
Barium, 46, 48, 68, 96, 132
Baseline condition/data, 5-6, 63-64, 78
Before federal income tax, 67
Bentonite, 60
Benzene, 68, 94, 132
Benzene/toluene/ethylbenzene/xylene, 49-50, 52-53, 68-70, 96-97, 106
Berm/firewall, 62
Beta particle, 75-76
Bioavailability, 45
Biodegradation, 103
Biological damage, 76, 84
Biological stimulant, 103
Bioremediation, 101, 103, 108, 113, 133
Birds, 91
Blending/compositing (soil sample), 52, 54
Blowout (well), 61
Boot tank, 28
Boron, 130
Brine contamination, 42, 44, 46, 61-62, 101, 112-113, 116, 120, 122, 126, 135, 137:

soil sodicity remediation, 112-113
Brine, 17, 28, 42, 44, 46, 56, 58, 61-62, 64, 101, 112-113, 116, 120, 122, 126, 135, 137
BTEX. SEE Benzene /toluene/ethylbenzene/xylene.
Bulk density, 42-43
Burden of proof, 20
Burial cell, 109, 111

C

Cadmium, 46-47, 68, 96
Calcium carbonate, 113
Calcium cation, 42-44, 112
Calcium nitrate, 113
Calcium sulfate, 112
California, xvi
Capital resource, 3
Case histories/scenarios, 115-140: scenario 1 (Rangoon-Dalek Eva Braun), 115-117; scenario 2 (Price field site #7), 118-121; scenario 3 (Price field site #12), 122-127; scenario 4 (Whopper site #1), 128-134; scenario 5 (Section D site #1), 135-137; scenario 5 (Section D site #2), 138-140
Cash flow, 2
Casing leak, 58, 60-61, 126
Cation adsorption, 42
Cation exchange capacity, 28, 43-45, 108, 113, 132, 136
Centralization, 3
Chain of custody, 54
Chain of title, 6
Characteristically hazardous, 14, 48
Checklist (audit), 33-35
Chemical injection, 103
Chemical inventory, 22
Chemical storage facilities, 62-63

Chloride, 45, 57, 68, 95, 105, 112, 118, 120, 132
Chlorofluorocarbons, 14
Chromium, 27, 46, 48, 68, 96, 132
Clay content, 41-44
Clean Air Act, xxi, 14
Clean Water Act, 13, 17-18, 21, 107
Cleanup cost, xviii, 7, 102-104, 107
Closure, 61, 75, 95, 109, 141-153
Code of Federal Regulations, 12
Commercial chemical products, 14
Commercial disposal facility, 107
Commitment by management, 8
Complexing, 45
Compliance auditing, 5
Compliance cost, 16
Comprehensive Environmental Response, Compensation, and Liability Act, 5, 17, 19-21, 23, 26, 135
Comprehensive Environmental Response, Compensation, and Liability Information System, 17, 20, 36
Compressors, 36
Concurrent remediation (soil/water), 114
Confined space, 94
Conflict of interest, 4, 8
Conservationist organization, xvii
Consultant, 9
Containment barrier, 103
Contamination plume, 28, 30, 69, 71-73, 103-104, 112, 136, 140
Corrosivity, 14
Cradle-to-grave management, 14
Crisis as opportunity, 4
Crude oil, 56-57, 61, 64, 94, 105, 111, 113, 120
Curie, 77

D

Dalek Eva Braun well (case history), 115-117

Decontamination (NORM), 85-86
Deforestation, 128, 130
Derived air concentration, 86
Detection instruments, 78
Developing countries, 2
Dewatering, 108
Diffusion, 30
Dilution burial, 109-110
Dilution, 21, 109-110, 112
Disaggregation, 42
Disclosure, 6
Disposal options (radioactive
    materials), 83-84
Drilling fluid, 45, 96
Drinking water, 18-19, 25, 55
Drum storage, 62
Due diligence, 26

E

Electrical charge, 76
Electrical conductivity, 44-45, 108,
    118, 120
Electromagnetic wave, 75
Emergency Planning and Community
    Right-to-Know Act, 21-22
Empowerment, 9
Encapsulation, 110-111
Enforcement, 14, 25
Environmental activists, xvi
Environmental concerns (oilfield),
    35-36
Environmental condition, xviii, 27
Environmental coordinator/manager, 3
Environmental impact statement, 27
Environmental liability, xviii-xix, 6, 26
Environmental management
    strategies, 1-9:
    United States, 1-3;
    organizational strategies, 3-5;
    auditing, 5-6;
    loss of status, 7;
    cleanup funds, 7;
    operated by others, 8

Environmental Protection Agency,
    12-14, 17-18, 20-23, 37, 67-68,
    82-83
Environmental regulation, xvii-xix,
    3, 12-13, 15, 25
Environmental risk, xviii-xix, 5, 25
Environmental site assessment, 37
Environmentalist movement, 11-23:
    environmental regulation, 12-13,
    15;
    Clean Water Act, 13;
    Clean Air Act, 14;
    Resource Conservation and
    Recovery Act, 14, 16;
    exemption/absolution, 16-18;
    Safe Drinking Water Act, 18-19;
    Comprehensive Environmental
    Response, Compensation and
    Liability Act, 19-21;
    Superfund Amendment and
    Reauthorization Act, Title III,
    21-22;
    Toxic Substances Control Act, 22;
    naturally occurring radioactive
    material, 22-23
Equipment decontamination, 52
Ethylbenzene, 68
Evaluation and risk analysis
    (groundwater), 63-64
Exchangeable sodium percentage,
    44, 108, 110, 118, 120
Exempt status/exemption, xviii, xx, 13,
    16-19, 21, 23, 48, 62, 96, 106,
    114, 126
Exodus from U.S. (majors), 1-2
Exposure, 77-78, 85
Extremely hazardous substance, 22

F

Facilities/installations, 126
Facility inventory, 62
Fate and transport analysis, 64, 69
Faunal diversity, 35

Federal Register, 16-18, 67, 82
Field work, 36
Financial risk, xviii
Fire hazard, 109
Flow lines, 35, 61, 79, 118, 120, 126, 128, 138
Flushing, 112
Food chain, 75
Free oil, 138
Free water knockouts, 36, 79
Friable sediment, 65-66

G

Gamma radiation, 75-78
Gas chromatograph, 49, 114
Gas separation platform (NORM), 87-89
Geiger-Mueller tube, 78, 85
Generic wastes, 14
Geological/geophysical expenditures, xv
Global warming, 12
Glossary, 179-183
Gravimetric assay, 49
Greenpeace, xvi
Groundwater considerations, 55-73:
    oilfield contamination, 57-63;
    evaluation and risk analysis, 63-64;
    groundwater sampling, 64-70;
    monitoring well network design, 71-73
Groundwater contamination, xvi, 17-19, 44, 57-63, 68, 91, 102-104, 110, 112, 130, 132-133, 135-136:
    subsurface contamination, 58-61;
    surface infiltration, 61-63
Groundwater monitoring, 18
Groundwater remediation, 26, 102-104, 106, 114:
    containment barrier, 103;
    chemical treatment, 103-104;
    interceptor/recovery wells, 104;

pump and treat, 104
Groundwater resources, 40
Groundwater sampling, 64-70, 73
Groundwater, 105, 109, 135 et passim
Gypsum, 112

H

Hazard ranking system, 21
Hazardous substance, 17, 21-22, 50
Hazardous waste, xviii-xix, 14, 16, 18, 21, 62-63, 102, 107-108, 111, 126, 136
Health and safety plan, 94
Health risk, 75-76
Heater treater, 28, 36, 75, 79, 115, 129
Heavy metals, 45, 56-57, 61, 64
Historical data research, 115
Hydraulic conductivity, 71
Hydraulic gradient, 63, 71-72, 102-104, 112, 140
Hydrocarbon fraction, 113
Hydrochloric acid, 45, 126
Hydrogen sulfide, 94

I

Identification/posting, 85
Ignitability, 14, 109
Illite, 44
Immobilization, 103, 110
Import tax, xv
Impounding, 103
In situ treatment, 101
Incineration, 102
Indemnity, 6, 128
Independent oil companies (U.S.), 2-3
Independent Petroleum Association of America, xv
Indurated rock, 65
Industry standardization, 36-37
Infiltration, 57, 103
Infrared spectroscopy, 49, 114
Ingestion, 75-76, 84-85
Injection well, 108

Innocent landowner defense, 21, 37
Innocent purchaser defense, 5, 26
Interceptor/recovery wells, 104, 112
International Committee of Radiation
    Protection, 84
Inventory control, 21
Investment value, xix
Ionization unit, 78
Isomorphous substitution, 42-42

J

Jastram vs. Phillips Petroleum, 17
Joint operating area, 8
Jug test, 35

K

Kaolinite, 44

L

Labeling requirements, 22, 85
Laminar flow, 71
Landfarming, 101, 107-109, 133
Leachate testing, 111
Lead, 46, 48, 68, 96
Leak, 28, 36, 71, 91-92, 101, 118,
    120, 129-130, 132-133, 136
Lease bonuses, 2
Liability, xviii-xix, 4-6, 17, 25-26, 116
Listed wastes, 14
Litigation, xx, 6, 8, 25
Lobbying/campaigning, 3, 12
Local Emergency Planning
    Commission, 22
Logging industry, 12
Loose contamination, 85-86
Loss of status, 7
Louisiana Department of
    Environmental Quality, 17-19, 36
Louisiana Department of Natural
    Resources, 13, 17, 19, 46
Louisiana Office of Conservation, 13
Louisiana Oilfield Site Restoration Law
    Act 404, 7

Louisiana, 13, 19, 23, 44, 46, 75, 79-
    80, 83-84, 95-98, 104, 106-109,
    111, 114, 118

M

Magnesium cation, 43-44
Major oil companies (U.S.), 1-3
Mapping, 36
Marginal producers, xv
Mass, 76
Material safety data sheets, 22
Maximum contaminant level, 18, 67,
    132
Measurement units, xiv
Mechanical integrity testing, 19, 58
Media culture, 12
Mercury, 46, 48, 68, 96, 132
Metal mobility, 45
Metals analysis, 69-70
Metals contamination, 45
Microorganism, 113
MicroRoentgen, 77
Migration, 30
Mineral scale, 75
Minerals Management Service, 84
Mississippi, 80
Mixture rule, 17, 21, 62
Mobile sources and clean fuels, 14
Moisture capacity, 113
Molybdenum, 130
Monitoring well design, 36, 65-67, 69,
    71-73, 127, 132

N

National priorities list, 20-21, 37
National Pollutant Discharge
    Elimination System, 13
Natural gas, 56
Naturally occurring radioactive
    material, 22-23, 36, 50, 61, 63,
    75-89, 95, 100-101, 104, 106,
    114-115, 118, 130, 132-134, 136:
    problem statement, 75-82;

EPA developments, 82-83;
disposal options, 83-84;
personnel training, 84-86;
problem analysis example, 87-89
Navigable waters, 13
Negotiation tool (audit), 5, 26
Netting (pit), 91
Neutralization, 103
New industry order, 1-9
New Mexico, 106
Nitrate, 113
Nitrogen, 113
Non-attainment areas, 14
Non-hazardous oilfield waste, 16-19,
21, 23, 49-50, 62-63, 102, 107,
126-127
NORM. SEE Naturally occurring
radioactive material.
Notification, 21-22
NOW. SEE Non-hazardous oilfield
waste.
Nutrient, 103

O

Off-site disposal, 102, 107
Oil and Gas Conservation Division,
Oklahoma Corporation
Commission, 19
Oil and grease, 49, 95-97, 109, 130,
132
Oil imports, xv
Oil price, 1
Oil reserves, xv
Oil spill, 25
Oil storage tank, 28, 36, 62, 122-123,
126
Oil well, 122-123, 126
Oilfield contamination, 57-63
Oklahoma Corporation Commission,
12-13, 18-19, 106
Oklahoma Department of
Environmental Quality, 18-19
Oklahoma, xvi, 23, 106
Operated by others, 8

Organizational strategies, 3-5
Orphan site, 7
Osmotic potential, 62
Outsourcing, 4
Overhead expense ratio, 8
Oxygen content, 41, 103, 113

P

Packing coefficient, 42
Painting wastes, 16
Particle emission, 75
Peat moss, 113
Penetration (radiation type), 76
Perched aquifer, 55, 57
Permeability barrier, 103
Permits, 14
Persian Gulf war, 1
Personnel training (radioactive
materials), 76, 84-86
Personnel training, 84-86: loose
NORM, 85-86;
airborne NORM, 86
Pesticide, 16
pH, 44-45, 47, 96, 105, 111, 126
Phase 1 audit, 26-29, 33-35, 37:
example, 27-29;
procedure, 33-35
Phase 2 audit, 27, 30-33:
example, 30-33
Phosphorus, 113
Photographic documentation, 28, 36,
79
Phyllosilicates, 42
PicoCurie, 77
Pipeline, 136
Pit analysis, 82, 92-98, 105, 107-108
Pit closure options/standards, 95, 98,
102, 104-111, 114:
off-site disposal, 107;
landfarming, 107-109;
road spreading, 109;
dilution burial, 109-110;
solidification/stabilization, 110-111
Pit evaluation, 98-100

Pit remediation, 104-106
Pit sampling, 94-98
Pit (production), 13, 17, 36, 61-62, 75,
 79, 91-101, 103-104, 128, 132, 138:
 pit analysis, 92-98;
 pit evaluation, 98-100
Point source, 28, 30, 71
Pollution Abatement Division, Oklahoma Corporation Commission, 19
Polychlorinated biphenyls, 22
Pore size, 41
Potassium, 113
Potentially responsible party, xix, 20-21, 102
Pressure integrity test, 35
Prestige (loss of), 7
Presurvey operational check, 79
Price field site #7 (case history), 118-121
Price field site #12, 122-127
Priority assessment, 20
Problem analysis, 28, 30, 87-89, 116, 120, 126, 137, 140:
 contamination, 28;
 audit, 30;
 example (radioactive materials), 87-89
Produced water, 16
Producing properties, 25-37
Production manager, 4
Production pit. SEE Pit (production).
Production well, 58, 60-61
Professional engineer, 13
Profit margin, 8, 25
Property transfer audit. SEE Transfer audit.
Proprietary file search, 36
Protective clothing, 85-86, 94
Public file search, 36
Pump and treat, 104
PVC sampling tube, 52, 95

R

Radiation absorbed dose (rad), 77
Radiation area, 85
Radiation, 75
Radioactive decay, 77
Radioisotopes, 96-99
Radium, 56, 68, 75, 95
Reactivity, 14
Reclassification (oil field waste), xx
Recommendations, 28, 116, 120, 126-127, 133
Recordkeeping, 21, 54
Regional aquifer, 55, 57
Regolith, 39
Regulatory action, 67
Regulatory environment, xx, 8-9, 79
Regulatory limits, 50
Regulatory requirements, 78
Release survey, 79, 81
Remediation options, 101-114:
 groundwater remediation, 102-104;
 pit remediation, 104-106;
 pit closure options, 107-111;
 soil amendments, 111-114
Remediation, 7, 17, 20-21, 33, 89, 101-116, 132:
 liability, 20-21;
 cost, 33, 89, 116, 132
Reporting requirements, 22, 50
Resource Conservation and Recovery Act, xviii, 14, 16, 18-21, 23, 35-36, 48, 62, 67-68, 96, 106, 108, 110, 114, 126, 135,
Responsible party, 19-20, 72
Restricted area, 84
Retroactive regulation, 2
Revenue source, 7
Risk analysis, 64, 69, 91
Road spreading, 109, 120, 127
Roentgen equivalent man (rem), 77
Royalty payments, 8

S

Safe Drinking Water Act, 17-19, 57, 67, 96, 132
Safety, 50
Salinity, 44, 64, 108-109
Salt content, 94, 96, 109
Salt damage indicator, 44
Salt water disposal, 13, 28, 58-59, 138
Salt water, 25, 56, 58, 79, 94, 111-113, 115-116, 122
Sample analysis, 154-177
Sample collection, 52, 54, 71
Sample handling/shipping, 54
Sample parameters (non-organic), 43-48
Sample parameters (organic), 49-50
Sampling equipment, 52
Sampling for contaminants, 94-98:
    pH, 96;
    metals, 96;
    oil and grease, 96-97;
    radioisotopes, 97-98
Sampling plan, 27, 50, 52, 94-95
Saturated paste method, 44-45
Scenario 1 (Dalek Eva Braun), 115-117
Scenario 2 (Price field site #7), 118-121
Scenario 3 (Price field site #12), 122-127
Scenario 4 (Whopper site #1), 128-134
Scenario 5 (Section D, site #1), 135-137
Scenario 5 (Section D, site #2), 138-140
Scintillation detector, 75-76, 78
Secondary recovery, 58
Section D site #1, 135-137
Section D site #2, 138-140
Selenium, 46, 48, 96
Separators, 36
Shutin well, 115
Sierra Club, xvi
Silver, 46, 48, 96
Site description, 30, 115-116, 118-119, 122-124, 126, 128, 137-138
Site identification, 118, 122-124, 126
Sludge, 36

Snapshot in time, 26
Sodic soil, 112, 130, 137
Sodium absorption ratio, 44, 108, 110, 118, 120
Sodium cation, 42-44, 95, 112-113
Sodium chloride, 44, 112
Sodium iodide thallium crystal, 78
Soil additive. SEE Soil amendment.
Soil amendment, 108, 111-114, 130:
    brine contamination, 112;
    soil sodicity remediation, 112;
    hydrocarbon contaminated soil remediation, 113-114;
    complications, 114
Soil analysis, 35, 39-54, 89, 125-126:
    soil development, 39-40;
    soil structuring, 41-53;
    soil sampling, 50, 52, 54
Soil borings, 30
Soil conditions, 30
Soil coverage, 118, 122
Soil development, 38-40
Soil pollution, 28, 75, 87-89, 118, 130, 135, 138
Soil probe, 95
Soil profile, 40, 91, 112, 120, 126
Soil remediation, 43, 102-104, 106, 120, 130
Soil sample parameters (non-organic), 43-48:
    cation exchange capacity, 43-44;
    sodium absorption ratio, 44;
    exchangeable sodium percentage, 44;
    electrical conductivity, 44-45;
    chlorides, 45; pH, 45;
    total metals, 45-48;
    toxicity characteristic leaching procedure, 48
Soil sample parameters (organic), 49-50:
    total petroleum hydrocarbons, 49;
    oil and grease, 49;
    total organic carbon, 49;

benzene, toluene, ethylbenzene, xylene, 49;
volatile organic analysis, 49-50;
reporting requirements, 50
Soil sampling, 27, 28, 35-36, 50, 52, 54, 58, 108, 116, 118, 120-121, 126-127, 130-131:
sampling plan, 50, 52;
sample equipment, 52;
sample collection, 52, 54;
sample handling/shipping, 54
Soil sodicity, 112, 130, 137
Soil structuring, 41-53, 112:
aggregation, 41-42;
bulk density, 43;
sample parameters (non-organic), 43-48;
sample parameters (organic), 49-50
Soil texture, 44
Solid wastes, 14, 18, 102
Solidification/stabilization, 104, 110-111
Soluble metals, 103
Solvation, 45
Solvents, 16, 56, 62, 107
Source-specific wastes, 14
Space entry procedures, 94
Spill Prevention Control and Countermeasure Plans, 13
Spillage, 92-93
Standard industrial classification codes, 22
Standardization, 36-37
State Emergency Response Commission, 22
Stock tank, 62, 79, 138
Storage tanks, 62
Storage tank, 75, 122-123, 126-127, 129-130
Structural integrity, 58
Subsurface contamination (groundwater), 57-61:

salt water disposal, 58-59;
waterflood wells, 58;
production wells, 58, 60-61
Sulfide, 103
Sulfur, 112-113
Sulfuric acid, 112
Superfund Amendment and Reauthorization Act, Title III, 21-22
Superfund sites, 19-22, 37, 83
Supply-side economics, xv-xvi
Surface drainage, 93
Surface infiltration (groundwater), 57, 61-63:
waste pits, 61-62;
oil/brine storage tanks, 62;
chemical storage facilities, 62-63
Surface owner, 118
Surface rights, xix, 8
Surface storage, 58
Surface valence, 42
Surface water, 13, 68, 91, 135-136
Surfactant, 62

T

Tank battery, 28-29, 62, 128-130, 132-134, 138-140:
audit example, 28-19
Tank bottoms, 36
Tar, 113, 118, 120, 122, 127
Tax abatement, xv-xvi
Tax credits, xv
Team relationship, 9
Texas Natural Resource Conversation Commission, 18-19
Texas Natural Resources Code ##91, 7
Texas Railroad Commission, xv, 12, 17-19, 36, 58, 60, 105
Texas, xv, 7, 18-19, 23, 61, 80-81, 83, 91, 95, 106
Threshold concentration/level, 21, 79
Threshold planning quantity, 22
Tied to the wellhead (waste definition), 16

Time/distance/shielding, 76, 85
Toluene, 68
Topographic map, 63
Tortuosity, 41
Total depth, 61
Total dissolved solids, 44
Total metals analysis, 45-48, 96
Total organic carbon, 49, 51, 118, 120
Total petroleum hydrocarbons, 49, 51,
     53, 96-97, 106, 113-114, 120
Toxic chemical release, 14, 22
Toxic Substances Control Act, 21-23
Toxicity characteristic leaching
     procedure, 17, 46, 48, 127
Tracer surveys, 19
Trade Expansion Act (1962), xv
Training program, 89
Transfer audits (producing properties),
     5, 25-37, 50, 89:
     purpose of audit, 26-27;
     audit example (tank battery),
     28-33;
     phase one audit procedure, 33-35;
     environmental concerns (oilfield
     facilities), 35-36;
     industry standardization, 36-37
Treatment/storage/disposal facility, 18,
     67-68, 102
Trouble log, 116
True total barium run, 46
Trust fund, 7
Turf wars, 18

U

U.S. Department of Commerce, xv
U.S. Department of Energy, xv
Ultraviolet radiation, 108
Underground injection, 19, 58, 61,
     101, 108:
     control, 19
Underground storage tank, 13

United States, 1-3
Unrestricted area, 85
Upstream industry, xviii
Utah, 84

V

Vegetation stress, 28, 30, 35, 61-62, 92,
     126, 128, 137
Visual inspection/site analysis (pit),
     92-93
Volatile organic compound, 49-50, 57,
     68, 109, 120:
     analysis, 49-50, 57

W

Washington, 84
Waste pit/storage, 61-62, 75, 83-84
Water movement, 41
Water sampling, 36, 127
Water solubility, 45
Water table, 55-56
Water treating, 102-104
Water well, 122-123, 126
Waterflood wells, 58
Weathering, 39, 93, 108-109, 113
Well classification, 19
Well plugging, 60, 126-127
Well spacing (monitoring), 71-73
Wellheads, 35
Wetlands, 91, 109
Whopper site #1, 128-134
Working interest, 8

X

Xylene, 68, 132

Z

Zinc sulfite, 78
Zinc, 46, 48, 92, 96